Harriot Mackenzie

Modern Science Unlocking the Bible

Or, the truth seen from three points

Harriot Mackenzie

Modern Science Unlocking the Bible
Or, the truth seen from three points

ISBN/EAN: 9783337035815

Printed in Europe, USA, Canada, Australia, Japan

Cover: Foto ©Lupo / pixelio.de

More available books at **www.hansebooks.com**

MODERN SCIENCE

UNLOCKING THE BIBLE;

OR,

THE TRUTH SEEN FROM THREE POINTS.

BY

HARRIOT MACKENZIE,

AUTHOR OF

"EVOLUTION

ILLUMINATING THE BIBLE."

LONDON : SIMPKIN MARSHALL, HAMILTON KENT & CO.,
LIMITED.

1892.

To the Memory

OF THE LATE

JOHN STUART MILL,

THIS VOLUME IS DEDICATED AS AN EXPRESSION OF
THE AUTHOR'S GRATITUDE FOR BENEFITS
DERIVED FROM WRITINGS OF HIS.

CONTENTS.

Preface.. 1
Introduction.. 3

PART I.

CHAPTER I.
The Discriminating Power of the Intellect 9

CHAPTER II.
Faith Expressing Itself in Practice................................ 19

CHAPTER III.
Jesus as the God of Humanity, or the Seed and Elect of God........ 23

CHAPTER IV.
The Effects Produced by Mind 30

CHAPTER V.
The Object of Justifying Faith..................................... 32

CHAPTER VI.
The Duty of Christians to Live Out their Professions............. 39

CHAPTER VII.
Christ as the Vicarious Sacrifice; and the Believer's Duty to Follow in His Steps, and accept Truth from All Quarters............ 46

CHAPTER VIII.
The Developed Religious Element, contrasted with the Fruits of the Vicarious Sacrifice.. 54

CHAPTER IX.
All Believers are Entitled to Eternal Life and may be Viewed as Saved 67

CHAPTER X.
Mind the Base for Christianity to Work on........................ 74

CHAPTER XI.
Man Presented before God as seen in the Inward Man 76

CHAPTER XII.
Christ Confessed, and the Value of Labour....................... 87

CHAPTER XIII.
In Reference to Pleasure Increasing the Vital Action 89

PART II.

CHAPTER I.
Does Christianity Admit of a Scientific Test?................... 101

PART III.

CHAPTER I.
Union with Christ Expressing Itself in Feeling 127

CHAPTER II.
The Two Types—The Old Man and the New........................ 131

CHAPTER III.
The Origin of the Objective Christ traced through many stages, and the Forces Employed in Building the New Man 137

CHAPTER IV.
The Impossibility of Proving the Existence of a God apart from Revelation... 147

CHAPTER V.
The New Birth Expressed in Feeling 152

CHAPTER VI.
The Soul as a Group of Sensations Proclaimed Immortal............... 154

CHAPTER VII.
The Theory of the Grouped Sensations brought out 158

CHAPTER VIII.
Christian Responsibility in the Light of Modern Science unlocking the Bible 162

CHAPTER IX.
A Theory applied in Reference to the Resurrection of the Body 169

CHAPTER X.
Two Sets of Truth contrasted in the Cerebrum Brain..................... 178

CHAPTER XI.
Clergymen responsible for Modern Scepticism........................... 183

CHAPTER XII.
The consequence of wasted energy in view of the Conservation of Energy.. 186

CHAPTER XIII.
The Responsibility attaching to a Christian profession................... 190

CHAPTER XIV.
The Freedom of the Will defined, and the effect of the organism...... 196

CHAPTER XV.
A Theory applied to explain Revelation and its effects 204

Conclusion 211

PREFACE.

THE work by the Duke of Somerset on "Christian Theology and Modern Scepticism," was greatly blessed to me in stimulating my thoughts. Trusting a blessing might be given to the effort, I am, therefore, induced to write the few simple pages of this work.

The opposition of the world in regard to natural and revealed religion, may be divided into two classes; those who, referring to the Bible, believe in miracles and those who, doubting, rest on the fixed laws of nature. The one class proves truth by faith in God's promises, the other by God's established laws of nature, thus confirming His revealed words in all that is absolute truth; so that, in the days that are to come, both truths shall be united in one, as part of a whole, and in this way an end be put to the controversy.

INTRODUCTION.

IT will be apparent at a glance that there is nothing of the culture of a trained mind in this treatise; and how it came to be written can be explained in a few words.

By the perusal of a review of a book by Professor Bain on "Mind and Body," where the nature of the Intellect was defined as Discrimination, Similarity, and Retentiveness, I saw in this group a basis for Christianity to work upon, and at once determined, in the strength of God, to define practical Christianity as seen in the form of Christian belief. In reply to *one question* put by the Duke of Somerset in a book published by him some years before, "Christian Theology and Modern Scepticism," page 148, namely, "Is faith in God the faith that Jesus taught? or, is Christian faith more complex in its manifold requirements?" I have tried to show that Christian faith is more complex in its manifold requirements.

That question I consider answered in the first few chapters on "Christianity reduced to Proof"; I continued, however, to write, as I felt desirous of adding something more to the treatise.

I intended to publish the work forthwith, but my

purpose was defeated; in consequence of which I cast the work aside, determining in a sense to make myself acquainted with modern science, and seek to establish the truth of revelation from that point.

The essay, "Will Christianity admit of Scientific Test"; and the other treatise, "The Christianity of the Future; or, the Union of two Systems of Truth," spring from the determination I had made. With this explanation of the object I had in writing, the book will go forth to the public, and I leave its readers to judge of its merits.

I have been obliged to treat the subject of "Christianity reduced to proof" in a way peculiar to revealed religion, because, if Christianity proper will not bear the test of criticism from all quarters, we have no right or authority to say it is a divine revelation, in which God revealed His will to man; but did not leave the subject sufficiently clear to enable man, when following God's direction, to prove for himself the absolute truth of revealed religion. (John vii. 17.)

As capable of producing the power implied in Christian influence, and of moulding the mind of man, which avowedly was Christ's object in coming into the world, He comes, with the authority of God, to deal with humanity as body and mind, to implant in man a new element by which man becomes convinced of a divine power; moulding his will and bringing it into

Introduction. 5

subjection to the will of God, or, to put it in other words, convincing mankind of the fact represented in eternal life, that the mind, individually, is to live eternally as a separate and distinct creation, and that, through the element implied in a revealed religion, man becomes convinced of a power represented in consciousness as a spiritual presence ; being the fruit of revealed truth, which, as it increases, becomes the strongest power in man, by creating new desires, as the effect of that spiritual experience implied in faith working by love. I have attempted to deal with mind as the recipient of the new influence that comes to us through belief, and so acts on the mind as that this influence becomes apparent to man in a spiritual experience, the unit of which is embodied in love to God and man. Thus man progresses into a perfect state, and the germ contained in the belief, realised as the perfect unit which is personified in the ideal Christ, is received into the mind as the medium of union with God, and thus becomes the ultimate cause of the change on the mind, as mind presenting our self-consciousness embodied in nerve-current* finds rest in the *Almighty*.

As a reply to " Christian Theology and Modern

* This phase of vibration, we may say, distinguishing the *human* soul. For what is the immaterial in the abstract, but a something we call matter, vibrating at certain periods, of which the colours supply the best example. he human organism takes on vibration and defines it in sensation as heat, light, sound, or colour.

Scepticism," I only pretend to deal with the question put in page 148—"Is faith in God, the faith which Jesus taught? or is Christian faith more complex in its manifold requirements?" and I hope I have been able to make it plain that Christian faith is more complex in its manifold acquirements, thus answering the one question put in page 148, by producing the state of consciousness necessary to create the other, referred to in page 143, as a faith which could combine the conviction of the intellect with the obedience of the heart; and by showing that the faith that Paul teaches is the same now as ever, and that the aspiration to the elevated doctrine of St. Paul means simply increased spiritual experience, which all may claim as the heritage of Christian belief.

The germ of the system of Christianity rests in Christ, and belief enables us to realise Christ as our Saviour. Christ in the heart germinates or causes love; love causes action; and thus Paul's experience becomes the heritage of each Christian, and may be realised as such. Christ as the centre of the system puts man in a position to act.

PART I.

CHRISTIANITY REDUCED TO PROOF.

Chapter I.

THE DISCRIMINATING POWER OF THE INTELLECT.

WORSHIP and Morality are possible when man possesses a religious and moral element, together with discrimination and similarity, the power by which he is enabled to recognise and classify differences: this power teaches him the nature of good and evil, and by it he knows the difference between a good action and a bad one; hence the knowledge as taught in the Bible, just before the fall of Man—"Ye shall be as gods, knowing good and evil." (Gen. iii. 5.) Reason or intellect in man may have been so weak when the revelation was first given, in consequence of his low state of civilisation,* that he could only receive the truth by figurative language, but, as intellect developed, God revealed truth as truth; though, in order to prove that, the Bible and mental science must join hand in hand, for truth in the Bible cannot contradict truth out of the Bible. The one is God's revelation of truth, the other God's expression of truth in mind; teaching man that God has given him an intellect so vast that, as it develops, it may comprehend more fully God, the eternal Creator, as God. Truth

* Civilisation will be understood to include a state in which the moral and religious element is highly developed.

will thus be tested by truth; for what is intellect, but the symbol of God's power in man?

The time has now come that truth in the Bible must be tested by proof, and Christianity treated as a science; for it is of the greatest importance to man that it should be fully understood, as much for his spiritual as his temporal benefit.

We Christians, holding the Bible as inspired, and given to man from God as His rule of life, when enlightened by God the Spirit through faith in the Lord Jesus Christ, may be fully assured that nothing can take from us the internal evidence of the spirit of truth, as revealed in the Bible. If we more fully realised what is meant in the 38th and 39th verses of the 8th chapter of Romans, we should be less concerned as to the way in which the truth is expressed in the Bible. The absence of this internal evidence is the reason why man, in his natural state, can see no beauty in the spiritual teaching of the Bible—hence the difference that has arisen between man in his natural state, and man in his spiritual state. In his spiritual state, he is conscious of the warfare going on in his mind between faith and reason; or, to put it more plainly, " his will and God's will," or the flesh and the spirit, as described in the 7th chapter of Romans, from the 13th verse to the end. Paul tells us why man in his natural state cannot receive or comprehend the things of the Spirit of God, as seen in the 11th and 14th verses of the 2nd chapter of 1st Corinthians : " the natural man receiveth not the things of the Spirit of God; for they are foolishness unto him : neither can he know them, because they are spiritually discerned ".

Man by his unaided mind can only see God in creation; he is thus searching out truth as revealed in nature, by the mighty power of his intellect bestowed on him by the Creator of the Universe, and called in the Bible the breath of life, by which man became a living soul: "And the Lord God formed man of the dust of the ground, and breathed into his nostrils the breath of life; and man became a living soul". (Gen. ii. 7.)

By this mighty power developing itself in man, we are surrounded by many luxuries and comforts of civilised life, as the product of man's inventive power; hence the power of mind over matter, and thus the pride of intellect. Scientific research can never take from man the truth as revealed in the Bible, which teaches man why he was born, and why he must die; and all that come to God, as reconciled by Christ, will find the God of the Bible a reconciled Father, leading and guiding them through life, and their sure hope in death; therefore taking the Bible, as it is open to proof, the Christian can lose nothing that is worth keeping. The Bible will thus become the guide book of the civilised world, when truth is recognised as implying God's expression to man in nature and in grace. The Bible will thus be useful to science and religion. Little good can come till this is done, and the sooner the better for civilised man.

My subject leads me to deal with the question how God, as revealed in the Bible, is made known to man. How far man, as man, endowed with reason or intellect, may realise the felt-presence of God, as the God of nature or creation, my subject does not touch; only we, as

Christians, are compelled to accept as truth whatever man can prove as absolute truth, because that must be God's expression to man in nature.

The Lord Jesus makes that very plain in the 37th verse of the 18th chapter of John's Gospel, where he expresses the cause of his mission to be to "bear witness unto the truth". We thus conclude that truth outside the Bible cannot be contrary to truth as revealed in the Bible : in so far as Christians refuse to accept absolute truth they act in opposition to Bible-teaching. Science and revealed religion unite here.

The truths, as revealed in the Word of God, are the truths contained in the leading facts of Christianity. The Commandments, as given in the 20th chapter of Exodus, only apply to man when he accepts the Bible as inspired by God, and as a revelation from Him ; and the reason to be given for this is very fully explained by Paul in the 24th verse of the 3d chapter of Galatians, in these words, "Wherefore the law was our schoolmaster to bring us unto Christ, that we might be justified by faith" (in consequence of Christ having fulfilled the law). Man by revelation thus becomes conscious, in the light of such passages as 2d Cor. v. 16-21, that in his natural state he can never approach God as a reconciled Father; therefore he now approaches the God of the Bible as a sinner desiring to be reconciled, feeling that an historical belief in Jesus, which he has held all through life, has failed altogether to give the peace of conscience he finds himself entitled to. He now becomes anxious to ascertain why he has failed to realise or experience the truth embodied in the Christian doctrine, and now becomes fully aware that Christian truth deals with the individual, and that he must receive as true, what God in His word reveals to be true. " But if the Spirit of him that raised up Jesus from the dead dwell in you, he that raised up Christ from the dead shall also quicken your mortal bodies by his Spirit that dwelleth in you," (Romans viii. 11.) Thus he enters into a new relationship with God as a God of Grace or favour, as revealed by the Lord Jesus Christ, and the sinner, thus voluntarily entering into a new relationship, becomes through it united to the Eternal " I Am ".

God thus becomes to man a centre of attraction, occupying the first place in his affections, and this feeling is strengthened by applying such scripture to himself as we find in Rom. iv. 5, " But to him that worketh not, but believeth on Him that justifieth the ungodly, his faith is counted for righteousness"; Rom. iii. 22, "Even the righteousness of God which is by faith of Jesus Christ unto all and upon all them that believe": for there is no difference; Cor. i. 3, "Grace be unto you, and peace, from God our Father, and from the Lord Jesus Christ"; Gal. iii., 11 and 12, "But that no man is justified by the law in the sight of God, it is evident : for, the just shall live by faith. And the law is not of faith : but, the man that doeth them shall live in them." The truth, being thus received into the heart, produces such fruit as is taught by Paul, Gal. v. 22-26, " But the fruit of the Spirit is love, joy, peace, long-suffering, gentleness, goodness, faith, meekness, temperance ; against such there is no law. And they that are Christ's have crucified the flesh, with the affections and lusts. If we live in the Spirit, let us also walk in the

Spirit. Let us not be desirous of vain-glory, provoking one another, envying one another."

This is the effect of the evidence which accompanies a belief in the truth of the Gospel as applied individually, and thus Christianity, embodied in the ideal of Christ, becomes a living power in the mind of man.

The Lord Jesus Christ, having thus revealed God to man and reconciled him to God, becomes an object of adoration and love; His words are treasured up in the memory, and act upon the life, and man feels that a new principle has taken possession of him, and he has thus become a willing subject of a new King, governed by a new power, which he finds defined in the Scriptures as "faith working by love". Gal. v. 6, " For in Jesus Christ neither circumcision availeth any thing, nor uncircumcision; but faith which worketh by love." Man, as an intelligent being, now realizes a change wrought in him so great that he feels himself to be indeed a new creature; "old things are passed away; behold, all things are become new". (2 Cor. v. 17.)

This is the internal or subjective evidence in the form of the Spirit of God, bearing witness with our spirits or mind, and testifying to the truth of the change produced. Rom. viii. 16, " The Spirit itself beareth witness with our spirit, that we are the children of God ".

The more God in Christ thus occupies the thoughts, and consequently moves the feelings of men, leading to the "Abba, Father" (" For we have not received the spirit of bondage again to fear; but we have received the Spirit of adoption, whereby we cry, Abba, Father." Rom. viii. 15), the more does man become conformed in heart and life to the truth, as revealed in the Scriptures. As the feelings thus become intensified, the motive power is strengthened, so that man becomes a *willing instrument* and a co-worker with God the Father, being created anew in Jesus Christ; things seen and temporal lose their power, and the unseen are realised as eternal. 2 Cor. iv. 18, "While we look not at the things which are seen, but at the things which are not seen: for the things which are seen are temporal; but the things which are not seen are eternal."

The soul in man thus finds rest in God, the eternal "I Am," as a reconciled Father; a new element of God is thus revealed through the Lord Jesus, and man is convinced of his immortality, as taught in the resurrection. (1 Cor. xv.)

Christianity presented in Christ is thus revealed *as the seed of God in the soul* of man *realising* God as a reconciled Father, for this new form is personified in Christ. It is thus the Lord Jesus becomes in man the hope of glory. Under this growing sentiment man begins to feel how weak he is, as he tries to follow the Lord fully, and applies to himself, as a rule of life, such portions of the Word of God as are contained in the fifth to seventh chapters of Matthew; the spirit of which is fully expressed in the forty-fourth verse of the fifth chapter, and twelfth verse of the seventh chapter, and thirty-seventh verse of the twenty-second chapter. Man becomes greatly humbled by a sense of his failures in heart and life, and feels for the second time that his safety and peace of mind rest on his *union* with God as a reconciled Father, revealed through and by the Lord Jesus Christ, *as he clings and rests on Christ.* Thus Paul's experience becomes his, and he is constrained to say, "For we are of the circumcision, which worship God in the spirit, and rejoice in Christ Jesus, and have no confidence in the flesh". (Phil. iii. 3.) Thus the teaching of the Lord Jesus becomes intelligent to man, for now he is enabled to see that the Christ of Christianity points man to his reason as his guide, when enlightened by divine truth, as taught in John vii. 17, viii. 12, 30-32 ; and this is proof to man of the truth of Christianity, *for he feels and knows* Christianity is proved to be absolute truth when it is accompanied by the fruit flowing from Christian experience, as made manifest by purity of heart and life. The believer, thus enlightened, is greatly comforted, as he *now understands experimentally* what is meant by the Saviour's promise to send the Comforter as a Spirit of Truth, revealing truth, and sent to guide His people into all truth. (John xvi. 12, 13, 14.) He can *now* sympathise with the spirit that prevailed among the disciples, as seen in the fourteenth chapter of John, when this truth was first taught by the Lord Jesus ; for the *sanctified* believer must confess that, like Philip, he has often said in Spirit, " Lord, show us the Father, and it sufficeth us," but did not till now realise that God, as the Creator and Father of Jesus Christ, was revealed in the mind of man. Thus, as he compares his past experience with his present knowledge, he feels that reason was given him as his guide, when enlightened by the Christ of Christianity as seen in the xiv., xv., xvi., and xvii. chapters of John. In the twenty-first, twenty-second, and twenty-third verses of the fourteenth chapter, the Lord makes it very plain that reason, when intensified by feeling as love to Christ, is the test of our adoption, that is, when the heart is full of love * to God in Christ.

How simple and yet how sure a test—the highest intellect need not err, and the meanest is moulded by this power!

As the power of mind over matter is revealed by the works of man, so the power of faith over mind is seen in the mind of man, as enlightened by the spirit, and can be reduced to proof as an evidence in the soul of man, as he is being moulded by a higher influence than that which governs the world of sense and reason, apart from revelation.

The Bible, containing the Word of God, is felt to be enough to meet man's spiritual wants when accompanied by the Spirit of God, as revealed in the heart of man, and tested by its fruit; the effect of which is always manifested by humbling man and exalting God, "Whosoever therefore shall humble himself as this little child, the same is greatest in the kingdom of heaven" (Matt. xviii. 4), and leading to purity of heart and life. For it is evident from the spirit of the Bible, that we are to accept nothing short of this teaching as a conclusive proof of acceptance and spiritual union with God. "Beloved, believe not every spirit, but try the spirits whether they are of God." (1 John iv. 1.)

Though man is thus entitled to judge himself, the Lord Jesus plainly tells us, his spiritual children, that the world is to know us by our *fruits* (Matt. xii. 34, 35); so that the world has no authority to accept our religious

* Love thus qualified is the finite put in possession of the essence of the Infinite.

professions, but only so far as our lives prove them to be genuine.

If our religion does not make us truer and better men and women, it is worthless so far as our fellow-men are concerned ; for the Master's command is, " Be ye therefore perfect, even as your Father which is in heaven is perfect " (Matt. v. 48). This striving after perfection is to be seen in our lives, and felt in our hearts.

Christianity is a new development, moulding man's mind through the power of truth as revealed through and by the Lord Jesus as absolute truth, and can only be reduced to proof, when the mind of man is brought into contact with the spiritual presence of the eternal God.

The truth of Christianity might be better understood by the intelligent thinking class of society, if expressed as a new development of the mind, only perceptible through the evidence of a new sense which connects the thinking part of man, or soul of man, with God as a spirit, by bringing it in contact with the spiritual power, or presence, of the God of creation, as a God of grace or favour, revealed in and through the Christ of Christianity. The truth of this new development was only to be made known to the world by the effect it produces in the individual believer, by showing in his life and conversation the fruit classified in 1 Cor. xiii. 3-13. Thus making good faith by works, it would then be felt that a Bible, containing the word of God, was enough to immortalise the truth of Christianity ; where reason intensified by feeling, as faith working by love, unites all the Christian graces in one great whole, as faith and practice.

CHAPTER II.
FAITH EXPRESSING ITSELF IN PRACTICE.*

IF faith and practice were understood to mean reason intensified by feeling, as faith working by love, would not the Protestant referred to by the Duke of Somerset, in page 145 (as he takes up his Bible he wishes to believe, he tries to believe, he feels ashamed of disbelief, he even debases his moral truthfulness by pretending to believe; all these efforts avail him nothing, and he is at last obliged in his own conscience silently to confess that he has been born some centuries too late), be greatly comforted if he realised faith and practice as the fruit of salvation, and feel it a great relief to know, that all that the Christian religion requires, is the willing mind, and that, beginning with the confession, "I believe, help thou mine unbelief," (Mark ix. 24), he will soon find by experience the truth of Luke xi. 13, where God promises to give the Holy Spirit to them that ask Him. Thus, by the power of the witness within, he shall be able to say, "for I know whom I have believed, and am persuaded that He is able to keep that which I committed unto Him against that day" (2 Tim. i. 12); "for God hath not given us the spirit of fear, but of power and of love, and of a sound mind" (2 Tim. i. 7). "Being confident of this very thing, that He who hath begun a good work in you will perform it until the day of Christ Jesus" (Phil. i. 6); "for it is God which worketh in you both to

* Practice here means work done, or feeling flowing from love to Christ.

will and to do of His good pleasure" (Phil. ii. 13), "according to the eternal purpose which He proposed in Christ Jesus our Lord" (Eph. iii. 11); "for the fruit of the spirit is in all goodness and righteousness and truth" (Eph. v. 9); "for we can do nothing against the truth, but for the truth" (2 Cor. xiii. 8). "That we henceforth be no more children tossed to and fro, and carried about with every wind of doctrine, by the slight of men and cunning craftiness, whereby they lie in wait to deceive; but, speaking the truth in love, may grow up into him in all things which is the head, even Christ" (Eph. iv. 14, 15). For all this will be found verified in the experience of every true child of God, "as a believer in Christ".

But, if such an experience as this is necessary before man can comprehend the Bible as containing the Word of God, it must be apparent to every one that man by his unaided intellect can never comprehend it; to man, as such, it must ever remain a sealed book. Therefore, man, as body and mind, may know much of God as a Creator, and be fully persuaded that the Judge of all the earth will do right, but can know nothing of the God of Grace or favour, revealed by the *God of humanity* as the Christ of Christianity; consequently this knowledge must come to man through the medium of a new sense, compelling the intellect to accept as true what God's Word declares to be true, as taught in the leading truths of Christianity, and as seen in the death and resurrection of the Lord Jesus Christ.

Seeing that the leading facts of Christianity may be as fully authenticated as any historical event of the same date, man, when true to himself, must accept them ; though the mystery involved must so far remain a mystery.

Inspired religion must thus be treated as a science in which the mind has to undergo a course of mental training, though the process is somewhat unusual.

Thus we divide mankind into two great classes. Both are the subjects of the one King, God the eternal Creator of the vast universe ; both adore God as the Creator. But the understanding of the one class has been enlightened by the power of divine truth, as revealed in the Bible ; and the Bible, thus enlightening the understanding, has awakened in this class a sense of the spiritual presence of God, the God of Grace, as a reconciled Father, in and through the Lord Jesus Christ, who "came not to be ministered unto, but to minister, and to give His life a ransom for many". (Matt. xx. 28.) " For the Son of man is come to save that which was lost." (Mat. xviii. 11.) But though this class has entered into a new relationship with God, as a God of Grace or favour, yet, as this relationship is of a spiritual nature, and is the line that divides the two classes, it can only be known to God (and man individually). Therefore, God alone can divide the sheep from the goats, (Matt. xxv. 32), (speaking of the church as a mass). In this connection take also the following passages, " He that shall endure unto the end shall be saved " ; (Mat. xxiv. 13.) " He that believeth on the Son hath everlasting life." (John iii. 36) ; " God is a spirit, and they that worship Him must worship Him in spirit and in truth." (John iv. 24.) But an experience of this nature is only valuable so far as it refers to man's relation to God, and though of the greatest importance to individual man, it is of no value to the world at large, except in so far as the command is fulfilled as given in Matt. v. 16, " Let your light so shine before men, that they may see your good works, and glorify your Father which is in heaven". Because all men, professing to believe in the leading doctrines of Christianity, are only entitled to be accepted as Christians in so far as their lives bear out their profession ; for the Saviour distinctly teaches this in Matt. vii. 14-23.

It is the motive that prompts the action that God will judge by; therefore the true motive can only be known to God and the individual, and man may not judge man. (Mat. vii. 1-6.) Those who have never entered into a spiritual relationship with God, as a God of grace and as open to all "to profit withal," (1 Cor. xii. 7.), by and through the God of Humanity, the Lord Jesus Christ, must allow that they have no claim to spiritual privileges ; and an inherent sense of truth will teach men that they only know God as the Creator, and that He who is the Judge of all the earth will do right; for God is to them as their Creator only.

When Christianity is received as the religion of mankind, and Christ accepted as the God of Humanity, it will then be allowed by all, that the motive which prompts the action, as seen in work done from love to Christ, divides the classes; for the time will come when there will be none but professing Christian men and women on this earth of ours. For the Lord Jesus Christ has not died in vain.

Chapter III.

JESUS AS THE GOD OF HUMANITY, OR THE SEED AND ELECT OF GOD.

THE truth that unites us with God is contained in the Saviour's life, death, and resurrection: once let these be fully realised and all becomes easy, because those truths, or facts, involve all that is really essential for our salvation. His death is a historical event, established on historical ground, and fully authenticated, and it is this that gives us the Jesus of history.

The resurrection is communicated to us through a different channel, and, though as fully authenticated, it was an event that was only witnessed by the professed followers of the Jesus of history, and through them communicated to the world, thus changing the Jesus of history into the Christ of Christianity. This event has been established by an unbroken line of testimony from that day to this; which truth is fully established, independent of Bible testimony. The different channels though which the truth has been communicated to us are very remarkable. The Jesus of history is accepted by all; but the Christ of Christianity is only accepted by his professed followers, as the God of humanity. "And, without controversy, great is the mystery of godliness: God was manifest in the flesh, justified in the Spirit, seen of angels, preached unto the Gentiles, believed on in the world, received up into glory". (1 Tim. iii. 16.) He is received first into the heart by faith. The laws that produce the resurrection are a matter of faith and above reason, being afterwards made manifest by the felt power of God in the soul of man; this is evident from the words of John, when he says, "He that believeth on the Son of God hath the witness in himself". (1 John, v. 9-21.) So that a profession in the belief of Christianity implies in reality a belief in Christ as the risen Lord, and through the medium of sense the soul of man enjoys the felt presence of God; for God, in this sense, is the eternal "I am" of creation and revelation; and the evidence of His spiritual presence increases in man, as his mind becomes moulded by this new spiritual element, "Which is the fruit of Christ in man, the hope of glory; even the mystery which hath been hid from ages and from generations, but now is made manifest to His saints: to whom God would make known what is the riches of the glory of this mystery among the Gentiles; which is Christ in you, the hope of glory". (Col. i. 26, 27). The fruit should be apparent to all in the Christian's outward life, bearing witness to those who are without of the moral and spiritual power of Christianity. Those without will here be understood to mean, those who honestly disbelieve in the Christ of Christianity as the Son of God, or, we may say, the God of Humanity; for it was to teach men humanity, and thus prepare them for immortality, that the God of creation has revealed Himself as the God of Humanity. The Christian religion will admit of nothing less; and this class of sceptics will be the first to allow that if Christianity admits of such a union with the eternal "I am," they have no claim to it: they may call it a superstitious belief, but they will never claim a right to any of the privileges derived from it. An inherent sense of truth will show this, for they are often men of great integrity, in sincerity of heart worshipping the God of Creation, but because they have rejected the God of grace, they refuse to enter into that new relation by which the sinner may approach God as a God of favour, with the "Abba, Father". God, thus wearing the mantle of humanity, is worshipped through the medium of sense or intellect in man. The mystery is great, that the God of creation has appeared as the God of humanity; thus in a double form revealing Himself to man; but this is no greater mystery than man finds in body and mind, when he tries to separate them. We Christians might understand the meaning of the double union, God as God the Father of all, and God as the God of grace; clothed in humanity, and through this medium known as the Jesus of history, and the Christ of Christianity, and the God of immortality, establishing, in the only way men as men could comprehend, the immortality of the soul: the mystery thus simplified is cleared away, and God, as God, remains the absolute "I am" of creation and grace, while the Christian worships God "through the evidence of a new sense developed in the mind," which is expressed as the influence of the God of humanity (or Jesus the Seed and Elect of God.) Thus governed by the law of love, Christians are responsible for purity of heart as well as purity of life. That is, the God of humanity, as their Master, comes to teach mankind through His Word and by His people, who are manifesting in their lives this purity; for to them an evil thought is accounted by God as sin; and nothing short of this earnestly striving after and longing for purity of heart can satisfy a soul in *communion* with God. Then the feelings become intensified, love operates in the mind in the usual way, and the soul in this state may be understood as guided more by feeling than by reason. This is beautifully brought out by the God of humanity, all through the Sermon on the Mount; but especially in the fifth chapter of Matthew, from the 37th to the 43rd verse. When we realise this fact that feeling, as love, is to stimulate, how plain Jesus' meaning becomes when He says, "Many that are first shall be last, and the last shall be first". (Matthew xix. 30)!

Those that act from this motive, "feeling," do indeed suffer loss in this world, but God is the Judge; and here man, as man, is silent, for we are under a new dispensation, and governed by a new law.

Fellow Christian, Christ is our Leader and Master: His field is the mind, His power is love, moulding the stubborn will, by creating in the meekest and the worst of the human race a desire so strong, that nothing short of immortality among the purest and the best, will satisfy their longing souls. With such a destiny in view as our union with Christ in God, it is easy to comprehend how reason ceases to be Master, and love rules supreme, where we cannot follow. We dare not condemn this in faith and above reason, and all that is left for man to say is, that the Judge of all the earth will do right. We see the risen Lord in the God of Humanity, as the seed and elect of God, and all as elected, when united to God in Him.

It would be wisest and best for us Christians, if we

realised more fully than we do, the field our Lord and Master, the God of Humanity, sent us to labour in. He died to win our love, and procure for Himself the first place in our affections. He found us estranged from God, as sinners outside of Christ. When most degraded man most dreads and fears God, as a God of truth and justice. Any place would be more desirable for such a man than a home among the purest and the best, so he must create for himself a hell, as the only place fit for him. Therefore a God of truth must, as he reasons, be true to His nature, and man that has sinned, must suffer again. Man when guided by reason, discrimination, or an innate sense of truth, striving to do his best, an honest man in heart and life, one whom saint and sinner dare to trust, may have no fear to meet God, as a God of truth and justice, feeling that God is not less just than man. And although the future is a vast unknown, yet he feels that the God of all the earth will do right, and he dare ask no more justice. It is now and here that the Christian finds it is not a book, though that book is the Holy Scriptures, he has to do with, but a Living Person, and in that person he can see God as the Creator, personified in the Christ of Christianity, dealing with the mind of man through the medium of a new development; moulding man's mind by the mighty power of love; a power more enduring than hope (2nd Peter iii. 13), more lasting than the heaven that now is (Rev. xxi. 1), and eternal as God (1st John iv. 7). "God is Love." The God of Humanity is now adored in the Christ of Christianity. Feeling that a place of worship is not heaven, and the Bible is not Christ, the soul in man melts in love to God who gave Himself for it, and thus gives itself back to Him, and finds rest in the arms of the Almighty. It is this, the mind, that Jesus our Lord came to purify; it is the field he sent us to cultivate. The tools he has provided for our use, are God's word of truth; the power He commands us to employ, is faith in God; and the end he sends us to accomplish, is purity of heart and life. (Mark vii. 21-23.) It is for the individual to ask—How am I to render an account of my stewardship? The promise is plain. "Whatsoever ye shall ask in my name that will I do. If you ask anything in my name I will do it." (John xiv. 13, 14.) What progress am I making? for the command is, "Love not the world, neither the things that are in the world. If any man love the world the love of the Father is not in him." (1 John ii. 15.) What does the heart witness? What do my friends see of the other injunction? (Mat. v. 44) "Love your enemies, bless them that curse you, do good to them that hate you, and pray for them that despitefully use you and persecute you." Do friends find us "bearing all things, believing all things, hoping all things, enduring all things". (1 Cor. xiii. 7.) Am I striving to do as I would be done unto? If the heart acquit us, (1 John iii. 21.) we must and shall be bearing fruit, and the world will add its testimony for to-day. And how the world shall testify we read in Matt. v. 16: "Let your light so shine before men, that they may see your good works, and glorify your Father which is in heaven". Because the sheep are not divided from the goats, and the tares and wheat are growing together, the Master was very careful they should not be separated. (Mat. xiii. 29, 30.) Except by the evidence of our lives bearing fruit, the world, as material, must always judge by the effect produced, though the motive power in this case is of God, and He is the final judge.

Christianity for eighteen hundred years has possessed the power of moulding mind. We see what Paul was in the first century, and we allow mind to be progressive, and the motive power to be faith over mind, established on a new principle, "faith working by love"; governed by a fixed law, "faith in God," made apparent by the power of faith* over mind; an influence all powerful, and lasting as eternity; and how is it that our men of science look in vain for results? We of Britain have spent millions sterling on a paid ministry, and millions more on churches, but where is the moral influence, that Light of the World which the God of Humanity came, in the likeness of man, to produce? The power He employs is to influence the mind of the individual man, hence every Christian, as an individual man, is responsible for the effect he is producing. It is the Pauls and Peters and Johns of humanity, that Jesus sends as lights to teach in the world. Such power employed will produce the result desired, wherever mind will yield itself a willing instrument. Thus man will become pure within and pure without, and Christianity will be accepted as the religion adapted to mankind, to mould, govern, and subdue the world of sense and reason.

* Faith in this sense will be understood to mean a belief in an objective existence not present to the eye of sense, as a thing that may be dissolved into parts, as we dissolve an object or a sentiment by reducing the concrete to the separate parts, or the sentiment to the separate states of consciousness which it springs from.

Chapter IV.

THE EFFECTS PRODUCED BY MIND.

THE mind in man that began to make itself felt in our first parents sewing fig leaves together to make themselves aprons, soon produced the coats of skin, and has now procured for the bride of Britain's Sailor Prince, that magnificent trousseau she carries with her to her adopted home, the wonder and admiration of many.

When man, as we know him, first appeared on earth, the command came to him to replenish the earth and subdue it. (Gen. i. 28.) The intellect or creative power of man is the instrument God has appointed and bestowed on him to accomplish that vast work. The material God created, and sent man to produce out of it whatsoever he will, by this mighty power of intellect, or soul, or energy of will, by which all may be subdued within and without man.

Within, this is effected by God, personified in the person of Jesus Christ, to whom man being united through faith enabled man to look up to God as a person to be adored and loved. Thus has man obtained the ideal God longed for by men in all ages, but not to be approached, for man is impure, and he knows it; an innate sense of truth teaches this, and this knowledge and longing may remain with man all through eternity, when he rejects the Christ of Christianity, because in Him alone God has appeared again the "second time without sin unto salvation".

This is the medium through which God is seen wearing the mantle of humanity, reuniting sinful life with sinless life in the band of love ; it is thus no presumption in man to approach God in adoring love through a crucified Redeemer, for this is the medium God appointed to subdue the will (or stronger power) in man, by the exercise of faith over mind, the God-appointed means to subdue it.

The power of mind over matter is seen in all that we do. By the mighty power of intellect man has subdued that subtle fluid, electricity, and sent it round the globe with the rapidity of thought, carrying man's message to man, and thus reuniting the human race by the first Adam presented in the experience of the race, mind, who yet liveth doing his God-appointed work, by calling all things by whatever name he pleases (Gen. ii. 19, 20). Moreover he continues to live in the embodied mind of the race, as an individual, and to teach men the perfection displayed by God in His works of creation, when God pronounced it very good (Gen i. 31), by showing mankind the precision displayed in the arrangement of the atoms of matter with which God formed the globe. Thus the first Adam continues to humble man and exalt God as the eternal "I am" of creation and grace. Man is thus silenced in mind, and dare not approach but with the "Abba, Father," in and through Jesus Christ.

Chapter V.

THE OBJECT OF JUSTIFYING FAITH.

WE see the magnificent effect produced by the first Adam, as mind in man, in accomplishing his work of subduing the material or visible world, and thus prove the power of mind over matter. What have we Christians, as the spiritual offspring of the second Adam, produced by the effect of faith on mind in subduing the will or carnal mind, which is enmity against God, and is the field our master God, personified in the Christ of Christianity, sent us to subdue? Yet the effect produced is as apparent in God's sight, as the effect produced in matter is in the sight of man. And we Christians, that profess to be practically united to the God of humanity, whom we hold to be the Christ of Christianity, as God and man, are through that union as responsible in God's sight for yielding to an evil thought, as those without, who disbelieve in the truth of Christianity as contained in justification through faith, are in man's sight for an evil act. But in all "God will be the final judge".

By accepting the credibility of the New Testament records, we are bound to submit to such a test as purity of thought, in so far as man may judge of thoughts by our actions, for now and here man is our judge. Our Lord and Master submitted to that test, and so must we; and although we are accepted as perfect in Him, and

The Object of Justifying Faith.

will be acquitted by Him as such at the final judgment, yet during the present dispensation we are sent to bear witness of the truth by purity of heart and life, and thus prove to man the power of faith over mind. According to Bible-teaching vicarious faith (John xiv. 13) is a power as liable of producing effect as the power of mind, and we are obliged to accept this faith as a power that governs the immaterial world in the same sense as the laws of nature govern the material world; for the teaching of Jesus will admit of nothing less. It is when we realise this that we are brought to feel, how little power man, as man, possesses over his belief. The Christian will be compelled to allow that in God's sight he is a great sceptic, and that every step of advance is to be fought and won by the "Lord, I believe, help thou mine unbelief".

The Jesus of history, as the Christ of Christianity, is seen in the God of humanity, who shows great compassion to man, in demanding nothing more from him than he does from his fellow man, which is the evidence of testimony to establish the truth of an historical event; and when the resurrection is established on that ground it gives us the risen Lord. With the risen Lord as an accepted fact, we have the proof of Jesus' mission. The "Lord, I believe, help thou mine unbelief," when uttered in sincerity of heart by man, as a sinner, to God, is the beginning of that mysterious power, faith; and is all that Jesus teaches as essential to reunite sinful man to God.

May we Christians be as merciful to man as God is to us, and not lay on Him the burden of believing the Bible, which we by the power of faith, have been enabled to do with Christ, in man the hope of glory! The power of faith over mind is established, and will make itself felt: Christ will be realised and glorified as a felt-power in the soul of man.

The prayer of faith will be answered, and the Darwins and Huxleys of our age will be united to the Lord and glorify the Christ of Christianity in a way we, the rank and file of Christ's followers, have failed to do. We Christians have driven men to unbelief by our lives and our teaching, for we have held up to man a dead Bible as sent from God to teach man purity of life, instead of a living Christ, making himself felt in the mind of man as an object of love, and the medium through which man may approach the mighty Creator as a reconciled Father. God, thus personified in the Christ of Christianity, becomes an active power in the mind. He created and bestowed on man a moral and religious element, which finds rest in the God of Humanity, personified in the Christian's God of Creation and Grace. When our sceptic men of science yield as willing instruments their great intellects to this mighty influence, God will reproduce the Pauls and Peters and Johns of the first century. The knowledge they have acquired of the mighty creations by the laws of nature, will qualify them well for such a work, for they can comprehend the value of the soul in a sense we have failed to do. Though eternity is incomprehensible to the finite mind, they can in some ways comprehend it better than we, and thus yielding to the power of God in and through Jesus Christ are created anew. Through this influence, realised as the Spirit of God in the soul of man, they will accept the Bible as containing the word of God, and we will rejoice together in one common Lord of Creation and Grace. Christ, in them the hope of glory, will produce the same fruit as Christ in us the hope of glory; for Christianity is the true and lasting religion for man.

We Christians of Protestant Britain, with an open Bible, recognised as the eternal Word of the living God, what progress have we made, for the world must judge by the effect produced? The Spirit or Comforter Christ bestowed on man at the resurrection (John xvi. 7), is as active and powerful now as then, and the means by which he is made effectual is plainly revealed by the prayer of faith, (Matt. xxi. 22.) "All things whatsoever ye shall ask in prayer, believing, ye shall receive". Now, that all work that a Christian may conscientiously be engaged in, is to be pursued in this spirit, is plainly taught in Ecclesiastes ix. 10 "Whatsoever thy hand findeth to do, do it with thy might"; taken along with Philippians iv. 8, "Finally, brethren, whatsoever things are true, whatsoever things are just, whatsoever things are pure, whatsoever things are lovely, whatsoever things are of good report; if there be any virtue, and if there be any praise, think on these things". God will have no sluggards in His vineyard, and this applies to the rich as well as to the poor, for all are stewards. Man as a free agent is responsible to God, and his duty is plainly revealed in the Holy Chart of the World, the very power of the Omnipotent Himself being pledged as a means to the end. It may be that

the gulf between the rich and the poor is widening year
by year. While heathen India is freeing itself from caste
differences, Christian England is making caste differences to be felt more and more. The rich and the poor
are inseparably united, and equally essential the one
to the other; the only thing needful being that mutual
sympathy which binds man to man. The poor do
not of necessity envy the rich, but the relation existing
between them can only be properly understood when
both are free to meet on one common platform as
equally independent, yet bound together by the one
common bond of humanity. Thus will the poor man
in his thatched cottage feel as independent in his manhood as the rich man in his palace: each as a man in his
own right, ready and willing to help his neighbours in
the common battle of life. Feeling that purity of
thought is the only real distinction, man will never envy
man. With an inherent sense of truth in man, a mighty
change is not only possible, but it is even now, and to-
day, in our power to produce an effect so marked that it
would surpass any feat of magic. Man would act towards
man the part of brother till all class differences should
melt away, like snow before the rays of the sun. We
only require each and all to apply to himself and herself
the spirit that is taught in one single verse of that book
which we, as a Protestant nation, believe to be inspired
of God, and given as our guide in life and hope in death
—Matthew vii. 12, " Therefore all things whatsoever ye
would that men should do to you, do ye even so to them,
for this is the law and the prophets ". The operation of
this spirit would effect the whole change in question. If

The Object of Justifying Faith.

asked, where is this power manifested? we would reply by asking, who else are to blame for the existing evils but we ourselves, the professing Christian men and women of Great Britain? *For is the evil not of our making?* Man possessing a moral and religious element may attain to this end apart from Christianity; for it is all which man, as man, has a right to expect from brother man. It is in this way that many in our day, who professedly disbelieve in Bible truth, are making themselves a felt power in the world. But if these people, who are without a religion having a risen Lord as its great cardinal fact, teach this high morality, how are we, the professed subjects of the God of Humanity, "Christ as God and man," to give an account of our stewardship? For the Master plainly tells us, that He came to purify those very people who are showing us such an example of moral excellence. Which are the most likely subjects of the kingdom of heaven, wherein dwelleth righteousness? The Master has said it is by their fruits His people are to reveal His character in the world, not by their religious profession of faith. James ii. 14: "What doth it profit, my brethren, though a man say he hath faith, and have not works? Can faith save him?" What are we to say then? Is our religion a sham? Is there no power as individuals given us from God to do His work, or is the power offered and refused? Will the Master at the great day say, Depart, or, Come? (Matt. xxv. 31-46.) Seeing then that the men Christ came to purify, are the very men who in many cases are now setting us Christians such an example—honest, true men, as much trusted by the saint as by the sinner—how dare we judge them, as long as we have the Bible open before us, and profess to believe that it was given to us by God, and contains that by which we shall be either acquitted or condemned at the final judgment?

On this point we have, in the seventh chapter of Matthew, the teaching of our Lord Himself, and we ask, Is the Bible bringing forth in us, the Bible-reading Protestants of Christian England, the fruit of this kingdom, purity of thought? Let each one judge himself and herself, for the Lord of Matt. vii. 21, 22, 23 will never save any one. The risen Lord is a felt power in the heart of His people; it is not the Bible, but Christ in the soul of man that opens the gates of heaven, while it is the fruit which proceeds from love to Christ that makes up the treasures laid up by the Christian in heaven, in obedience to Christ's command. (Matthew vi. 20, 21.)*

* Christianity all ends in this : union with God in Christ creates love, love expresses itself in feeling as action ; action, thus generated, is spent in Christian work, and work done from this motive appears in God's sight in heaven in the shape of treasures laid up, in the form of works done from love to Christ. Thus we see the action and counter-action as the fruit of revealed religion.

CHAPTER VI.

THE DUTY OF CHRISTIANS TO LIVE OUT THEIR PROFESSIONS.

THE time has come for us, the Bible-reading people of Britain, to decide whether we or our sceptic men of science are to lead the moral and religious thought of our day. They have shown us how far they can go, by teaching that great lesson—to do to others as we would have others do to us. That is their limit, and is what Christ calls the teaching of the law and the prophets; for reason can carry us no farther. Beyond this faith alone can go. Now if this is all we have to offer, why condemn them? They have as good a right to judge as we. If we believe in a risen Lord, what of that? They do not; but they point to the practical lessons involved in the principle of the law and the prophets, apart from faith in a risen Lord. Is man as perfect without a living Christ in the living soul as with Him? Where and what is the difference? If we have nothing higher to offer, we have no right to teach that they are cast out from the presence of the Eternal God, and that we are accepted. What need was there of Him, who was the child of Mary, but the Son of God, going through the garden of Gethsemane to the cross of Calvary, and from the grave of Joseph ascending to heaven as the God of Humanity, possessing the attributes of God, and at length being personified in the Christian's God of Creation and Grace? What, we ask, does the Bible teach all this, and teach nothing more? Or, does the Bible only begin to teach where man without it leaves off? And what? Before we, the Bible-reading people of England, condemn, we have this plain and pointed question to answer, each one for himself and herself, or keep silent; for we are not called to teach others if we have not learned for ourselves what the Bible was given us for. Did the founder of the Christian religion say in vain as He ascended from Galilee (Matthew xxviii. 18), "All power is given unto me in heaven and in earth .... and lo, I am with you alway, even unto the end of the world"? Did the early Christians require the most powerful navy in the world, and a standing army, such as ours, to protect their homes and their children? How few of us have been able to say, in the strength of an open Bible and a risen Lord, for us our Saviour exists, *in the felt power within!* Let might be right, trusting in the Lord as we do, we feel how secure our home is in glory, and that death to us is indeed gain. To many of us this may look like fanaticism; but Christianity will admit of nothing less. The Vicarious sacrifice was intended to lead to the Vicarious* faith; as we resist not evil, otherwise it gives to the world nothing better than the world may have without it. Christ died for us, to teach us to die for others; and our Moffats, our Burns, our Williams, and our Gardiners, and many others, have lived, and, living, have died, to prove to us that profess so much and do so little, that they did indeed believe Bible truth, and that Christ is as much a felt power to-day as when He ascended from Galilee, more

* Seen in the fruit of our lives as we represent Christ in the world.

than 1800 years ago. This is the power that has given to Protestant England such men as Richard Williams, surgeon and missionary to Patagonia, who, with Captain Gardiner and five others, died from starvation in the year 1851. To show the character of the man, I quote a few extracts from his diary.

"After describing his sufferings on Saturday, March 22, he observes of his rest the night following : ' It was, I think, the most refreshing that I ever enjoyed ; not so much because it was a balmy restorative to my poor debilitated body, but because if ever the whisperings of Almighty love spoke tranquillity to the soul of man, and breathed a continued flow of divine consolation upon his heart, I felt them that night. I was, so to speak, talking with the Lord ; and His grace diffused such an influence around me, that I could very well have thought I was in Paradise. I might have thought so, but the subject-matter of my communings with the Lord was the services, the joyful, heartfelt services, I should render unto Him in this my lifetime, and period of sojourn here on earth. My heart seemed to tell the Lord how willingly, how gladly, my poor all should be given unto Him, to spend and be spent for Him alone. And whilst such were my thoughts, the Lord seemed to pour upon me the blessings of His Grace, so that he was unto me as the dew unto Israel. Communion, heavenly and blessed ! Earnest of joys to come, and foretaste of that inheritance undefiled and that fadeth not away, where I shall see Jesus face to face, yea, behold Him as He is, not even the transparent veil of a divine faith being betwixt Him and me ! And how transcendently glorious is the further assurance, that when we do see Him as He is, we shall be like Him, partakers of His divine nature, and sharers of His glorious image. O God, my Lord, for ever be thy name adored'.

"*April* 14.—Seeing the sunset once more (for it is long since I beheld it), my soul aspired towards the plains of light, and I could conceive some such portal as yon bright scene, only brighter, brighter far, and cloudless, opened into the paradise of our God. Thither my happy spirit bent its way upon the wings of hope, faith pointing out the pathway to the golden gate, and love desiring and hastening on the soul to win so priceless an inheritance among the saints in light.

"*May* 23.—This evening I have been so allured by the love of Jesus, that I have not been able to refrain from asking the Lord to permit me to come to Himself. Nothing on earth could hold back my wishes from transporting me at once into His presence. I felt it could be no sin to desire thus eagerly for heaven. Its light, its atmosphere, its peace, its joys, yea, and its holiness, were around my soul, and earth to my eyes seemed a dreary place. But am I ready to go? O yes; Jesus has made me ready. I could not be more ready than He can make me, were I to live a century longer. His blood, His precious blood, I bear upon my heart; His righteousness declared of God, I hold for my title-deeds.

"*May* 27.—My soul rejoices in the Lord, and I would not exchange my dying hopes, surrounded as I now am with all earthly discomforts, for the greatest luxuries, and all the blandishments the world could set before me; nay, nor could it stop one minute my onward flight to

God, were the whole realm of nature, and every monarch with his crown, inviting me to linger for a while, and taste of honour, power and earthly good. No, oh, no! All that is vanity and a delusion. There is no other happiness but in knowing God, and Jesus Christ whom He has sent; in knowing Him as our merciful, gracious, long-suffering God; forgiving iniquity, transgression, and sin: and Jesus Christ as——no words can say what Jesus Christ is, when you know Him. This is the white stone, inscribed with a new name, which no one knows but he to whom it is given.

"*June* 12.—Ah! I am happy day and night, hour by hour. Asleep or awake, I am happy beyond the poor compass of language to tell. My joys are with Him whose delights have always been with the sons of men; and my heart and spirit are in heaven with the blessed. I have felt how holy is that company; I have felt how pure are their affections, and I have washed me in the blood of the Lamb, and asked my Lord for the white garment, that I too may mingle with the blaze of day, and be amongst them one of the sons of light."*

If the child of Mary, but the Son of God, is the author of such joy, when the world has taken back almost all it has to give, and before the soul enters glory, are we, as belonging to such a family, purchased at such a price, justified in the sight of God or man in living as we are doing?

* Any one that will make himself acquainted with modern science will see, in such an experience as this, the reflex action of the cerebrum brain that has been shaped through the influence of revealed religion, by one that has dedicated all to the Master's service, as the material soul vibrates in unison with the redeemed in glory.

With such a power within man, what may not man do? Is it too hard for us, when smitten on the right cheek, to turn the other also; for us, who are followers of the Lamb, heirs of glory and joint-heirs with Christ? The sceptic men of science have a perfect right to demand from us such proof; for the sciences are established on proof; and we have no authority from our Master to hold up a Bible and call it the Word of God, except we are prepared to live out its precepts. This will admit of proof. For the Bible does contain truth that may inspire man with the strength of a hero, enabling him to run into danger and to death, and in death to die a conqueror. This power must be felt by the men who are to lead the religious thought of the nineteenth century, if religion founded on Christianity is to take its place as one of the sciences established on truth, which is eternal. But if so, it must in this respect be reduced to proof, seen in the lives of the men professing to believe it, in whom purity of thought leads to purity of life, as seen in all their actions. Thus only will Christianity be established as the permanent religion of man, with the child of Mary, who is also the Son of God, as a risen Lord, reigning in the heart of His people, and operating as an active power, subduing the world as a silent conqueror. Thus shall we teach men that an open Bible is indeed a living Christ.

The Reformation gave us back an open Bible, but taught man to believe that revelation had ceased. By this we gained much; but at the same time we lost much. For the Christian religion was established on the promise that a Comforter was to come, who was to remain with the Lord's followers for ever as His felt-presence on earth, to reprove the world of sin, of righteousness, and of judgment. As Christ Himself said, " I have yet many things to say unto you, but ye cannot hear them now" (John xvi. 12), and man has no authority from God to explain away Christ's teaching, which, for all we know, may contain a new revelation, as the human soul holds communion with Christ. For, if Christ is not now and ever a felt-power in the spirit of man, our religion is a delusion, and the Bible no better than any other book, even though it contains many a "thus saith the Lord". But we Christians feel and know that Christianity, including the ideal Christ, is a heaven-born thing, and is the seed of God in the spirit of man, revealing truths to him.

Christianity is established on the Jesus of history as the risen Lord; on this, and this alone. The Bible without this is nothing, and with it, it may be called the chart of heaven, even though God is in the world, as well as in the Bible, teaching man what is truth. Christ, in man the hope of Glory, is the " Mystery which hath been hid from ages and from generations, but now is made manifest to his saints". (Col. i. 26.) This is the germ the Bible contains ; with it, we have the promise of all things becoming ours, and without it, the Bible would be no better than any other book ; for without this, it insures no certain future in the world to come ; but with Jesus occupying a point in space, as the Redeemer, a certain future is established in Him ; and where He is, thither we shall follow in course of time.

Chapter VII.

CHRIST AS THE VICARIOUS SACRIFICE; AND THE BELIEVER'S DUTY TO FOLLOW IN HIS STEPS, AND ACCEPT TRUTH FROM ALL QUARTERS.

IN this our day, when Bible truths are attacked on every hand, it is necessary for us who believe that the Bible contains the revealed Word of God, and that it is thus inspired, in a sense in which no other book is, to know what is the absolute truth which it does contain; for in the Bible there is eternal truth; the very truth which separates the human races, and divides it into two great classes, called the saved and the lost. The Bible is given to reveal God's character to man as a God of Grace or Favour in Jesus Christ, the vicarious sacrifice, the sinless man revealed in the Bible as the Saviour of the world. This, and this alone, is the absolute truth which the Bible does contain, and does reveal to sinful man. When we add to this Christ's resurrection as a great cardinal fact, which admits of proof, the character of God, as revealed in the Bible, remains absolute truth, whether man accept it or reject it. If we accept it, we receive all the benefit that flows from it, and are accepted as perfect; for the God of humanity, the God man died for us as sinners; and we are accepted as perfect* in His stead. (1 Tim.

---

* The operation of this realised perfection is manifested in the forces held together by the complicated generalised ideas which have combined to produce this effect, as in thought we take possession of all Christ has procured for us. The effect produced through this means is graphically

iii. 16.) "Without controversy great is the mystery of godliness ; God was manifest in the flesh, justified in the spirit, seen of angels, preached unto the Gentiles, believed on in the world, received up into glory." This is truth, absolute truth. When man accepts this as truth, he is united to God as a God of grace; whether he feels it or not, it is the truth that saves, and gives us the Christian's God, as the Creator and Father of Jesus Christ. Man, as a free agent, may accept or reject God thus revealed. Where he accepts, the "Lord, I believe, help thou mine unbelief," as the prayer of faith, will be soon followed by the realization of belief on man's part ; and Paul's experience will be his own, and he will be enabled to say (2 Timothy i. 12.) "I know whom I have believed, and am persuaded that he is able to keep that which I have committed unto him, against that day". Sinful man, with this experience within him, and the Bible in his hand, can rise above earth and the things of earth, as a sinner saved by grace; and rejoices in the one only true God, as the God of creation and grace. Man is thus prepared to accept absolute truth as God's expression to man from all quarters.

The Darwinian theory, if proved, must be accepted as truth, though we may feel humbled at the thought of having come from a jelly fish; or of being obliged to

described in the 36th question of the Catechism used in Scotland, in "Assurance of God's love, peace of conscience, joy in the Holy Ghost, increase of grace, and perseverance therein to the end." Through this medium, we shall say, the action and counteraction of the cerebrum brain makes itself felt in the form of reflex action, as it manifests the effect the forces communicate to it, in producing the food we employ in feeding the brain.

accept spontaneous generation. Consequently, the first Adam was not created, that is, called forth then and there, in the form of the Adam of the garden of Eden, as a perfect man, and yet he may have been evolved, and may gradually have attained to that perfect state of innocence in which we find him, when Eve was given to him as a helpmate. That is to say, Adam may have been evolved, and, through the influence of the moral and religious elements present in humanity, have attained in his generation such a condition as God was pleased to call perfect.

In this way, then, it is free to suppose that Adam attained to that perfect state. And how very easy and simple all this seems to be, when perceived in the light of our present knowledge. To many, this will seem the most natural way to render the Bible intelligent to a large class of liberal-minded Protestants that accept the miracles (say the resurrection) as established on the evidence of testimony, received from the time of the Lord till our own day. With us it will be a very easy matter to suppose, that Eve was formed by supernatural power, in a miraculous way, as a helpmate to Adam, and thus bone of his bone and flesh of his flesh; that is, both formed in the same mould; and might we not suppose that, when temptation came to her, because of the formation of her character, as being mostly guided by feeling, she was not able to resist the temptation so effectually? And might we not also suppose that her influence on her husband was very hurtful? How natural then does the explanation seem which was given as an excuse to God; the temptation was gone, the effect alone re-

Christ as the Vicarious Sacrifice. 49

mained, and now the voice of the Lord was heard in the garden in the cool of the day. (Genesis iii. 8.) From first to last, the story is one which all might comprehend to some extent. But, when it is compared with what we find in Matt. v. 28, we see that there is a still higher Christian life, which can only be understood by the class represented by Paul in Titus i. 15, where he says, that " Unto the pure all things are pure ". This class alone can comprehend the full meaning of such a life.

To the class which regards Adam, the first historical man, as the absolutely first man, the Bible, as it always has been, is sufficient. But there is a large number who believe that the earth teemed with multitudes, hundreds of thousand of years before the time of historic man; and these may see reason in the explanation which we have offered. However, where and how we came to be formed is a question of very little importance in comparison with that of being fully persuaded as to the place to which we are going. This, it must be admitted, is a matter of the deepest moment to men who are to live for ever. For if the doctrine of evolution is fully established, man must give up the old mode of rendering the Bible, and begin with the second Adam, the risen Lord. Furthermore, he must confess that, though he cannot tell where he came from, he knows where he is going to, which is a matter of greater necessity, and of much greater importance to him, a sinner saved by grace. For all will allow that evil is in the world ; and Christians, in accepting the credibility of the New Testament records, see in Christ's vicarious sacrifice God reconciling the world to Himself, as the design He had in view in originating the laws that have produced humanity as we find it. 2 Cor. v. 18, 19, 20: "And all things are of God, who hath reconciled us to Himself by Jesus Christ, and hath given to us the ministry of reconciliation; to wit, that God was in Christ, reconciling the world unto Himself, not imputing their trepasses unto them; and hath committed unto us the word of reconciliation. Now then we are ambassadors for Christ, as though God did beseech you by us: we pray you in Christ's stead, be ye reconciled to God." The reconciliation spoken of here necessitates and will produce purity of life, that we may realise the great Apostle's exhortation, " Be blameless and harmless, the sons of God, without rebuke, in the midst of a crooked and perverse nation, among whom ye shine as lights in the world; holding forth the word of life" (Phil. ii. 15, 16); and thus reflect Christ's character. For it is clearly revealed in the New Testament records, that this is the God-appointed means whereby these attributes of the Saviour of mankind are to be made known to the world; especially is this made clear to us in Phil. ii. 12, 13, 14, where the command is given, "Work out your own salvation with fear and trembling, for it is God that worketh in you, both to will and to do of his good pleasure. Doing all things without murmurings and disputings". This, when reduced to proof, and seen in the believer's life, is the God-appointed work which the followers of Christ are left in the world of sin and sorrow to accomplish, realising His presence as a felt power within, leading them on to glory and to God. So the Comforter, which was to reprove the world of sin, and reflect Christ's character, as it is revealed

Christ as the Vicarious Sacrifice.   51

in the New Testament records, teaches the world what He means, when He says in John xvi. from the 7th to the 15th verse, that He had many things to say unto the people, which His disciples at the first could not bear. This is just what every Christian man and woman must learn for himself and herself from God, and in this sense each and all are inspired of God, and prepared by Him for the work He hath appointed them to do. For while sin remains, the world will demand that the just die for the unjust, as a sacrifice for sin, and Christ's redeemed ones are accepted as just in Him, their Head, who died for them. Each one is His representative, sent to convince the world of sin, and of righteousness, and of judgment, by striving after the perfection He has enjoined, where He says, in Matt. v. 48, "Be ye therefore perfect, even as your Father in heaven is perfect". The Bible, as inspired of God, will admit of proof nothing short of this—it is either thus, or Christianity is a myth; it is either Christ as the Saviour of man, reconciling the world unto Himself by and through His redeemed ones, or the world is no better of the Christ of Christianity as a vicarious sacrifice, reconciling the world unto Himself by not imputing to them their trespasses. Man is thus left a free agent,* and may accept Christ as a sinner, saved by grace, striving unto death to attain perfection, or purity of thought and life, and thus entering eternal bliss. Or he may reject Christ, and meet God as a just Judge; feeling that the "Judge of

---

* A term intended to represent a state of consciousness present in every one as he *feels* he has power to choose between two courses of action.

all the earth" will do right. Every man and woman, with an open Bible, has his and her choice to make, and must appear as rejected or accepted of God. Man, by a profession of Christianity, accepts God as a God of grace or favour; and the world has a right to demand from such purity of life and thought, as the evidence of belief, the fruit of Christ's death. Are we not then all to be blamed for the evil that threatens us, by men everywhere saying, show us the Lord (or what is truth)? These fail to recognise Him as the felt-power in the soul, presented in conscience, convincing them of sin, and so they resist and refuse to yield to the influence of God manifested in the flesh—flesh here being understood to admit of the double meaning, as the feeling and the felt—and revealed in the mighty power of faith (taken in the scriptural sense) over mind* which is seen and felt by all men, by prince and peasant, by master and servant, by mistress and maid. Moreover, in the Christian this mighty power manifests itself unto death; for Christ died for them that they might die to save others, not resisting evil, Matt. v. 49, but submitting rather to be wronged. Thus they make their calling and election sure, holding forth the Word of life, and revealing "Christ in them the hope of glory". Nothing short of this will prove to man and woman that the Bible is true. When all are doubting, this, and this alone, is absolute truth, or the fruit springing from the absolute truth of revealed religion. Moreover, it admits of proof, as the power of God, a God of grace in the soul of

---

* I deal with the material *human soul* capable of receiving impressions from God.

sinful man. As sinners, saved by grace, we enter glory, and as such we shall be known throughout all eternity. No man can be better; and no man in Christendom need be worse, for Christ came to seek and save the lost, as the fruit of His vicarious sacrifice.

Chapter VIII.

THE DEVELOPED RELIGIOUS ELEMENT, CONTRASTED WITH THE FRUITS OF THE VICARIOUS SACRIFICE.

THERE is a party that are not Christians, but worship God as the God of truth and nature. Thus they worship the Christian's God, but do not recognise Christ as the Son of God, and have therefore no right to be called Christian, for they only are Christian who accept the Christ of Christianity as the risen Lord. All that deny this are false to themselves and their God, if they accept for themselves, or demand from us the name of Christian, even while they may be more pure and holy, so far as man can judge them. There are many who are Christian in heart and profession only, but that gives them no title to the claim of being Christians; we are Christians for what Christ did for us, and not for what we are striving to do for Christ, from a sense of gratitude and love, in return for what He has done by reconciling the world to Himself as a God of grace. We accept salvation first, and then do His work to show our gratitude; this and this alone secures for us the name of Christians; and when men disallow this, and take to themselves the name of Christ to distinguish them for their deeds of charity and love, they are false to themselves and false to their God, whether they feel it or not. For if the Jesus of History did not rise from the dead, there could have been no Christ of Christianity, and therefore no society formed in His name, and by this power doing the God-appointed work of charity and love. It looks as if this new religion which relies on the Divine presence in the nature of man, "this religious element, established on scientific ground,"* and called absolute religion, wished to claim for itself all the deeds of charity and purity which Christ's death and resurrection have accomplished in Christendom.

This mistake has arisen in consequence of Christ having worked by His people, though unperceived and unfelt on their part ; in consequence also of his followers not having had clear views of Christ's character and works, and having therefore seemed to do good for the sake of goodness. They are, thus far, false to themselves and false to their God of grace, and many of them, from this mistake, are all their lives subject to bondage. They are indeed safe for eternity, though they do not realise it ; "Christ is in them the hope of glory," though by reason of unbelief they fail to see Him with the eye of faith ; and thus mistaking the Bible for Christ, they cling to it with the despair of drowning men. But, for all this, it follows that they place themselves and their friends of absolute religion in a false position : the one set clinging to the Bible because it reveals the God of grace, the God that "so loved the world, that he gave his only begotten Son, that whosoever believeth in him should not perish, but have everlasting life" (John iii. 16); the other set clinging to the Bible, because it teaches more of purity and charity than any other book ; and, as they say, because the Jesus of history was the greatest

* In the expression of the sentiment universally present in the race.

religious genius of the race. But they have no risen Lord to adore and love. The Christ of Christianity, as the Son of God, is nothing to them; they have nothing to lose by losing Him as a divine being, and heaven is as full to them without Him as with Him. God is to them only as the God of truth.

Their redeemer is within; they call it conscience and reason; charity and purity are life to them. This is absolute religion; God is everywhere, but nowhere in particular. For them Christ has not gone to prepare a place, but He has gone to prepare one for us Christians, (John xiv. 2), and He has left with us the Comforter, promised in this chapter, as a felt power to prepare us. Our Redeemer died on the cross, rose from the dead, and is now in heaven, as God and Man: He is without us, preparing a place for us, as well as in us, preparing us for the place. Charity and purity are the fruits of His work in us, in the cultivation of which He is preparing us for his kingdom; and we, in so far as we strive after this charity and purity, are preparing ourselves for the place we are to occupy in that kingdom. They of this party of absolute religion are doing for themselves what Christ, the Son of God, did for us; they are redeeming their souls, but Christ has redeemed ours, and sent us to do this work for Him in the world; that is to say, by a vicarious sacrifice to redeem the world to Him. But what a poor bargain He has made in the case of many of us! for we are much more our own than Christ's. We want the world to live in and enjoy, but Christ to die in, and appear before God as His.

They of absolute religion are better than we in

some respects; for they do good for the sake of goodness, and thus leave the world better than they found it. "They build wiser than they know, for God will reward them according to their works." We take eternal life and sometimes give nothing, and thus leave the world worse than we found it; for Christians sometimes lead others into sin: they do evil, and call it good to save themselves; and thus we reverse the law established by Christ as absolute Christianity, as seen in His vicarious sacrifice. The new life is a life of faith; for it unites us to Christ, and therefore this sentiment is eternal as God. Charity and purity, as the fruit of the religious element in the other class, is life to them; it may or it may not insure eternal life. They would thus take away the children's bread, and give them in return a stone. They can rise no higher than hope, only hope; still the world is the better of them in as much as they do good for goodness' sake. We, as the fruit of Christ's vicarious sacrifice, may rise, and many of us do rise to certainty; but how little do we possess of the new life, that vicarious sacrifice, that "faith which worketh by love," and "which overcometh the world"! This mysterious power Christ describes when he says (in Matt. xvii. 20), "If ye have faith as a grain of mustard seed," nothing would be impossible to you. What of this faith do we show, by works accomplished in God's strength?

Scientific research has proved that vicarious sacrifice, death giving life, is the law that governs the material world, and Christendom is produced to prove, by the effect of that great Vicarious Sacrifice, that God has done for man what man could not do for himself. Man, without Christ, in striving after perfection, is striving to do for himself what the first Adam lost at the fall; whatever that may mean, for God is absolute purity and truth; and evil is in the world, as all will allow. Life, as the fruit of doing good for goodness' sake, is only hope at the best; but the life of the Christian, the life that procures in him the fruit of charity and purity, is the life he has derived from that great vicarious sacrifice, and is eternal; for it is God in him saving man, because he is a sinner. Man refusing to be saved as a sinner, though he feels that he is a sinner, and, while allowing that God is perfect, despising offered grace, and willing to accept no favour, will have to meet God as a judge, who will render to all their due, and take what comes of it; for God says, he must either be served by Christ or not saved at all in the scriptural sense of being saved, that is, a sinner saved by grace—nothing less and nothing more.

If the two classes would accept their proper position before God and man, it would be well for the world and well for themselves; the one class are sinners saved by grace, the other class are sinners not saved by grace; they leave their present and their future to all eternity in God's hands. As one of them has said, "I indeed believe with Jesus of Nazareth, that I shall ascend to His Father and my Father, to His God and my God"; thus taking the Jesus of history as an Example, but not as a Substitute. Herein lies the difference that divides the human race.

It is a difference of God's making, and man has his choice to belong to the one class or the other. We Christians, however, have no authority to call the members of the other class bad men. Many of them are good, doing God's work, and we are enjoying the fruit of their labours in many ways. For many of this class are our men of science; and, nex tto Christ's vicarious sacrifice, science has done most for the world, being the God-appointed work which the first Adam was set to perform. (Eccles. i. 13.) That is to say, the men of science make known to us God's character in the uniformity of the laws of nature present everywhere, manifesting a universal power. From God they came, so to God they will go, and take the place prepared for them by their search after truth. They worship God as a God of truth; we worship Him as a God of grace, in and through Jesus Christ as the Son of God.

When the first Adam and Eve sewed the fig leaves together to make themselves aprons, and hid themselves from the eye of God, they realised their state, that they were impure, and they felt it, for they had disobeyed a command. We may suppose they procured for themselves the coats of skin, when they offered the first sacrifice, as an offering for sin, to reconcile themselves to God. The God of grace may have been preparing sinful man to accept the great Vicarious Sacrifice, the God-appointed means by which sinful man is reconciled to God as a God of grace. The Bible, as containing the inspired Word of God, reveals this to man, a sinner, and Christ's resurrection is the great cardinal fact to prove to him that God has prepared for him reconciliation, in and through Jesus Christ, who is that vicarious sacrifice. We see the effect of faith over mind in subduing and conquering the affections and lusts, by binding the heart of man to God in adoration and love, as the God of grace, and in thus preparing man to glorify Him, as such, through all eternity. When we see the spirit or soul of sinful man thus clinging to God as a reconciled Father, or to the Christ of Christianity as the God of humanity, as God and man, taking on Him our nature, and dying in our stead, we are made to feel that faith gives life; that God hath indeed made coats of skin, and clothed Adam and Eve, when he procured for man this Vicarious Sacrifice, called in the Scriptures the righteousness of God. The influence of this sacrifice is seen in faith which, working by love, is the fruit of Christ's death, which hath procured on earth all the works of charity Christendom has produced. Christianity says, God as a God of grace has provided a sacrifice for us, which we may accept, and thus appear before God as sinners saved by grace. It is thus that all Christians stand in the sight of God, whether they feel it or not. As for the other class, those who believe in an absolute religion, they will stand or fall by their own merit; for the moral and religious element which is in man, procures for him, without the vicarious sacrifice, the fig-leaf aprons; for God is justice and truth. Their Redeemer is within; they will abide by the consequence, and through all eternity they will remain what they make themselves. Hence they must remain a separate and distinct creation. An innate sense of truth can procure the fig-leaves for covering, and God will not despise them though he procured for others of the same race coats of skin, by the vicarious sacrifice of Christ. These have made their choice, so have we Christians; therefore, let us now live together in this understanding, that they are God's children of nature, but we are God's children of grace. Believing this, let us gladly serve each other in our day and generation. We are safe for eternity. Let us live above the world, as the Master himself has told us— " Ye are not of the world, even as I am not of the world ". (John vii. 16.) Natural religion assuredly was never intended to drive man from Christ, but we Christians, by living as we are doing, have had that effect, and we now suffer the consequences, in seeing so many of our number asking in despair—what is truth ?

I cannot do justice in describing the class we have had under view. I will, therefore, close this part of my subject by placing before my readers the 6th and 7th chapters of a book by Theodore Parker, entitled, " A Discourse on matters pertaining to religion ". This eminent writer is one of the class with which this chapter has been dealing, and though he is no Christian, all must allow that he displays much beauty of character in the book I have named. But Christ as a risen Lord is nothing to him, and, indeed, another of the same party, Charles Voysey, in the preface to this work, very honestly repudiates the name of Christian being applied to his party ; for that name is only applicable to those who are united through Christ to God.

This party has an Idea wider and deeper than that of the Catholic or Protestant, namely, that God still inspires men as much as ever; that he is immanent in spirit as in space. For the present purpose, and to avoid circumlocution, this doctrine may be called SPIRITUALISM. This relies on no Church, Tradition, or Scripture, as the last ground and infallible rule ; it counts these things teachers, if they teach, not masters; helps,

if they help us, not authorities. It relies on the divine presence
in the Nature of Man; the eternal Word of God, which is
TRUTH, as it speaks through the faculties he has given. It
believes God is near the soul, as matter to the sense; thinks
the canon of revelation not yet closed, nor God exhausted. It
sees him in Nature's perfect work; hears him in all true Scripture, Jewish or Phœnician; feels him in the aspiration of the
heart; stoops at the same fountain with Moses and Jesus, and
is filled with living water. It calls God Father and Mother,
not King; Jesus brother, not Redeemer; Heaven home;
Religion nature. It loves and trusts, but does not fear. It
sees in Jesus a man living manlike, highly gifted, though not
without errors, and living with earnest and beautiful fidelity to
God, stepping thousands of years before the race of men; the
profoundest religious genius God has raised up, whose words
and works help us to form and develop the idea of a complete
religious man. But he lived for himself; died for himself;
worked out his own salvation, and we must do the same, for
one man cannot live for another more than he can eat or
sleep for him. It is no personal Christ, but the Spirit of
Wisdom, Holiness, Love, that creates the well-being of men;
a life at one with God. The divine incarnation is in all mankind.

The aim it proposes is a complete union of Man with God,
till every action, thought, wish, feeling, is in perfect harmony
with the divine will. The "Christianity" it rests in is not the
point Man goes through in his progress, as the Rationalist, not
the point God goes through in his development, as the super-
naturalist maintains; but Absolute Religion, the point where
Man's will and God's will are one and the same. Its Source
is absolute, its Aim absolute, its Method absolute. It lays down
no creed; asks no symbol; reverences exclusively no time nor
place, and therefore can use all time and every place. It
reckons forms useful to such as they help; one man may com-
mune with God through the bread and the wine, emblems of
the body that was broken, and the blood that was shed, in the
cause of truth; another may hold communion through the moss
and the voilet, the mountain, the ocean, or the Scripture of
suns, which God has writ in the sky; it does not make the

means the end; it prizes the signification more than the sign. It knows nothing of that puerile distinction between Reason and Revelation; never finds the alleged contradiction between Good Sense and Religion; Its Temple is all space; its Shrine the good heart; its Creed all truth; its Ritual works of love and utility: its Profession of faith a manly life, works without, faith within, love of God aud man. It bids man do duty, and take what comes of it, grief or gladness. In every desert it opens fountains of living water; gives balm for every wound, a pillow in all tempests, tranquillity in each distress. It does good for goodness' sake; asks no pardon for its sins, but gladly serves out the time. It is meek and reverent of truth, but scorns all falsehood, though upheld by the ancient and honourable of the earth. It bows to no idols, of wood or flesh, of gold or parchment, or spoken wind; neither Mammon, neither the Church, nor the Bible, nor yet Jesus, but God only. It takes all helps it can get; counts no good word profane, though a heathen spoke it; no lie sacred, though the greatest prophet had said the word. Its redeemer is within; its salvation within; its heaven and its oracle of God. It falls back on perfect Religion; asks no more: is satisfied with no less. The personal Jesus is its encouragement, for he helps to reveal the possible of man. Its watchword is, BE PERFECT AS GOD. With its eye on the Infinite, it goes through the striving and the sleep of life; equal to duty, not above it; fearing not whether the ephemeral wind blow east or west. It has the strength of the Hero; the tranquil sweetness of the Saint. It makes each man his own priest; but accepts gladly him that speaks a holy word. Its prayer in words, in works, in feeling, in thought, is this, Thy will be done; its Church that of all holy souls, the Church of the first-born, called by whatever name.*

Let others judge the merits and defects of this scheme. It has never organised a Church; yet in all ages, from the earliest, men have, more or less freely, set forth its doctrines. We find these men among the despised and forsaken. The world was not ready to receive them. They have been stoned and spit

---

* It is unnecessary to enlarge on this scheme, since so much has been said of it already. See Book I. ch. vii. § 3, and Book II. ch. viii., and Book III. ch. v. vii.

upon in all the streets of the world. The "pious" have burned them as haters of God and man; the "wicked" called them bad names and let them go. They have served to flesh the swords of the Catholic Party, and feed the fires of the Protestant. But flame and steel will not consume them. The seed they have sown is quick in many a heart, their memory blessed by such as live divine. These were the men at whom the world opens wide the mouth and draws out the tongue and utters its impotent laugh; but they received the fire of God on their altar, and kept living its sacred flame. They go on the forlorn hope of the race; but Truth puts a wall of fire about them and holds the shield over their head in the day of trouble. The battle of Truth seems often lost, but is always won. Her enemies but erect the bloody scaffolding where the workmen of God go up and down, and with divine hands build wiser than they know. When the scaffolding falls the temple will appear.

Now then, if it be asked, what relation the Church sustains to the religious Element, the answer is plain: The Soul is greater than the Church. Religion, as Reason, is of God; the Absolute Religion, and therefore eternal, based on God alone; the Christian Churches, Catholic and Protestant, are of men, and therefore transient. Let them say their say; man is God's child, and free of their tyranny; he must not accept their limitations, nor bow their authority, but go on his glorious way. The Churches are a human affair quite as much as the State; ecclesiastical, like political institutions, are changeable, human, subject to the caprices of public opinion. The divine right of kings to bear sway over the Body, and the divine right of the Churches to rule over the Soul, both rest on the same foundation—on a LIE.

The Christian Church, like Fetichism, Polythesim, like the State, has been projected out of man in his development and passage through the ages; its several phases correspond to Man's development and civilisation, and are inseparable from it. They are the index of the condition of Man. They bear their justification in themselves. They could not have been but as they were. To censure or approve Catholicism, or Protestantism, is to censure or approve the state of the race which gave rise to these forms; to condemn Absolute Religion called by whatever name, is to condemn both Man and God.

Jesus fell back on God, aiming to teach absolute Religion, absolute Morality; the truth its own authority, his works his witness. The early Christians fell back on the authority of Jesus; their successors, on the Bible, the work of the apostles and prophets; the next generation on the Church, the work of apostles and fathers. The world retreads this ground. Protestantism delivers us from the tyranny of the Church, and carries us back to the Bible. Biblical criticism frees us from the thraldom of the Scripture, and brings us to the authority of Jesus. Philosophical Spiritualism liberates us from all personal and finite authority, and restores us to GOD, the primeval fountain, whence the Church, the Scriptures, and Jesus have drawn all the water of life, wherewith they fill their urns. Thence and thence only, shall mankind obtain Absolute Religion and spiritual well-being. Is this a retreat for mankind? No, it is progress without end. The race of men never before stood so high as now; with suffering, tears, and blood they have toiled, through barbarism and war, to their present height, and we see the world of promise opening upon our eye. But what is not behind is before us.

Institutions arise as they are needed, and fall when their work is done. Of these things nothing is fixed. Institutions are provisional, man only is final. Corporeal despotism is getting ended; will the spiritual tyranny last for ever? A will above our puny strength, marshals the race of men, using our freedom, virtue, folly as instruments to one vast end—the harmonious development of Man. We see the art of God in the web of a spider, and the cell of a bee, but have not skill to discern it in the march of Man. We repine at the slowness of the future in coming, or the swiftness of the past in fleeting away; we sigh for the fabled "Millennium" to advance, or pray Time to restore us the Age of Gold. It avails nothing. We cannot hurry God, nor retard him. Old schools and new schools seem as men that stand on the shore of some Atlantic bay, and shout, to frighten back the tide, or urge it on. What boots their cry? Gently the sea swells under the moon, and, in the hour of God's appointment, the tranquil tide rolls in, to inlet and river, to lave the rocks, to bear on its bosom the ship of the merchant, the weeds of sea. We complain, as our fathers; let us rather rejoice, for questions less weighty than these have in other ages been disposed of only with the point of the sword, and the thunder of cannon—put off, not settled.

If the opinions advanced in this Discourse be correct, then Religion is above all institutions, and can never fail; they shall perish, but Religion endure: they shall wax old as a garment; they shall be changed, and the places that knew them shall know them no more for ever; but Religion is ever the same, and its years shall have no end.

CHAPTER IX.

ALL BELIEVERS ARE ENTITLED TO ETERNAL LIFE AND MAY BE VIEWED AS SAVED.

GOD, as a God of mercy and grace, reconciles man to Himself, through Jesus Christ; all that are putting their trust in Him as a God of this nature are Christians, and are to be received as such. The distinction which God has Himself made is clearly laid before us in the two following passages, John iii. 3-6, "He that believeth on the Son hath eternal life;" and Heb. iii. 16, and some "could not enter in because of unbelief". By this we are bound to regard all, without exception, who profess belief in Christ, as saved men and women; this is evidently what Christ means in the sermon on the mount, when he says, Matt. vii. 12, "Judge not, that ye be not judged, for with what judgment ye judge, ye shall be judged, and with what measure ye mete, it shall be measured to you again". Christ came to save sinners as such, and unbelief is the only sin that a professing Christian can be condemned for. Good and bad, rich and poor, old and young, are all included in God's promise "Whosoever believeth in Him should not perish, but have everlasting life" (John iii. 15); and it is in opposition to His command that we judge and condemn any. If some of us have attained to the assurance by faith, which all are entitled to, we are no better in God's sight than the very weakest believer. Whatever our state may be, it is Christ's death that hath saved our soul. Man is either saved or lost, in a scriptural sense, because Christ died for us. God did not send us here, and give us strong faith, to judge and condemn our weaker brother, but to bear his infirmities by taking him by the hand as a sinner, saved of grace, as much entitled to heaven as any of us. For Christ died to save all as sinners, and though any one should fall seventy times seven, if he says he repents, the Master's command is, forgive him; and He, the Lord Jesus, is not less merciful than He would have us to be. This also is surely what He means when He says, " He that is greatest among you let him be your servant ". It is much more difficult to get men, as sinners, to believe that they are saved, than that they are to try to save themselves; they think that because Christ condemns sin, He hates the sinner. A sense of the iron grasp of sin often keeps men silent; because they feel sin so strong within them, they fear God, and will not trust Him. But when they once draw nigh to God, with the " Lord, I believe, help thou my unbelief," the light begins to come, and the sinner thus approaching, will soon realise in his inmost heart the promise fulfilled in his case, that " He that worketh not, but believeth on Him that justifieth the ungodly, his faith is counted for righteousness " (Rom. iv. 5); and with joy and gladness he will feel the truth of the Gospel, and hail the glad tidings as the source of the new joy he possesseth. As a sinner, saved by grace, he will hate sin now; because he is saved, and not because he is lost or may be lost. Oh that we Christians that know this would teach men and women to realise it, and treat all as Christians who profess the name of Christ, and do our duty to them as Christians, thus doing to others as we would have others to do to us! Then the spirit of Christ would be seen and felt amongst us; envy, and malice, and evil-speaking would disappear. The same eternal home is to belong to all that believe; then why not act as if we felt it here, and now, seeing this is truth, and we cannot change truth? We are all one in Christ; Christ is our only hope; we are acccpted in Him; it is Christ on the cross that saved us; we are all saved or lost alike. We that enjoy much of the Master's presence, should have stronger faith than some; and though that does not make us any better in His sight, it makes us happier here, and it ought to make us more useful; for what we take in of life by faith, we ought to give out by energy in sympathy: we have got much, and much therefore shall have to account for. We may well ask ourselves, is not that text in Matt. xvii. 30, where the Master says, "Many that are first shall be last, and the last shall be first," applicable to us? You, who do not know that you are saved, though saved as much as we, little know what we have to strive against, and how often we feel just like the Pharisee, though we are no better than the vilest that are trusting to a God of mercy. Nay, we sometimes feel and act just as if God had given to us authority to make the distinction, by saying this one is saved, and that one is lost, which is just assuming the part of God, and judging man; we have no authority for that. We may reprove each other of sin, as Christians; that is all God would have us do: He alone can condemn or acquit. The world must take us as it finds us: that is to say, the world that Christ came to save, it is to be our judge and must judge us by our actions; now and here it is the Master's command that it be so. The righteous and the wicked live together, and God alone can or may separate them. It is in this way only that strong faith can be of any use to the world; not to condemn, but to acquit. We have authority from God to call all Christian brethren and sisters that profess the name of Christ, and to tell them that it is their belief in Christ that saves them; and because they believe they are indeed saved, John iii. 36, and are as much entitled to heaven as any saint on earth. Being saved because Christ died, we have no merit in ourselves, and can have no merit. Christ came to save sinners; and when that is accepted we receive the benefit of His death. It is the weakest and the worst that the Christian of strong faith is sent to comfort; not to condemn, but to acquit on the ground of their belief, and that alone. When we act thus we are indeed ministering spirits, doing His work in His name, not judging, but acquitting. For God sent not His Son into the world to condemn it, but to save it. (John iii. 17). We must get men to believe that first; and when they realise it, their own consciences, thus enlightened by the Comforter, will reprove them of sin. We that have found mercy may direct them to this power within them, as the evidence of Christ in them, and as the fruit of their belief causing the spirit to war against the flesh. Further we may show that, in so far as they yield to this influence in striving against what they feel to be wrong, they are working with Christ as heirs of glory. Christ must convince of sin first, and in His strength they and we all are to strive against it, but we have no authority to dictate to any man what course he is to take; we are rather to direct him to the Word of God (John xvii. 17), and leave his own conscience to teach him his duty. Some Christians condemn one thing, some another, and seem to forget that we as Christians are each, for himself and herself, to ask God to teach us, and to act according to our own sense of right or wrong; having the one broad rule as our duty to man, namely, to do to others as we would be done unto. For God will have willing servants and not bondmen, but free men who feel that to their own Master they stand or fall; for, as Christ frees men, they have a right to tread His earth as men accepted by Him. Not only so; they are entitled to demand from their *fellow-Christians* that they should be recognised as such, for what they believe and not for what they do. All unrighteousness is sin, the evil thought,* in God's sight, as much as the evil action; "be ye perfect," is His command to all. It is not the proud Pharisee as he says, "stand by, I am holier than thou," but the publican with his humbler "Lord, be merciful to me a sinner," that the Lord acquits, and accepts.

By setting up a standard of righteousness, as is done by many true children of God, they tempt the weak

---

* An evil thought is meant to imply cherishing an evil sentiment in any form, always bearing in mind we are not responsible for the expression of thought as the reflex action of the cerebrum brain; it only becomes sin when we cherish the sentiment by permitting the feeling to rest and generate in the conscious mind.

brother either to act the hypocrite, by professing more love to God than he feels, or drive him away from Christian influence, which if less tyrannically exercised might and would have helped forward. But he is too honest to be a hypocrite, and will not profess more than he feels. I would therefore plead for others what I demand for myself as a Christian, freedom of thought and freedom of action; to serve God according to my sense of right; and only expect to be taken for a Christian by the world in so far as I prove my faith by my works; to worship God where and how I please; this is the freedom I believe Christ has bought for all His redeemed ones; and we that believe have a right to act as Christ's redeemed ones, free as the air we breathe; and ready to help our weak brother by taking him by the hand and lifting him up in Christ's stead till we convince him that Christ came to save sinners, and showing him that only as a sinner, and only because he is a sinner, can he claim to be called christian; for Christ has no mercy to offer except *we* we come as such. We that have strong faith may help many thus, but only thus. We do not want to make mankind hypocrites but honest, taking Christ for what he is to them as sinners, and believing in a God of mercy, able and willing to save.

What I say here I believe to be truth, and have faith in God that He will give me strength to act on it: to my own master I stand or fall, feeling I am responsible alone to Him; taking the Bible as His written Word, and His promised presence as a felt-power within me, teaching me to do His work by taking all professing Christians, however sinful, as erring Christians, but not lost, and therefore as much entitled to the benefit of Christ's death as I or any of His redeemed are. For we all are accepted on the ground of what He is, and not of what we may ourselves be. I thus regard the weakest and the worst in faith as Christians, and lead them back to God. That God, who "so loved the world as to give His only begotten Son" to save it, has not cast them off; and I dare not, believing as I do that the vilest and the worst are most longed for and pitied by Him, just because they are least willing to approach, in consequence of the deep load of sin that seems to separate them; for they have not yet learned by experience that He loves the sinner though He hates the sin. But this is just what my strong faith has taught me; this is the advantage of knowing God as a God of love, willing to save all that trust Him through Jesus Christ.

In a religion where belief is life, and where the evil thought is sin, how dare men, professing the same belief, judge fellow-men to condemn them? I take my stand here, and all that profess His name I accept as His redeemed ones; and hope to win many of the worst back to peace and happiness, not as bondmen but free men; free because Christ died for them; and man is responsible alone to God, who saves all that come to Him in Christ's name.

Belief, as a state of the mind, can be known directly only to the individual, so that, as professing Christians, all have a right to the benefit of the doubt, and to be accepted by fellow-Christians as believers, and therefore saved.

Chapter X.

MIND THE BASE FOR CHRISTIANITY TO WORK UPON.

CHRISTIANITY comes to man with the authority of a divinely-inspired religion — dealing with humanity as body and mind, the soil prepared of God to receive it. Man thus formed of intellect, feeling, and will is in a prepared state, and Christianity comes to him as such to create in man humanity as an instinct, and the love of liberty as consuming.

In dealing with the intellect as composed of the three faculties, discrimination, similarity, and retentiveness, Christianity teaches man by reason the change that is taking place in mind through the moulding influence of the Spirit of God in the soul of man. Christianity presupposes that man is capable of conceiving God, or perceiving that there is an intelligence at the heart of everything; but my subject deals with the Bible as inspired, and man as believing in the facts of Christianity, and thus worshipping God as the Father of Jesus Christ, through a crucified Redeemer, by whom sinful men are to approach God as reconciled children, with the Abba, Father. The Bible deals with the mind of man, teaching that, though he has no control over what thoughts may come (Matt. xv. 19), yet, as a free agent, he has the power of rejecting or accepting at will what thought he will retain in conscious memory. The Bible and mental science agree on these two points, that men have no control over what thoughts may come, but that we may accept or reject at will by occupying our mind with the subjects that we prefer.

The prayer of faith is the means we are to employ on Bible authority. By accepting the facts of Christianity as the seed of God in the mind of man we become a new species, with man as the genus, and belief as the distinguishing quality. The facts referred to are intended to imply the life, death, and resurrection of the Lord Jesus Christ : on these facts Christendom rests, and they will admit of proof, by the evidence of testimony ; with this the intellect is satisfied. Now feeling, in the shape of love to God and man, may and must take the lead when humanity is to become an instinct (1 John iv. 18), and with the resurrection of the body in view, accepted in faith, it is no more than Christ has a right to expect of His people. In the resurrection body we shall understand the meaning of John xii. 24: " Except a corn of wheat fall into the ground and die, it abideth alone : but if it die, it bringeth forth much fruit " ; and this is further explained in the doctrine of the conservation of energy.

Thus is it that science lends its aid in unfolding the full significance of Bible teaching. The men of science, on the other hand, need Christianity in order that by the love of God, revealed in it, they may have the emotional side of their nature stimulated and fully developed.

CHAPTER XI.

MAN PRESENTED BEFORE GOD AS SEEN IN THE INWARD MAN.

IF absolute religion and absolute Christianity are to be accepted in the world for what they really are, then both are of God, though worshipping Him through different mediums. The one, worshipping God through nature, does good for the sake of goodness, asks no pardon for its sins, but gladly serves out its time, its redeemer being within, where also is its heaven and its oracle of God. The other worships God as the God of grace or mercy, regarding the Bible as containing His revealed will, Jesus Christ as both God and man, the God of humanity as the ideal God of the human race, the great Vicarious Sacrifice, the medium through which death temporal gives life eternal; and this life eternal is faith realised.

Again, faith is the power employed by God to operate on the mind of man, to subdue and mould it into willing submission by striving to overcome the defilement which dwells therein, and which Christ condemns in Matt. xv. 19, 20, where he says "out of the heart proceed evil thoughts, murders, adulteries, fornications, thefts, false witness, blasphemies: these are the things that defile a man". Faith thus purifies the world through the energy of life by making its influence felt in deeds of kindness.

They of absolute religion appear before God for what they are or do themselves; we of absolute Christianity for what Christ has done for us.

But we appeal to the world to test us individually by our actions; a man's belief is a thing between himself and his God; the world is to judge us by our actions, and that alone. Matt. vii. 20: " By their fruits ye shall know them ". This then is the test which the Master himself, the Lord Jesus, applied to all the human race, and in accordance with it any judgment may be pronounced between man and man.

We Christians, that have the Lord Jesus Christ as a felt-power within, and an object of worship here and also in heaven, have a motive power high enough to carry us above time and sense.

Well, how do our spiritual teachers stand in this respect? Are they true to their profession, and do their hearts acquit them in the sight of God as teaching the doctrines they are teaching, not because the Bible says so, but because they have experienced the truth of it in their own souls, as teachers sent from God, with a message to man; for all truth comes from God; and it proves itself as such, when it exalts God, and humbles man, and leads to purity of thought and life. And no man has a right in God's sight to possess more than he feels. If he preaches faithfulness in all things, do we find him faithful and true when we trust him with no more religion in the pulpit than out of it. A false profession cannot be accepted as service rendered to the God of truth and righteousness; for man is false or true according as he appears to God in his inward man.

Again, what of our Christian judges, as they judge in their Master's name, doing justice between man and man? If the universal rule may be applied anywhere with effect, surely it is here, where the judge for the time takes the place of his Master, the great I Am of the universe, to see that justice is done, as a centre of gravity; for here we ask not for mercy, but only for justice in the Master's name, in all things doing whatever he would that men should do to him, knowing that he is entirely responsible for his own conduct, and that the case, as dismissed by him from the bar, will be judged again where all will be real, where man will appear what in his heart he really is.

Well, what are we to say of the summing up of the Lord Chief Justice in a recent famous case? We do not ask, is the claimant Arthur Orton or is he Roger Tichborne? that is settled for this world. But it is not the last scene, as the journals of the day call it; there is one other scene where all will be real, though it may be a long way off. Yet nothing is really old in eternity, where the judge and the claimant will stand side by side at the final judgment as men, each responsible to God for the deeds done in the flesh. Sir Alexander Cockburn, the gifted judge of '72, will be what his heart proves him to be, and in his case Matt. vii. 12 is surely applicable. If his Master, while reading his heart, can say, "Well done, thou good and faithful servant, thou hast been faithful over a few things, I will make thee ruler over many things, enter thou into the joy of thy Lord" (Matthew xxv. 21), then it is indeed well with him. With God within, with God overhead, and with

God as judge throughout eternity, it must be well. God shall judge.*

Well, what of our men of wealth and influence, that hold the Bible to be inspired of God, are they rendering to all their due by doing the part to the weak and the

* This part was written [after the so-called Arthur Orton was condemned to two terms of seven years' servitude—that is to say, to fourteen years in which he is compelled to generate so much energy a day, as work done for the British nation in the shape of retribution for his previous conduct, so that when he takes his place at the judgment-seat of Christ along with Sir Alex. Cockburn, the energy thus generated and presented in his muscles will be a precise measurement of the judge's penalty for the offence committed. Therefore, if cause and effect can thus be measured with certainty, little will be left for Christ to do as judge, while the words of Matt. vii. 2, "For with what judgment ye judge ye shall be judged," stand out to all eternity as God's word delivered by the God-man, and destined to be fulfilled at the final judgment-day when all await their sentence.

To the above I would add a few remarks in reference to the Penge case. We hear there are two men and two women condemned to death for a murder, though no murder is proved to have been committed. As we listen to the summing up of Justice Hawkins, and see the jury return with a verdict of guilty (when no murder is proved to have taken place), we may well ask is the jury a cat's paw to the judge: as we hear the judge pronounce the sentence in the most heartless manner ever adopted by an English judge; as he brands the four, thus condemned to die, with the crime of the murder of a child not certainly proved to have been murdered; as he thus stands as judge, apparently without one ray of human sympathy in his breast; as we see the prisoners leave the bar, we ask is this British justice? Is this the voice of the nation making itself felt in the final judgment that Alice Rhodes should be reprieved while the other three are consigned to a life without hope. As we see the wife separated from her husband, the infant torn from the mother's breast; as they dress her in the convict garb and lead her in despair to the convict cell, for this we are tempted to ask, are we to be ruled by a modified British Inquisition, and will the nation stand aside in silence while the three condemned ones live on without hope? But the time for Christ to judge as God is coming, when as a nation we shall be judged as we have judged.

outcast that God has a right to demand of all, to do as they would be done to? Are the daughters of the oppressed and the poor as safe when in their power as their own daughters? God is their judge, for now they are the strongest power. It will not be always so, and a time will come when with what measure they mete it shall be measured to them again, and man will stand before God as what he is in his heart. Then again, what of the mercantile class? Are capital and labour equally reckoned and esteemed, and do men act the part of men to each other? The world is the witness that they are neither better nor worse for what they have, but for what they are, equally independent and equally responsible, and in accepting the Bible, bound by one common rule. (Matt. vii. 12.) In Christian Britain, where the Bible is almost universally received as the inspired Word of God, how are we to account for the universal complaint among all classes that no one is to be trusted, and that integrity has gone out of the land? Now, if the revealed Word of God, bringing forth fruit in man, is to be a power in the world, its power must first be felt by the individual realising Christ as the ideal God of humanity, dwelling in man as man's guide and example through life.

What have mothers and daughters to say to this general rule of doing to others as they would be done unto? Does the fine lady, as she holds her Bible, surrounded by all the luxury that wealth or position can give, think of this, when she demands more from the meanest in her household than she can say before God she would be willing to give, if she changed places, either in service or respect? Though money will buy service, integrity alone will demand respect, and both parties are what they have made themselves; they are here before God to serve Him by doing His work, as mistress and servant, in His strength.

And they of the middle-class, what of them? Money will buy service, but are they not expecting more than they have paid for? Is it the servants or the daughters that in God's sight ought to pull down the blinds, light the gas, add fresh coal to the fire, or hand a glass of water? The kitchen is on the low floor, but what of that? Is not the bell at hand? In all this does either love or justice rule? Again, what are the ways of society? Is it governed by the general principle of universal love? Of course in this I refer to the Bible-reading section of the community, which Christian influence has been moulding for over eighteen hundred years. This Christ, the ideal or mental God of humanity, has been striving all that time to make His influence felt as the ideal of the soul of man, that men might be filled with all the fulness of God. (Eph. iii. 19.) And what of the fruit does society present to the world? Let the general public speak here. Do we always find those that make the greatest profession of godliness ready to take the lowest place, so that they may help some weak brother? Or do they pass him by without recognition when it serves their purpose best, though elsewhere and at another time they professed to be eager for his friendship, because some bye-end was to be served, or his acquaintance was a convenience and might serve some purpose. But because he is not of their class they may cast him off when and how they please, and when it seems most suitable. He has no right to feel resentment: he is poor, or he has no position, and therefore may be pushed aside at pleasure. The Master as the Carpenter, the Child of Mary, would be treated in the same fashion, for they only recognise Him as the exalted Son of God. The ideal God of humanity is nothing to them, for He came to teach every man what true manhood is, and to manifest Himself as the perfect example of the human race.

It must appear to all how shallow that feeling is in many in our day—I mean that sentiment of Christian sympathy, that love of the brethren pointed to by John in 1 John iii. 14, as a distinguishing mark of Christian experience; for how often do we find that a friendship, which professes to be based on that very feeling of union in Christ, is ignored as soon as it turns out to be a hindrance or an inconvenience, in the shape of requiring the recognition of an acquaintance holding an inferior social position? How often does it happen that such an one is thrust aside, or passed unrecognised till another time, when the so-called Christian friends meet in a humble place, or when the humble friend is one that it may be a convenience for the time to know; or one with whom it would be profitable to resume the acquaintance. But for all this, they reason that the injured one has no right to be indignant; he has no social position. The Master would (as I said before) now be treated in the same way by such people, for they know only the exalted Son of God; the Carpenter, the Child of Mary is nothing to them.

Again, what of the general public, among whom the Bible is held as the holy chart of the world to guide man from earth to heaven? Let us ask, what advance is man making in his knowledge of the eternal "I Am"? God as a universal power has sent His commands to the human race by means of a written book, telling man where he is going and supplying him with a medium through which man may know God's will. Surely a general community holding this belief may be taken as a guarantee for the genuineness of the book, because, however pure a Darwin or a Huxley may live, if they refuse to accept the Bible though they believe in God and eternal life, they are condemned without mercy. That a book such as this is of infinite importance to the human race cannot be doubted, but the value of the belief in any given fact is to be measured by the effect it has on the mind of man. For it is a universal rule that belief prompts to action. Well, let us examine society where this belief prevails, and test it in respect of that charity which is spoken of in the thirteenth chapter of 1 Cor., and which is the principle that is to mould our lives; for I am one of the number that holds the Bible to contain truth that will divide the human race into species. Well, what fruit do we present to the world? for the world is willing to believe if we prove our doctrine; an innate sense of truth in man impels him to this. Are the peculiarities of absent friends explained away in the spirit of love, and covered over by the gentle touch of friendship, so that a stranger may be favourably impressed?

Is a man's general character that by which his worth is measured?

Is a neighbour's good fortune rejoiced over because the God of the Bible saw fit that he should succeed and we fail?

Are all that love the Lord dear to us in a general way? Do we prefer them just because they love the Lord, though their sense of truth may lead them to choose different pursuits, or to frequent a society different from ours and opposite to our sense of right? Are our servants treated as fellow-heirs with us of glory? And do they render to us what their sense of truth teaches them we have a right to expect from them?

Is charity the governing principle which is to set all things right between us? As members of one great family, do our servants find that in families where the greatest profession of godliness is made love towards all is the prevailing rule in the house? Are children in such families taught, by precept and example, that an unkind word spoken of an absent friend is worse in God's sight, and may be more injurious to the absent one, than if they stole his purse? His purse may easily be replaced, but the influence of an unkind word may follow to the judgment-seat of Christ, and determine the place the one who used it is to occupy in the kingdom of glory through all eternity.

Though the Vicarious Sacrifice, as seen in the God of humanity when He died on the Cross, opens the gate of heaven, yet the labour of love and the single eye are to be rewarded, though the reward is only promised when the motive that prompts the action is love—(Matt. xxv. 34-40)—love, that is to say, to the ideal God, the God of humanity, seen and felt in the Jesus of history and the

Christ of Christianity as the great human model of the race. But how can we expect men to believe, except where they see the fruit of this great Vicarious Sacrifice produced in us His professed followers? If we are true to this ideal God of mercy and truth, and give up our wills hearts and souls to be purified by the influence of His indwelling power, then we shall guard the truth of the Bible in the only way God expects us to guard it, and the Bible will hold its place in the world, while Christ holds his place in the heart of man as their ideal or mental God, in the form of a transfigured realism, teaching the human race their duty to God and man by worshipping the one and serving the other. It will no longer be a question of importance how sin came by the first Adam, if we only are true to the second Adam by honouring God in all we do; for we can only *feel sure* that we are doing so in living God-like, because in following Christ as an example we have the life which absolute religion demands as the fruit of the Spirit of God manifesting His presence in man, and thus *freeing body and soul from the power of the second death.* We must bear in mind that it is *only* those who shall rise at the *first resurrection* that the second death has no power over. (Rev. xx. 6.)

In our present state of knowledge we can understand the quality of matter in which the disembodied spirit is presented. Therefore we must look at the meaning of many texts as applying to the state of existence which intervenes between death and the Universal Resurrection and Judgment. We can now fully comprehend the meaning of Our Lord's words in Luke xxiv. 37-41, where He said "A spirit hath not *flesh* and *bones* as you see me have". The words must refer to the *inward man* as the body or *nerve force* which has been evolved through the natural body, and must be held to imply the ever-conscious part which survives death.

Now, in this state of existence where the individual is a believer in intellect and profession, but one whose life has not been consecrated to Christ in love, such an experience may *induce* suffering in the form of repentance in the state of existence between death and the resurrection.*

* In applying Matt. vii. 2—"With what judgment ye judge, ye shall be judged" to the believer, we must understand the text to refer to the place or state in heaven he or she have fitted themselves for in their life on earth, as one of the species of which man is the genesis and belief the distinguishing quality.

Chapter XII.

CHRIST CONFESSED, AND THE VALUE OF LABOUR.

WE as Christians with all our glaring defects honour God in one way which is peculiarly our own—that is, by honouring the Son (John v. 23), and thus securing the love of the Father. (John xvi. 27.) By partaking of the holy communion, the weakest and the worst believer confesses Christ; and thus makes his own the promise made in Matt. x. 32 : "Whosoever, therefore, shall confess me before men, him will I confess also before my Father which is in Heaven."

We can have some conception of how broad Christ's church is, when we realise that His followers range from all the various grades of belief, so to speak, implied by Jesus in John xi. 25-26, where He says : "He that believeth on me, though he were dead, yet shall he live, and whosoever liveth and believeth in me shall never die." To such an one as the last death is only a change of place, but no change of state; for Christ is the centre of attraction here and there.

In the experience of advanced believers Christ is realised as a state of consciousness in three ways—that is, 1st, as the Jesus of the Christian records; 2nd, as a symbol of the Jesus present in consciousness as the ideal object of love; and 3rd, as the Jesus now existing in the place He has gone to prepare for His people. Christ is thus realised in consciousness according to the first description as the child of Mary; and the Son of God, in the second, as the ideal Christ, the elect of God; and according to the third, as the real personage with the marred visage and the pierced hands and feet, so well known to His followers when on this earth of ours as the "Man of Sorrows and acquainted with grief". It is this Jesus whom we confess before men by our profession of faith in baptism and the Lord's Supper.

There is one relationship which we Christians seem to overlook, and that is the fact that this Jesus came to sanctify labour. This is proved by the greater part of His life spent as one of the sons of toil, so that he was generally known as the Carpenter, the child of Mary. (Mark vi. 3.) How often do we fail to realise that the energy required of our sons and daughters of toil, in providing for their daily wants, is work done for God (1 Tim. v. 8); that is, in the case of a mistress and servant, both believers, the mistress must spend as much energy in the shape of necessary labour of one kind or another as her servant spends, before she can take her place on the same platform in God's sight; that is, before the 'well done good and faithful servant" can be applied to her in the same sense as to the other.

This is a fact we all need to comprehend, and it will be well if we do so here and now, because each and all are fitting and preparing themselves for the place they are to occupy in that other world where Jesus has gone before us.

CHAPTER XIII.

IN REFERENCE TO PLEASURE INCREASING THE VITAL ACTION.

IN the foregoing pages I trust I have been enabled to make it plain what we Christians mean by faith. For I have striven to show that, though this faith is so simple that a child may comprehend it, in as much as it demands nothing more than the willing mind, yet so comprehensive is it, that a Tyndall or a Herbert Spencer will find in it something too high to be accounted for without the sense of a spiritual presence, as a state of consciousness, realised as the actual spiritual presence of God, and made known as a felt power within, in the feeling of joy that follows belief. Nevertheless, the evolution theory, which claims to deal with only body and mind, explains the meaning of Jesus' interview with Nicodemus, in the course of which he referred to the new birth. In the sixth verse of the third chapter of John Jesus explains the full meaning of his teaching in these words : " that which is born of the flesh is flesh, and that which is born of the Spirit is spirit ". He thus cuts man off from a spiritual experience as a state of consciousness, in the sense that many believers enjoy it apart from union with Him. And science confirms His teaching in this respect, so that there is no need for our men of science to reject Christianity merely because they hold the evolution theory, or because most Christians believe in special acts of creation. It is not how this world came to be formed (Genesis ii. 4-5), but man as an intelligent being, and Christ in man the hope of glory, represented in consciousness, that constitutes Christianity ; and thus Christ becomes all in all (Col. iii. 11), for we will only have one Christ given to the human race.

There is one fact which as yet I have omitted to refer to that may help to explain much in connection with our subject. I allude to the force known as vital action. Science has proved that pleasure increases vitality, and the Bible teaches us that the action of the Spirit of God represented in consciousness involves love, joy, peace, &c., &c. (Gal. v. 22), proving that the vital action has only one meaning, however differently it may be applied.

It will thus be seen that union with Christ and increase of vitality is one and the same thing. Through Christ we comprehend and love God as a reconciled Father, and thus enjoy pleasure of the highest kind and in the highest degree. The vital action is increased to the highest degree when this union is completely realised ; then life is fullest. But all this might be a delusion if we had not the resurrection as a great cardinal fact to rest upon ; at least, as intelligent beings, we might be quite unable to believe in it and trust our eternal all to it.

We thus see how eternal life is fused with temporal life, and, *vice versâ*, temporal life fused with eternal life. The words of Jesus are thus proved, when He says in John xi. 26, " Whosoever liveth and believeth in me shall never die. Believest thou this ? " We thus comprehend how the religious element in man becomes perfected by his union with Christ. This is the peace represented in consciousness, and the fulfilment of the promise given in John xiv. 27, 28. The last clause of the 28th verse is very expressive in this respect, that Christ as a part is less than God as a whole, and the Christ represented in consciousness as a part is less than the whole.

When we comprehend vitality to imply life eternal as well as life temporal, and pleasure as increasing vital action and pain as diminishing it, the Bible becomes intelligent to all classes, and Christ's teaching may be understood in the fullest sense. I refer in particular to His teaching conveyed in the following passages: Matt. x. 39 and xvi. 25; Mark viii. 35; Luke ix. 24 and xvii. 21-33; John xii. 25. We thus see that in giving away energy or life for His own sake, or in His service, we increase our capacity for enjoyment in the life that is to come. (Matt. v. 11, 12.) This is the fruit of His vicarious sacrifice. That is to say, by temporarily lowering vital action in His service we increase it eternally. In the light of this, how different does the Sermon on the Mount become, so comprehended! And how easy is it to understand how we may become the salt of the earth, and what He means when He says, Matt. v. 39, "I say unto you that ye resist not evil: but whosoever shall smite thee on thy right cheek turn to him the other also". In such teaching Christ shows us in what relation we stand toward the world, as in it but not of it. (John xv. 19.) We thus comprehend His meaning when He says, Matt. vi. 20, 21, "Lay up for yourselves treasures in heaven, where neither moth nor rust doth corrupt, and where thieves do not break through nor steal: for where your treasure is there will your heart be also." We are thus to learn to labour and to wait, knowing that pain here is in effect loss of vital action, and leads to death temporal but life spiritual. Or we may speak of it as the conservation of nerve energy in the spiritual body which survives death temporal, and carries the redeemed soul from earth to heaven (the place where Jesus waits us), there to witness the redemption of the body proper, the organism of which will be rendered capable of sustaining enjoyment of the highest degree; in this respect being very unlike our present bodies with their frail organisation altogether unfit to bear excessive joy.

We must thus have a pretty clear conception of what is stated in the Bible in reference to both worlds before we can adjust the molecules properly in the brain, and then decide which world we are to labour for: as sinners saved by grace we have our choice. And it is manifest, when we compare the Bible as seen in Matt. xii. 36, 37, Rom. xiv. 12, 2 Cor. v. 10, with science, that by adding moment by moment to that first dawn of consciousness (that eternal sequence) we are building up that inner man who will survive death, and hold the forces together all through eternity as the self-conscious ego of the individual, representing that spiritual body referred to by Paul (2 Cor. iv. 16) as the inner man who was renewed day by day, and will be known in that self-conscious ego as the beginning of the life "in me" in us having been derived by the law of inheritance through our parents (John iii. 6), and in that respect being the first cause of all our actions. The conservation of energy presented in the forces included, when applied to the spiritual body, must be understood to be in like manner applied to the spirits of children presented in the energy of life, locked up in the brain, or somehow fused into the infant as the soul, or spirit, presenting the energy of the ego, and referred to by Paul in 1 Cor. vii. 14, where he says, " else were your children unclean ; but now are they holy ". In our present state of knowledge we are thus able to trace out how the living germ comes from the parents, presented in their lives as the medium through which the vital forces are fused into one, where the individual life presented in this form must be known as such all through eternity, in its connection with the two lives that gave it an existence.

If the energy of life were understood as nerve current, presenting the subtle fluid in which the ego is embodied, and the ego in intelligent beings were understood to represent the activity of life, the vital principle of which is ever increased by pleasure, pleasure would be courted in consequence of its life-giving property, manifesting itself as the strongest power in man, and, in consequence of this life-giving property being diminished by pain, pain on that account would be avoided or shunned. To the properties of the mental life thus defined Christianity is capable of imparting a new influence in the shape of a disturber of elements, which, through the operation of this influence increasing, man is enabled to *counteract*, thus reversing the law of his nature manifested in the formation of his organisation and compelling his choosing pleasure to increase life. Whereas this new or

Christian influence is manifested in inducing him to choose pain, suffering, and death as the visible proof of that yet stronger power working through humanity, representing the expression of the Spirit of God, as God in Christ, enabling man to overcome the flesh (or burn out the original structure), which is the term employed in the Scriptures to distinguish man in his natural state. So that through this process Christ's kingdom might be increased on earth by Christ's race being increased on earth; in consequence of man convincing fellow-man in the only way that eternity can possibly be realised by him; so that God is through this glorified in having given His only begotten Son to redeem the race, always bearing in mind the fact that all that was of the earth, earthly, in Our Lord came by Mary, and was made under the law. (Gal. iv. 4.) What I would say is, that His organisation as perfect man came to maturity through the Virgin Mary on this earth of ours as the form that is to redeem humanity. In the light of known truth we are perfectly justified in holding, that nature, as the fruit tree bearing fruit after its kind, could not have produced one capable of having lived the perfect life Christ lived, and God, the Father of the race, gave the beginning—the germ—in the shape of a perfectly organised brain, and that such implies that our Lord's divine nature could act and react through it, and thus produce the Jesus of history and the Christ of Christianity as God and man.

We might represent life temporal and life spiritual in another way—namely, in the self-conscious ego embodied in a subtle fluid called light as the most likely emblem, when we know light to be a disturber of elements and the possible origin of organic life, whereas I would define intelligent life embodied in the word. Life is hope, being the cause and effect of intelligent life, and the highest point in view of the future the natural man can rise to in his reasoning on the immortality of the soul; for all such reasoning must end in this—namely, man lives, and he hopes to live—hope, nothing but hope. Nature can go no further, can rise no higher. We require the Christ of Christianity to open up the way beyond, and reveal the source of the new development (Acts xix. 2) felt in the self-conscious ego as a spiritual experience whereby we can say *God is love, I know I feel*. The Spirit of God is thus acting in the shape of a disturber of elements apparent to the inner man. Thus we comprehend hope as life to be realised as eternal life by means of a felt union with God, bestowing on Jesus' race peculiar grace and glory too.

Holding as I do that the Bible is inspired of God, and contains truth that will decide the human race, and having in comparatively early life experienced the change which takes place in mind when the truth of the Gospel as "the glad tidings" is first realised, and Christ is perceived as holding a definite place in consciousness in the shape of a conception grounded on the truth of Christianity, that is, offering Himself as a substitute for sinners; when I was first enabled to individualise myself as one of the species concerned in the revelation, and as willing to be saved by Him; I can now in a pretty general way single out the succeeding state of consciousness that followed this conception, and thus point inwardly to the transfigured realism as the effect produced by belief in or through the facts of Christianity. That is to say, the Christian experience realised in the term faith working by love, and presenting a full thought as the cause and effect produced by the condition implied, has enabled me to comprehend the truth, taught as plainly in the Bible as out of it, that before any one can come to a clear understanding of the truth of any subject the mind must undergo a special course of training, and that Christianity is a subject in regard to which this is peculiarly true, for this is one of the greatest strongholds of its system, if indeed it is not the greatest stronghold of it.

What I would have clearly understood is, that the state of consciousness which succeeds a belief in the leading facts of Christianity applied individually, is of such a nature experimentally as to confirm the truth of the Christian doctrine.

In this connection it is very evident that John's experience in after life in this respect qualified him to comprehend the Saviour's meaning in a way quite impossible to the other disciples, who lacked the aged disciple's experience. He alone, so far as we know, understood experimentally the full meaning of John vii. 17, where the Saviour says, " If any man will do his (God's) will, he shall know of the doctrine whether it be of God, or whether I speak of myself". As contrasted with the assertion made in 1 John v. 10, where John takes the state of consciousness or experience of each believer as a guarantee of the truth of the doctrine.

The succeeding veres (1 John v. 9-12-20) are full proof of this, that John pointed to the witness within. And here I would particularly draw attention to the full meaning of the word *understanding* as it is used in the 20th verse. It will be clearly seen that we are to judge of our right to eternal life by the former knowledge which we have acquired in the experience of life in following out the course enjoined; and it is also evident that our serial states of consciousness constitute the knowledge which our understanding is to be guided by in establishing our individual right to eternal life. We shall thus find ourselves guided by the principle of love that animated John nearly nineteen hundred years ago. My object in quoting the former verses from the fifth chapter of 1 John was to show John's mode of reasoning, as proof of the truth which is taught in our day, namely, that mind is formed by the serial states of consciousness of each individual, which are bound together by laws eternal as God Himself, and must endure as that by which individual humanity is to judge and be judged. That which undergoes this experience is the part of humanity that will survive the body, and thus it will come to pass that each man may be his own judge.

I would end by adding one word to the class that treat the Bible with indifference. If Christianity is what those of my opinion believe it to be, then the other class, if *true to themselves*, must make up their mind to face the consequences of rejecting Christ as the objective part of the universal power which we call God, and known to man as the individual that is to judge humanity; for since the experience of Jesus Himself is made up in part of the serial states of consciousness which He underwent during his sojourn on earth, and while He had a human form He is qualified in an especial manner to act the part of Judge of the human race.

In the simplicity of an untrained mind I have written the foregoing remarks, feeling that there is a Christian culture more valuable to the individual than that which all the learning in the world can give without it. Thus I leave the subject, asking the Lord's blessing upon my efforts.

PART II.

CHAPTER I.

DOES CHRISTIANITY ADMIT OF A SCIENTIFIC TEST?

IT must be apparent to all that this is the question of questions of our day; and that, unless Christianity will admit of a scientific test, belief in it can only linger for a little while, but cannot last. We that claim for it a divine origin, and regard it as containing supernatural power, can assuredly have no objection to submit such a religion to such a test. Let us try to realise, therefore, wherein Christianity proper consists, and how it differs from all forms of natural religion.

Christianity comes to mankind by the authority of God, and dealing with humanity as a form of body and mind seeks to implant a new state of consciousness, known as a spiritual experience, which gives a new direction to thought and action, and creates desires unknown and unfelt before.

Mind is regarded by our men of science as one great organic growth containing a moral and religious element, man in the form of body and mind being the evolved unit. Christianity comes by divine authority to deal with this unit, which we find that Christ defines as one substance, calling it flesh. In John iii. 6 we read "that which is born of the flesh is flesh," so that to this extent at least science and revealed religion are in agreement, but only science has proved what Christ revealed nearly two thousand years ago. We have no right, however, to quarrel with science for thus proving the truth of Christ's words, as is done by so many in our day.

It is with men as such that Christianity has to do, and out of this structure seeks to evolve a new state of consciousness, with Christ as leader and centre. Such is the teaching of Jesus Christ, and such also is the science of Christianity. Christianity is doubtless a religion of belief, but of belief of such a nature that it rules and reigns in us, and at length becomes the strongest power in man.

I assume nothing as essential to substantiate the claims of Christianity, except the evidence of history from the Lord's day till ours. The death of Jesus is an historical fact, and rests on historical ground. His resurrection was witnessed by His disciples aud followers—the class that knew Him best, and could recognise Him. They were startled by the resurrection, for we nowhere read that they expected it ; that is, they doubted as long as doubt was possible, and when it was no longer possible they believed. And thus from the church of the first born we have received the resurrection on the evidence of testimony from the Lord's days till our own, of which testimony the Roman Catholic Church may well claim to be a part. The Christian records in some form as a production of the first century, most professing Christians admit, and I suppose I may add, that most accept them as written by the men whose name they bear. The question now to be answered is, will the doctrine taught in the Christian records produce the effect implied—that is to say, a new state of consciousness which will endure, and at length raise the believer above the things of time and sense, and enable him to realise things spiritual and eternal. (2 Cor. iv. 18.)

I now assert that a belief in the life, death, and resurrection of Christ is essential to salvation as viewed from the Christian point I am dealing with at present. Now let us try to comprehend what is to be saved as a something that exists in an unsaved state. Here we must call in the aid of science to enable us to understand Christ's teaching in John iii. 6, where he tells us that "that which is born of the flesh is flesh"—that is, all that lives in us comes from our parents in the shape of two lives fused into one, and is the origin of an organisation like to that from which we have sprung, with structure and functions prepared for definite work. This life is realised in the first dawn of consciousness as the beginning of those serial states of consciousness which survive death, and hold together our individual experience all through eternity. Now this individual I, this unit of consciousness, possessing a moral and religious element, is the *unit* of that great organic growth which our planet has produced in ages gone by; and observe, it is this unit that revealed religion deals with. It teaches what I think all will allow, that we as individuals have failed in our duty to man and to God, and that as rational beings endowed with intellect—that is, with powers of discrimination, similarity, retentiveness, along with feeling and will—we are responsible beings, and must be judged according to our merits. I think that all will admit that human nature is fallible, and that the best have not in all ways and at all times done the *best they could.* It is here and now that revealed religion in the shape of Christianity takes effect, by dividing the human race into two species, with man as the genus and belief the distinguishing quality, and there is produced a new development which enables man to worship God in the Spirit, rejoice in Christ Jesus, and have no confidence in the flesh. (Phil. iii. 3.) To trace out how this state of consciousness is produced is the object of this paper.

The most extensive view or idea we get of the great First Cause is obtained in realising that there is an intelligence at the heart of everything. What this intelligence is we learn in the 16th verse of the 3rd chapter of John, where Jesus tells us that "God so loved the world that He gave His only begotten Son, that whosoever believeth in him should not perish but have everlasting life". Therefore, just as we realise this Intelligence to be the father of Jesus Christ, do we get the most comprehensive view of God possible for us to have. We can now pray to a something special, a something definite, and ask for what we want, while we are also in a position to realise the spiritual presence of the great I Am. For we are told that "the natural man receiveth not the things of the Spirit of God: for they are foolishness unto him: neither can he know them, because they are spiritually decerned. But he that is spiritual judgeth all things, yet he himself is judge of no man". (1 Cor. ii. 14, 15.) In the resurrection we find enough to substantiate all this —and observe, we do not take it on faith, but on proof substantiated by the evidence of testimony.

We will now suppose a case very common in a society of believers such as ours, namely, an individual born of Christian parents, trained in the Christian religion, but failing to realise the state of consciousness which his religion entitles him to, and such as was Paul's experience as stated in 2 Timothy i. 12 : " I know whom I have believed, and am persuaded that he is able to keep that which I have committed unto him against that day." Though the structure is complete it fails in the work assigned to it, that is, Christ is not realised as the seed of God in the spirit of man, nor recognised as the elect of God, a state of consciousness which Paul explained in Col. i. 26, 27, as " the mystery which hath been hid from ages and generations but now is made manifest to His saints : to whom God would make known what is the riches of the glory of this mystery among the Gentiles; which is Christ in you, the hope of Glory ". It is this state of consciousness that we are to suppose it is the aim of each individual in life to attain.

As to what is to be believed, Jesus Himself teaches us in John iii. 16 : " For God so loved the world that He gave His only begotten Son, that whosoever believeth in Him should not perish, but have everlasting life." It is further fully explained by Paul in Romans x. 8, 9, 10 : " But what saith it ? The word is nigh thee, even in thy mouth, and in thy heart ; that is, the word of faith which we preach : that if thou shalt confess with thy mouth the Lord Jesus and shalt believe in thine heart that God hath raised Him from the dead, thou shalt be saved. For with the heart man believeth unto righteousness ; and with the mouth confession is made unto salvation." By " the word," as used in the eighth verse, we are to understand the work of Christ as Mediator between God and man. Man professing to believe is to approach God as a sinner saved by grace, desiring to realise that he is indeed saved. Now for the first time the prayer of faith ascends from a heart that feels its need in language such as, "Lord, I believe, help Thou my unbelief". The mind tries to grasp, tries to realise the state of consciousness desired, a state which every Christian man feels, and knows, on the authority of God, he has a right to possess as a sinner, and because he is a sinner. On every occasion that he repeats in thought or word "Lord, I believe, help thou my unbelief," while his mind is striving to grasp, is striving to realise the state of consciousness desired (that he is indeed saved because he believes), he is gaining strength, and as he repeats the prayer of faith he gradually begins to realise the meaning of such passages as that contained in Rom. iv. 5 as applicable to himself individually; that is to say, "to him that worketh not, but believeth on him that justifieth the ungodly, his faith is counted for righteousness". Once the believer realises the full meaning of this the conquest is won, the prayer of faith is answered; and as a sinner saved by grace he approaches God as a reconciled Father in and through Jesus Christ. His intellect is now satisfied, for he *feels* and *knows;* his emotional nature is in full play; the real Christ is transfigured as the Ideal Christ of his soul, adored and loved, as the Mediator between God and man, while God is adored and loved as the Father of Jesus Christ. This is the Great I Am of Creation and Grace, comprehended as that intelligence which is at the heart of every thing. Thus also does the mind of man find rest in the arms of the Almighty, and realising love as the unit of that in-

telligence is made conscious of the spiritual presence of
God as a something known and felt. In this way the
Word of God, in the shape of a revealed religion, which
discloses to us a future state of existence and our relation to God in it, is fulfilling its mission to man by supplying food which serves to satisfy that spiritual nature
in him, which is the structure that has been evolved,
and is now being brought to perfection through the
agency of divine influences.

As how to know God as a God of grace was the great
concern of the individual when he first felt his need, and
offered up the prayer, " Lord, I believe, help Thou my
unbelief," so now that has been realised in the state of
consciousness expressed in Rom. v. 1-5, according to
which, being justified by faith, he now stands in grace,
and rejoices " in the hope of the glory of God," his great
concern will be, how to serve the object of his love
as God in Christ. It is thus that Christianity becomes
the strongest power in man; the individual is now in
possession of a state of consciousness which is called
faith, and which worketh by love. But as he tries to
fulfil his mission to God and man by regulating his life
in accordance with Christ's teaching, it is then that he
feels his weakness and a need of a stronger power. For
though his life may have been throughout its whole
course all that man could desire, it is with the thought of
the heart that the Saviour concerns Himself. Thus He
reproves him that is angry with a brother without cause
(Matt. v. 22), and points out that impure desire is sin.
(Matt. v. 28), For the individual is now building up
that structure of consciousness, which is to be his gar-

ment in heaven, and in which he is to appear before the judgment seat of Christ, as seen in Matt. xii. 36, 37 : " But I say unto you, that every idle word that men shall speak they shall give account thereof in the day of judgment : for by thy words thou shalt be justified, and by thy words thou shalt be condemned". It is when this is realised, that the world and the things of time lose their hold, and purity of heart becomes the great aim of life. The Christian in this alone realises the truth of a doctrine that is applicable to all, and as he goes forward in the strength of the Lord, as a sinner saved by grace, he conquers even when he seems to fail. When old habits and old desires come upon him and seem likely to lead him away, guilty and erring, yet as a sinner saved by grace, as one that Christ is substitute for, and possessing the spirit of a penitent child, he finds rest and strength in God, being saved through that which Christ did for him, and not through what out of gratitude he, the sinner saved by grace, is striving to do in overcoming sin. Here we Christians stand and are strong, here and here alone. As sinners saved by grace, all who are followers of Jesus and spiritual children of God, take their stand on this, and as such, that is, as sinners saved by grace, they will be known as a new development all through eternity, having Christ as the *centre*.

Christianity, as a religion of belief in which even an evil thought is sin, excludes man from the right to judge his fellow man, for belief being a state of the mind can be known directly only to the individual. In this realm then God alone may judge, the ground being that which is stated in John iii. 16. But to this belief all the human race are invited, the invitation being given in these words: "Whosoever will, let him take the water of life freely." (Rev. xxii. 17.) Therefore in a society of Christians, which regards justification by faith as essential to salvation, there is given to every individual member of it the right to be accepted by the society as entitled to the benefit that flows from Christ's death, whatever may be the character of the life of each individual.* The justice of all this will be seen when we try to realise the different classes that are included in that general invitation implied in "Whosoever." When we consider the structural differences that exist between an individual born of Christian parents, trained in a family where to do justice, to love mercy, and to walk humbly with God (Micah vi. 8), is the constant rule, and an individual who is born and brought up in the haunts of vice, where theft is reckoned an honourable profession, and where lust rules supreme; the direct influences of revealed religion when brought to bear on two such minds must be taken into consideration. In seeking to trace the effects of this influence, we must remember that a life of faith is a life of trial, sometimes apparently of failure, whilst the old structure is being burned out, and in its place there is being gradually developed a new structure, the possessor of which slowly rises in the moral and religious scale, going onward and forward in the strength of the Almighty. Thus it may happen that the poor child of vice may be striving and progressing in

* God provided the substitute, the condition being believing and the performance of works for the sake of Jesus, which are laid up as treasures in heaven. (Matt. vi. 20.)

the sight of God, while we in our ignorance seek to cast her off as a worthless thing, forgetting that Jesus Himself took one of that class which we call the worst, and assigned to her a place in the first rank of the saints in glory. (Luke vii. 37-50.) This God alone, Who can weigh and measure the force of human energy, and knows who is striving with greatest effect against sin; it was He alone Who gave the promise expressed in Matt. xxi. 22: "All things whatsoever ye shall ask in prayer, believing ye shall receive," and He *knows* who is grasping that promise with the strongest hand, and going forward in the strength of it. For He who taught Peter to be merciful, saying that he was to forgive until seventy times seven, is Himself not less merciful, and will show Himself infinitely merciful, so that we shall find many of the first last, and the last first. But though to show this charity in judging is the duty of each believer when thinking and speaking of a fellow believer, nevertheless the world at large, whether believing in the Bible or not, has no authority to judge individuals in another way than by their fruits.

That is a test which we all must submit to. "Ye shall know them by their fruits. Do men gather grapes of thorns or figs of thistles? Wherefore by their fruits ye shall know them." (Matt. vii. 16, 20.) Here we can be accepted by none as saved and one with Christ, except it be by those who are our fellow-believers; all else must judge us by our lives, and can only accept our profession of Christianity as genuine, in so far as our lives prove it to be so. The world is to judge us, and we are to judge ourselves by the standard Christ has given in

Does Christianity admit of a Scientific Test. 111

Matthew vii. 12—" Therefore all things whatsoever ye would that men should do to you, do ye even so to them, for this is the law and the prophets ". And it would be well to notice, that Christ's teaching applies directly only to his professed followers, the code of laws as promulgated in the Christian records being addressed only to believers, for to them only was it given to know the mysteries of the kingdom. (Matt. xiii. 11.) As subjects of a new King, the Lord Jesus Christ, professing to be guided by a new principle, faith working by love, we are in that respect to be recognised by God as in the world, but not of the world. Therefore the impure thought is sin to us, who profess a religion in which belief insures life eternal, a life which is realised as a state of consciousness in the spiritual experience of all Christians. When we try to understand Christ's teaching in the light of our present knowledge, this will become very plain. Science teaches us that the instinct of self-preservation, though pleasure increases the vital action, is the strongest power in man. Starting from this basis, we are able to take in a view of life as a whole —that is to say, proceeding on the fact that the vital action is increased by pleasure and diminished by pain, we feel that we have all that we need to know, in order to substantiate our claim to eternal life as a continuation of the present life. For we find that vitality essentially consists of that which is the fruit of our spiritual experience as expressed by Paul in Romans v. 1-5, where in the fifth verse the climax of all is represented to be " the love of God shed abroad in our hearts by the Holy Ghost which is given unto us," love being the highest state of happiness, or pleasure, or enjoyment known to us at present. Thus then would we prove our claim to eternal life on scientific ground. And not only so. We would in the same way also show, that it is impossible that Christ could have intended His teaching to apply directly to the world at large, as it undoubtedly demands self-sacrifice in the highest degree; the whole tenor of His teaching being to lower the vital action of the individual in the present life, while the world at large, lying outside the Church, might be saved through the instrumentality of His own people walking in His footsteps. The sermon on the mount points directly to this, and such a passage as is to be found in Mark viii. 35 leaves no doubt of Christ's meaning. There we find him saying, " Whosoever will save his life shall lose it; but whosoever shall lose his life for My sake and the gospel's, the same shall save it ". Of course we are to understand life here to mean energy, and we naturally ask, how could mankind give away life or energy in the service of one who has not been accepted as king. It is thus perfectly clear, in the light of present knowledge, that Christ never intended His teaching to apply to unbelievers. Neither will they be judged by it, for how could those who do not recognise His claim as a redeemer be expected to give away life, in striving to fulfil the code of laws He left for His followers. We, on the other hand, who realise the benefit of His death in the shape of a felt power within us, have at our own disposal, and in our own power, all that the energy of life includes, and this we may consecrate as a free will offering to His service; and indeed in so far as we are living up to our professions we are doing so. Nevertheless it must be apparent to all that, in the light of recognised truth, the Christian records only apply to professing believers, and just in proportion as they exert an influence on their lives and through them on the world at large. Thus we see the whole scheme centres in the principle of causation—that is to say, the warfare which continually goes on between the flesh and the spirit, as described by Paul in Rom. vii. 15-25, and elsewhere, can be fully understood only when we realise the fact that self-conservation, as the strongest power in man, wars against the higher law of faith working by love, first made apparent in revealed religion as a spiritual experience, and represented by a warfare going on between the flesh and the spirit.

But this opens another question which we Christians are constrained to answer. Has Christ made it possible in a Christian sense for a man to save himself? To this I reply without hesitation in the affirmative, understanding, however, that salvation coming in this way is not the rescue from sin by means of grace, but by another way in which the sinner in *virtue* of *Christ's vicarious sacrifice* has salvation made possible. What this other way is, we find revealed in the seventh chapter of Matthew at the 12th verse, where Christ distinctly announces what is implied in "the law and the prophets". His words are these: "Whatsoever ye would that men should do to you, do ye even so to them, for this is the law and the prophets". In these words we may hold that there is laid down a standard of righteousness equivalent to obedience, and that where truth and justice rule within and without salvation is made possible. Compare with this what is contained in the first verse of the fifth chapter of Jeremiah : " See now, and know, and seek if ye can find a man, if there be any that executeth judgment, that seeketh the truth; and I will pardon it ".* We have always to bear in mind that Christ came to reveal the character of God as a God of love, of truth, and of justice, and that, although Christ opens the gates of Heaven to the most depraved, and although it is such that the angels of God rejoice most over, because Christ " came to save that which was lost," yet the ninety and nine just persons, who in one sense need no repentance, are represented as a class in glory. For Christ never came as a substitute for sinners in such a way as to exclude them from Heaven, because, like Thomas, they would not believe except they put their fingers into the prints of the nails and thrust their hands into His side ; for doubtless, like Thomas, when they perceive the real Jesus in glory, the exclamation of " My Lord and my God " will burst from them only, alas ! to be received with the cold rejoinder of " because you have seen me you have believed ; blessed are they that have not seen and yet have believed ". There can be no doubt that Thomas represents a class, and that the blessing just mentioned, with all that it implies, will distinguish the redeemed of the human race, dividing them into species, among which many that we have branded with the name

---

* This passage applies directly to the Jewish race, God's covenant people, as the seed of Abraham. It may, therefore, not bear the broad rendering I give it in applying it to the Gentile world. From the law of inheritance, doubtless, the Jews derive many advantages peculiar to *their race.*

of sceptic will find a place, and there worship him who is at once the sinner's friend and the one who made it possible for them to enter—the Jesus Christ. In this belief I go forward on my Christian course, trusting there to meet with one, an Author whom I have learned to admire and revere, in whom truth and justice ruled. It is indeed the case that John Stuart Mill has here been branded as a sceptic, nevertheless I trust to meet him among the redeemed—not indeed as a sinner saved by grace, but as a sinner to whom Christ made salvation possible. The class, however, which I have more particularly in view here are our men of science, who spend their lives in the search after truth, and so consecrate their best energies to Him who is the God of all truth. We may well say that the words in Eccles. i. 13 are applicable to them: "I gave my heart to seek and search out by wisdom concerning all things that are done under heaven; this sore travail hath God given to the sons of man to be exercised therewith". Therefore those who despise such men, as many do in our day, must be held to set at defiance the Word of God. For a truth outside the Bible is as much His word, or sign, or token, or laws as that which is revealed within it, and we shall be held responsible for the use to which we may apply all our knowledge of the former description. Moreover, as Protestants we claim the right of private judgment for ourselves, and an equal right we should be prepared to yield to others.

In rejecting the sacred Scriptures this class cuts itself off from the assurance of eternal life, which is a fruit proceeding from a belief in Christianity, and substantiated by a psychological experience that is within the reach of every believer, and may be taken as a fulfilment of the promise given by Jesus in John vii. 17, where he says : " If any man will do his will he shall know of the doctrine, whether it be of God or whether I speak of myself". Thus it is Christians alone who can hope to rise above the world, and, soaring through the regions of space, reach unto the presence of the Absolute, where they shall assert their claims as heirs of eternal life through Jesus Christ ; for the glorified body of the risen Lord is the point where they will gravitate to at death, when they will be for ever with the Lord and know Him even as they are known by Him. Christians are saved because they believe on Christ, and works done by them in His name and for His sake, whether many or few, are the fruit referred to by Christ in Matt. vi. 20, where He says : " Lay up for yourselves treasures in heaven, where neither moth nor rust doth corrupt, and where thieves do not break through nor steal ". But on this point much confusion is apt to be begotten in the mind of the individual believer by reason of his not sufficiently regarding the distinction between this injunction of Christ's and that contained in the immediately preceding verse, and trying clearly to understand what is implied in the terms used.

Those that reject Christianity live, and they hope to live ; but they can rise no higher, they can go no further, than merely to hope on. But hope is the life of the race, and in their case it will be realised in eternity, when every effort that they may have put forward in the cause of truth will be accepted as work done for Him who is the God of truth and the Father of Jesus Christ.

Many of the class I represent, sinners saved by grace, will be doubtless shocked by the material way in which I treat this subject, not wishing to realise that Christ came to save man as a form of body and mind, and of mind and spirit ; that, in fact, the Christian man is saved as body, mind, and spirit together, and is an individual possessing a spiritual experience.

We must observe that in Genesis we have as it were two creations, and that we may understand the first to mean something like this, that the highest intelligences on this planet, when they had attained to a sufficiently high state of development, were enabled to guide their actions by feeling, intellect, and will—and observe this class are presented as male and female—as described in Gen. i. 26-31. But this being regarded as the first creation, we may go further and say that in the course of time some individual man of a class, possessing a moral and religious element, at length attained to that state of perfection which is described in Gen. ii. 7, as the result of God breathing into man's nostrils the breath of life, so that he " became a living soul ". And we must observe here that, as we nowhere read that the first creation ceased to exist, therefore those who in our day believe Adam to have started up all at once at the word of the Lord have yet a former creation, if they choose to call it so, to point out as existing along side of Adam ; though I fully believe Eve to have been produced by miraculous power as a helpmate to Adam, bone of his bone and flesh of his flesh, by that infinite Intelligence whom I hold to be at the heart of everything, helping man everywhere, upward and onward, heavenward and homeward, and who gave His only begotten Son to save mankind. Moreover, I firmly believe that Adam and Eve, having God as a felt power within them, lived in that perfect state of innocence which we read of in the Bible until by the fall Adam became father of the human race, as has been made known to us by divine revelation; for doubtless the miracles of the Old Testament were as fully authenticated to the people then living as the Resurrection is in our day. However, let that be as it may, it is Christ, the chosen one of God and the redeemer of the world, who reigns in the mind of man, dividing the human race as is indicated in Col. i. 26-27, where he is spoken of as the mystery which was hid from ages and from generations, but is now made manifest to the saints as Christ in them the hope of glory. Thus, therefore, it all ends in causation, God being understood to be the author and finisher of all, and man, in the form of body and mind, being moved by the strongest power which enables him to build up and pull down.

In conclusion, I would add one word in reference to the Son of Man as the God of Humanity. In Jesus doubtless we can trace the history of the race, recognising in the root and the offspring of David (Rev. xxii. 16) the germ which was brought to maturity through the Virgin Mary, and then called to occupy a place in time and space as the carpenter, the son of Mary and the brother of James and Joses, and of Juda and Simon (Mark vi. 3), at first differing from his contemporaries only in being endowed with a power which enabled him to refuse the evil and choose the good (Isaiah vii. 15). For we cannot but believe that the Jesus of history was prepared for His work by realising in Himself the Messiah of the Jews, and being therefore the saviour of man. The voice that greeted him on the threshold of his public ministry with the words—" Thou art my beloved Son ; in thee I am well pleased " (Luke iii. 22), must have left an impression which enabled Him to realise His relationship and his mission in such a way as he had never realised them before. And it is because of all this that the Christ of Christianity became what he was when he lived upon earth, and what he now is, the centre of attraction to all Christians, so that they may finally attain to a resting-place in the universe of space—that is to say, find a home in Heaven. The glorified body, as the material part of Jesus, being the point towards which the evolved human soul of the believer must gravitate to at death, we have here mass and distance, the two conditions necessary in gravitation.

If some of us Christians have been so moved by the tumult from without as to have lost for a time the conscious feeling of the vital process which is the expression of union between the soul and its redeemer, and have therefore found it necessary to examine the evidences of Christianity to secure a foundation for the objective structure, and have thus, as it were, laid hold for the second time on Christ as the ultimate unit ; we can only say we have suffered because we doubted, and that we now rejoice because we believe.

I therefore trust this essay may be useful to a class who are even now doubting, and that it may help to establish them in the faith, so that they may experience the freedom Christ points to in John viii. 32, where he says, "Ye shall know the truth, and the truth shall make you free," for Christianity was never intended to fetter the intellect of man.

NOTE.—The apparent inconsistency appertaining to the statement in this essay referring to the vital action as being increased by pleasure, which pleasure is derived from our union with Christ, and yet at the same time as being manifestly lowered by the course of conduct which was prescribed by Him as the course to be followed by His people—for instance, in the Sermon on the Mount—demands a word of explanation.

In the first place, love or joy is the expression of the action and counter-action that takes place in a soul in union with Christ, the embodiment of love; therefore, when we speak of the fruit of Christian belief from this point of view; we mean that an increase of vitality makes itself felt in the wave of feeling issuing from a soul in union with Christ, realised as love, while at the same time it is the case that the soul gives out energy in the performance of the work prescribed by the Christ of humanity, as the work His followers are to devote their lives to for His sake while they are in the world. But this is a work of self-denial, and therefore tends to lower the vital action in so far as our temporal life is concerned; afterward being realised in the spiritual body, it becomes a cause of quickening to that body through intense joy, in consequence, we may say, of its having been put to death in the flesh, but raised to life again in the spirit. Thus the contradiction was only one in appearance, and admits of a rational explanation.

NOTE.—The foregoing essay was written in May, 1875, and was intended to make its appearance in one of the magazines, but this idea was not realised.

Before publishing it now, I feel an explanation is necessary in reference to a point or two not so fully wrought out as I could wish.

First, it will be necessary to explain the meaning attaching to the phrase "being saved" or "redeemed," as used by Protestant Christians. The phrase "being saved" is applied to the soul as being the inward life of the individual which has been, or is being, evolved through the body, and retains an individual existence when separated from the body at death. Now, a soul in this condition is saved when it has been relieved from the consequences attaching to sin or conscious guilt; and it is thus that Christ's redemption-purchase affects the soul of the Christian by redeeming or saving it from the consequence of sin, and procuring for it the assurance of a happy eternity. Thus the highest form of Christian life is developed through the individual believer becoming converted or born again; and from the time this change takes place, the believer having realised his pardon and title to eternal life through Christ, he is animated by a desire, generated by love, to serve Him; so that every act of service, arising from love to Christ in God, is accepted by Christ as service done for him, and includes the treasures laid up in heaven referred to in Matt. vi. 20, and explained more fully in the cup of cold water mentioned by our Lord. (Matt. x. 42.)

By my mode of reasoning it will be apparent that it is the motive prompting the action that will determine whether the work is accepted or rejected of God in Christ.

In the second place, I would allude to the remark previously made by me, that Christ's atoning sacrifice, viewed in a universal sense (1 John ii. 2), does enable that man to save himself in whom truth and justice rules. As to such individuals, when the soul is separated from the body they will realise their title to a happy eternal existence, which they have been enabled to earn for themselves in consequence of the fruit of Christ's atoning sacrifice. But this class can have no treasures laid up for themselves in heaven, for they will only learn to love Christ as they come to realise the eminent obligation he has conferred on them in thus securing them salvation or deliverance.

But the shallowest intellect must see the enormous difference existing between the two classes in respect of the relationship which they bear to the individual through whose agency both classes have attained to an eternal well-being. The important distinction that separates the two classes will be of infinite moment, and may really determine almost everything in their progress onward through eternity. Yet I rejoice to feel that we all are one with Christ in God, and that the best of the race will mingle and rejoice together in Christ, the Head, throughout eternity.

ABOUT # PART III.

THE CHRISTIANITY OF THE FUTURE

OR

THE UNION OF TWO SYSTEMS OF TRUTH,

AS THE SCIENCE OF CHRISTIANITY IN RE-
VELATION AND MODERN SCIENCE.

CHAPTER I.

UNION WITH CHRIST EXPRESSING ITSELF IN FEELING.

IF the laws of nature are God's thoughts, and revelation is given to reveal the future destiny of the race to humanity, we must read both systems of truth in the light of the one explaining the other, and both of God. Consequently, the truth in the form I present it can only be realised by the Christian Church viewed as the representative of revealed truth, in the form of the body of Christ. For the Church springs from Christ's person, and works as the product of His life and death ; while the individual, as the unit of which the Church is formed, is made responsible to Jesus for the light his character presents, the Saviour being the Master he professes to serve. Further, every unit of this Church possesses the power of enjoying felt communion with Christ, expressing itself in a new state of consciousness as the fulfilment of Our Lord's words in John xiv. 21, "I will love him and will manifest myself unto him".

Viewing feeling as man's ultimate criterion, as we are bound to do in the form science presents him, and as that sensitive thing to which our Lord addressed these words, I insist upon this personal experience as an absolute necessity before man is in full possession of revealed truth, and therefore may with safety use the language of Paul (2 Tim. i. 12), "I know whom I have believed, and am persuaded that he is able to keep that which I have committed unto him against that day". And it is in this personal experience that Paul has revealed truth demonstrated as God in Christ addressing *him*, having been enabled to realise revealed truth for himself in the union that unites the soul of man with Christ. With his feet fully established on the rock, and the risen Lord occupying the point of space where the wave of motion originated which expressed itself on his conscious soul, there was manifested the union, as a Christian experience, of which the objective Christ was the origin, and toward which the individual believer will gravitate at death. Possessing revealed truth in this form the individual believer may meet the sceptic man of science half-way as he declares the immortality of the soul, and asks to be instructed in the laws of nature, as recognising that in them his God speaks, so that thus he may more freely understand his Master's words as revealed in the sacred Scriptures. In reference to that passage in them (Joshua x. 13) where we are told that the sun and moon stood still at Joshua's bidding, I confess I know not how that may be; but one thing I know, that the God I serve had the power to affect nature so, for He rules supreme, and as His servant I would prove all things, holding fast that which is good. (Thess. v. 21.) For this reason then I would be taught of you, and glorify God through the truth as you men of science present it. It will be observed from this that the believer alone has power to combine the two sets of truths expressed in nature and in grace.

Starting from this ground, all knowledge must take the form of the feeling; and the felt as presenting the subject and the object, and therefore all our knowledge must appear in the form of contrasted ideas, just as we see the truth of nature presented in the truth revealed, wherein the contrasted ideas stand for two objective existences.

For example, we have man presented in John iii. 6 in the form of body and mind; that which is born of the flesh as flesh (which the material school of thought has taught us to comprehend) being placed in contrast with its opposite—namely, that which is born of the spirit as spirit. Thus is presented the new element which is got in our union with Christ, and the full thought is realised in the Christian as a form of body and mind and spirit. Thus do we pull the idea to pieces and build it up again, to find in it the full thought as presented by our Lord. When we speak of the soul we mean the thing formed and the process employed in forming it, and the future work of the Church, as Christ's body on earth, will be to present the future of the race as seen in the light of revealed truth illuminated by science, with our Lord as its developing intelligence.

It will be seen from what I have said that I boldly assert that matter presents man in the ultimate form of body and mind; and that the unit of humanity who contracts a union with Christ, made apparent by a new state of consciousness, has felt the effect of a wave of feeling issuing from the very person of Christ, defined as the spirit of truth. Through this medium the believer becomes possessed of the essence which includes the spirit of God, so that with this meaning attached to this experience I would have it distinctly understood that the

Christian is to be regarded as composed of body, mind, and spirit. Further, I hold that in this wave of feeling that issues from the Saviour we ought to include a something which represents the Godhead, received through our union with Christ in God; in this sense Christ is to be taken as the objective existence presented to the eye of sense.

Chapter II.

THE TWO TYPES—THE OLD MAN AND THE NEW.

FROM my starting point it makes no difference whether the race was evolved or created, taking the latter term with the meaning usually attached to it. For anyhow it was created, in the sense that the word of God produced the race, either as the effect of the laws of nature—namely, the thoughts of God—or otherwise. Therefore this unit which presents itself before us in the form of body and mind is the unit which revealed religion has to deal with, as well as the unit in which the vital action expresses itself in the form of conscious life as the function of the structure. Therefore we must view the individual being as a unit possessing a continuous existence, whose vital action will ever be increased by pleasure and diminished by pain, and consequently we must hold that pleasure and pain are to us life and death. Life is increased by the vital actions put forth to secure a pleasure and avoid a pain. Man is thus stimulated to self-preservation, which indeed becomes the strongest power in him, and may be said to govern his actions almost, if not quite, entirely, rendering him an automatic machine as he grasps a pleasure and avoids a pain. With this we have to include the individual as possessing a moral and religious element, and as capable of reflecting on the consequences of his actions at the same time that he has the conscious feeling that to act or not to act is within his power (how far this feeling may be *actually realised* is a very different matter). It remains, however, that to man, a rational responsible being, self-preservation is the spring of all his actions. Now, this self-regarding instinct, where there is a due respect had to the rights of others, is a legitimate and right feeling in the individual *unbeliever*, because his ultimate is understood to consist in making the best of life as we now know it, and his eternal destiny will depend on what use he makes of his present opportunity. Man, therefore, as the highest intelligence presented in the form of body and mind is, we maintain, quite justified in acting according to his nature, provided he manifests a due regard for the rights of others. But all this becomes changed immediately we admit the power of Christian influence, for Christianity strikes at the very root of this self-regarding interest as regards this life, calling it the work of the flesh and the cause of enmity to God. Moreover, it was that very self-regarding interest which led to Adam's fall, and constituted the germ from which all evil springs. It was this ingredient present in humanity which necessitated a saviour being provided (in one sense) to redeem the race by converting a rebel into a friend and co-worker with God, where every unit of humanity, as the consequence of being saved, will cease from this self-regarding interest, and henceforth only desire a separate existence in union with Christ. Otherwise there would be presented two opposing forces, which would tend towards man's destruction, and ultimately effect it. For herein lies the whole germ of man's *controversy* with God. And here we see God's foreknowledge manifested in providing the Saviour as the medium through which humanity may be subdued by the power of love. Thus men are raised above what is known as the doctrine of necessity, and are stimulated individually to actions arising from love to Christ, each one devoting his *energy and conscious life* to the service of Christ in God, this being his God appointed work upon earth. For, taken in his Christian relationship, a man is not of the world, but one that Christ has chosen out of the world as in a special sense destined for eternal glory, therefore not of the world though in the world. From this reasoning, the motive that prompts action in the two classes of individuals which I have described arise from quite different and opposite sources, and will produce fruit altogether unlike. The Christian so animated is storing up treasures in heaven, as the fruit of his redemption, in service done for Christ; in other words, as an individual he ceases to live, and is only desirous to have a continuous existence in union with Christ; to be one with Christ is the only life which he would now know. The other, on the contrary, is desirous to maintain his separate and individual existence, and is perfectly justified in using all lawful means to attain a lawful end. Action thus springing from this idea, the two-fold motive of securing a pleasure and avoiding a pain, is the germ from which self-preservation takes its rise. In the other class, however, this self-regarding instinct has been overcome in consequence of a new principle, in the shape of a *dominant idea* taking possession of the mind, inspiring love to Christ, together with a desire to serve Him in grateful return for service rendered by Him. In this way the individual's mind is raised above the self-regarding instinct, and is stimulated to action as the fruit of a passion or emotion—namely, love for Christ. In the light of present knowledge we are thus enabled to divide the human race into two classes, whose actions proceed from entirely different motives, and therefore produce fruit eternally different. We find the noblest types of the one class, as fully developed in their natural state, to be noble, generous, high-minded specimens of humanity, just and righteous in all their ways, acting according to reason and conscience, perfect men. Yet only men, born of the earth, earthly. They are perfect models of what the world can produce, *nature's very noblest work*, and as such we would present their disembodied spirits as they escape from the tenements in which they have been evolved, and now leave dead on the ground, and would present them before Christ the judge as the noblest portion of matter the earth and its surroundings can produce. In contrast with this we would present the other. Probably we find him poor and obscure, for his calling may be a humble one, perhaps that of a ticket-collector at some central terminus. He is always to be found at his post, and little does one think of the self-denying life he leads as he provides for a large family, and devotes every moment of his spare time to the service of Christ, his master. His heart is full of love to Him, for he has been born again, and with a feeling of deep gratitude would he now consecrate all to Him, while he labours to bring others to the knowledge of Christ (happily in Scotland the Sabbath is mostly his own, and therefore that day is wholly consecrated to his Master's work). You watch him as he devotes every moment of his time to the service of his Lord, and you find that the self-regarding instinct has been overcome in him by a nobler feeling, as he follows in the footsteps of the Master. In all this you see the effect of faith working by love, as he feels his eternity secure. Does he look for a reward? Mark the expression on his face, if you broach the possibility of any profit arising from this service he is rendering. How puzzled he looks! He cannot understand you! His labour is the fruit of gratitude and love; he already has his reward, for has not Christ saved his soul, and is not his life the effect of Christ's sacrifice, for which he would thus show his gratitude? Press the point of reward a little further, and all the brightness that before animated his face has disappeared, either in pity for your ignorance regarding the way of salvation, or from the feeling of uncertainty that would attach itself to his future did he think that his eternal happiness depended in the least on his efforts to secure it through the medium of good works. These are indeed performed, but only as the fruit of a something he already is in possession of—namely, the consciousness of being a sinner saved by grace, who seeks to express his soul's emotion in this form. But as for the notion of any reward being attached to works so rendered, that is wholly absent from his mind.*

---

* The labour of love proceeding from the inner circle in its highest form is simply the effect of the new principle that is animating the individual in the form of the wave of feeling which proceeds from Christ and includes the spirit of God. A new wave is thus in turn generated which, returning to Christ, presents the individual experience in heaven as the soul or angel

From the two examples just offered of the noblest of the race, it will readily be seen that there is not one point in common between them. The source of action in both individuals is entirely different : the self-regarding interest, which is the just and legal feeling, animating the one, while the other, having ceased altogether to think of self, has his conduct controlled by love to Christ, and that feeling of gratitude which the prospect of eternal happiness in and through Jesus, his Lord and Master, has inspired.

of the redeemed. In this way a constant action and reaction in the form of the feeling and the felt is taking place between Christ and His body or Church on earth.

Chapter III.

THE ORIGIN OF THE OBJECTIVE CHRIST TRACED THROUGH MANY STAGES, AND THE FORCES EMPLOYED IN BUILDING THE NEW MAN.

LEAVING my two possible types of the last chapter, I would try to present the Christianity of the future in the light of known truth, by building a new structure out of the material which may be said to be the effect of that self-regarding feeling or instinct of self-preservation which has been seen to be the strongest power in man. The soul of the infant I would regard as though the forces in the little brain of the child had been in equilibrium. Furthermore, as the product of the joint conscious beings from whom it has sprung it may be looked upon as embodying in a manner the experience of the race, and as having stored in its brain the ideas which have been evolved in the process of time, and of this experience the soul of any such dying in infancy may be taken to be in a measure the expression. The souls of the imbecile or idiot may be viewed in a similar way, only I cannot help thinking that their souls have a special claim on the Almighty, and in this idea I would cling to the old Scotch saying, that they are the children of the Almighty, implying that He keeps a special watch over them. And indeed I am sure that He does so, knowing them to be irresponsible creatures, whom His own laws have produced. All the insane, therefore, seem in my opinion to be specially cared for by God, and to have before them a future very splendid indeed, as possessing much of the experience of the race without any responsibility attached. We may say that their's are souls fresh from the hands of the Creator, as being the product of His laws, and this would be a good reason to offer for such an opinion or belief, through the latter may also partly have arisen from the sympathy I feel for all such in the treatment they often receive. Anyhow, in the spirit of the old Scotch saying I would address one and all, and say, Behold the offspring of God—the offspring of the Almighty—which He has committed to the care of mankind, and in regard to which we will have all of us to render to Him an account of our stewardship.

To return to my subject as relating to the power that Christian influence exerts on the individual life, I would first deal with the germ which I perceive to present itself as the original Christ, understood to represent the God Man. And I would begin by stating that I hold the religious and moral element in humanity to be a fact which is apparent to all. Therefore, understanding this to be an element existing in the race, I would take hold of Abraham as that one in the race who in his generation displayed the religious element in the highest form, and in consequence of the developed state of this element was chosen by God to fulfil His design, and to become the medium through which the future Saviour was to be produced. In this way came the effect that the revelation given by God was intended to produce, which was destined to be accomplished by God revealing Himself from time to time to Abraham and his seed. It must be observed here that the revelation thus made by God is understood to include an entirely new element, namely, that of God specially presenting Himself to man. No matter how high and exalted and utterly beyond our reach it may be, modern science presents a first cause, while as believers in a revealed religion we are dealing with facts, and must conclude that Abraham and his seed were specially called of God, and in this form presented a new development, which was destined to produce eminent and glorious effects, through the influence of this new element of God revealing His will to man. It was this that taught Abraham's race to fear and adore Him, as the Self-existing, Eternal, Omnipotent One, who chose thus to make Himself known to them by this wave of feeling issuing from the Eternal, and making itself felt in truth communicated through this medium.. Man was brought to the knowledge of God, and the forces thus united eventually assumed the form of definite ideas, in which God's character was revealed, and through which God ordered that man should perceive his need of a Saviour. The result of the laws thus originated through the forces employed has been the production of a germ, in the shape of an idea, which includes God's will to save and man's desire to be saved. This is the germ from which the future Saviour was destined to be produced, and to which as made apparent in the light of our present knowledge our Lord traces His origin when he alludes to the root and offspring of David, implying by His language that David's united contrasted ideas in revealed truth, which, when united, formed a full thought, and became the word of God. Thus was presented to us the germ which afterward appears in the form of the Lord of Hosts, who is to be called the God of the whole earth (Isiah liv. 5), and which, being in due time brought to maturity though the Virgin Mary, is known to our age as the Jesus of history, and the Christ of Christianity —the child of Mary indeed, but also the Son of God, and the God of humanity, by whom as God-Man our race is redeemed. Thus we have the medium of the organism and its environment presented in the subjective and objective, the feeling and the felt, and expressing itself in the wave of ether, which in this sense includes the embodiment of the spirit of God uniting sinful humanity, as conscious life, with the eternal, in the expression of the "Abba Father" which is the Christian's birthright. Thus we have found the Jesus of history in the first revelation made by God to man, and have followed the cause presented till we see Him seated on the judgment seat, and recognised as the God of the whole earth, and the only one able to weigh and measure human energy, that is to say, what is seen in the possible to man in his efforts to mount up higher and yet higher, bearing the image of God. In all this I would have it observed that I have not stripped Christ of His divine nature. For every unit of the forces thus employed existed in the form of the Godhead before they were presented in the way we have seen. To show this we need only quote the words of Jesus Himself, "And now, O Father, glorify thou me with thine own self with the glory which I had with thee before the world was." (S. John xvii. 5.) Such language can only refer to that previous state of existence which included Christ's divinity, and which you and I as Chiistians believe in. By doing so we become sharers in that wave of feeling that units us with Christ, and which John speaks of as the spirit of truth. Therefore let us glorify God with our bodies and spirit, which are God's.

From my reasoning Christ must have existed first of all in the form of the original Godhead, and then as a separate existence in the germ presented to us in Revelation xxii. 16, where He speaks of Himself as the root and offspring of David, which germ was afterwards brought to maturity through the Virgin Mary, being the fruit of miraculous conception. And again having presented itself as the Jesus of earth, it afterwards appeared as a disembodied spirit, which preached to the spirits in prison. (1 Peter iii. 19.) Lastly, having taken possession of His body, it appeared as the risen Lord. And now we point to the form as it occupies a point in space, where the soul of each believer desires to gravitate. And I feel perfectly confident in saying that Jesus will yet again appear on the earth as the Messiah of the Jews, when Jerusalem will be rebuilt, and the ordinance of circumcision be once more demanded as a sign of the chosen seed. Then shall the prophesy of Zechariah be fulfilled, and " Ten men shall take hold of the skirts of him that is a Jew, saying, we will go with you ; for we have heard that God is with you." (Zechariah viii. 23.) My theory then is, that Jesus during the millenium will take up His abode now at one time on the earth, and now at another on one of the nearest planets of less dimensions than the earth, for we are told in Revelation xx. 9, that "They went up on the breadth of the earth, and compassed the camp of the saints about". Here the reference is made in regard to the last rebellion and final battle as the gathering of Gog and Magog. The consequence of this battle is, that the end and consummation of our earth will be determined and brought about through its effect, as the *combined will of the race* is manifested by the inhabitants of the earth whom the self-regarding instinct will prompt to an act of rebellion in surrounding the camp of the saints as their last struggle, when the devil who deceived them is to be cast into the lake of fire, events which will immediately precede and determine the final resurrection and judgment. From the 10th verse to the end we see the last judgment described, but during the intermediate period—including the millenium and the time of falling away which will succeed the millenium—I hold His people, who are raised as the fruit of the first resurrection, will be present on either one or other of the neighbouring planets, while the souls or disembodied spirits of His people, not yet ready for this change, shall enjoy His conscious presence while they are being prepared for the second and final resurrection. Anyhow, whatever may be the future of the race in this respect, there can be no doubt that the Jews will find every promise of the Lord's fulfilled to themselves, and so we may leave the future, feeling assured that the Lord of all the earth will do right.

Having followed Jesus in this way through many different stages, I would have you see the influence which the ideal Christ is destined to produce on the race, for it is this influence which rebuilds the structure of this, mostly automatic, machine which we have seen to be produced as the result of self-preservation. The Saviour cuts at the root of this self-regarding interest in His rebuilding, and the Scriptures call the individual believer who acts under its influences as "at emnity with God, and not subject to the laws of God". But it must always be borne in mind that the meaning which I attach to this language is, that the vital action is increased by securing a pleasure and avoiding a pain. This I hold to be an illegal course of action for the believer to secure vitality by, as he goes forward through life bearing his cross in the service of his Redeemer. And I would also have it understood that I do not regard the pleasure arising from felt communion with Christ as included in this form of speech; that pleasure is the believer's ultimate, and is derived from a legal and proper source—the source that bestows eternal life. Consequently it is worldly pleasure that I refer to, of which the enjoyment has no longer become a necessity to the believer, as one of the class to whom Jesus speaks in John xvi. 33, "In the world ye shall have tribulation: but be of good cheer, I have overcome the world." Thus the believer is bound to seek his enjoyment elsewhere, as not of the world, but of them whom Jesus has called out of the world. (John xv. 19.)

The significance to be attached to our Lord's teaching in this respect is very apparent in the light of present knowledge, according to which we see the whole individual structure to be evolved through the influence of an opposite law, that finds expression in every feeling of the human heart or soul. And it is when we view these two contrasted interests that we recognise Paul's teaching, as expounded in his contrasted ideas presented as flesh and spirit warring against each other. We thus get at the root of his meaning, when he made objective his conscious self in the graphic description to be found in his epistle to the Romans vii. 14-25. In the view there maintained to be going on we see the fire that is burning out the old structure, while the new form is made to take its place. The effect of this opposing current is very plainly and fully defined in Galatians v. 15-26. Here the meaning is as manifest as is the effect of an organism built up through the principle of self-preservation and ready to grasp at a pleasure, and from the possession of which a man feels how strong he is in the full flow of life, while the vital action is rising even higher and higher. · It is to the individual so constructed that Jesus addresses the Sermon on the Mount, and expounds the process through which His followers are to be moulded. We thus realise how often Paul's expression, Romans vii. 19, "For the good that I would I do not; but the evil that I would not that I do," will represent the state of consciousness experienced by the believer, as he rebuilds the structure after the form of the teaching of Jesus. As the organism he will joyously welcome his Lord in whom he shall have confidence, and not be ashamed before Him at His coming. (1 John ii. 28.)

We have in our day the teaching of Jesus fully demonstrated before our eyes, as we see the formed structure, and perceive the process employed in forming it

Origin of the Objective Christ Traced. 145

plainly, confronting the teaching of Jesus Christ as brought out in Paul's philosophy, the counter current answering to the definition of Paul's description so graphically given by him in Galatians v. 17. "For the flesh lusteth against the Spirit, and the Spirit against the flesh: and these are contrary the one to the other: so that ye cannot do the things that ye would." We now fully comprehend the words of Jesus to Nicodemus. (S. John iii. 7-8.) "That which is born of flesh is flesh, and that which is born of the spirit is spirit. Marvel not that I said unto thee, ye must be born again." In this new birth we see the action of the new set of forces applied to the conscious mind, and producing a movement totally different from the previous movement, in which the external actions are felt to vibrate in unison with the Lord, as He proclaims His power over the structure which His influence controls, for it is the unit which His sacrifice has redeemed, and in which He now takes up His abode as the ideal Christ presented by Paul, (Colossians i. 26-27) as "the mystery hid from ages, which is Christ in you the hope of glory". Thus we trace the internal movement to its source, finding it in the power which this ideal Christ produces, in directing and enabling the individual to rise above the things of time and sense, as the fruit of God's spirit in this new state of consciousness making itself felt according to Galatians v. 22-23, in love, joy, peace, long-suffering, &c. Thus the human soul finds rest and peace in Christ.

The natural experience of such a soul is manifested in the joy derived from the consciousness of being reconciled to God, and being in felt communion with Him, as the individual's future is realised in union with Christ, and this though the battle of the counter forces sometimes rages. Yet, while the eye is directed to Jesus as the sinner's friend, the renewed soul is sure to conquer.

Thus modern science enables us to see our strength and our weakness, as we follow the Master, and get at the Lord's meaning in His saying, " Ye must be born again". Then we see an entirely new element making itself felt in the process which this implies, being the movement of the Spirit of God, and as I have said the leading features of this movement is the feeling of security attaching itself to the consciousness of being reconciled to God, and for this reason enabled to approach Him with the Abba Father of the Christian God.

Chapter IV.

THE IMPOSSIBILITY OF PROVING THE EXISTENCE OF A GOD APART FROM REVELATION.

THE very ground work of Christianity arises from the accepted fact of the existence of a Self-existing Eternal Being defined as God, and revealing Himself in and through Jesus Christ as the objective part of Himself, and arising out of the forces that were from time to time employed in revealing the presence of the Almighty Power in whom the Jews trusted, and from whom they received the law. In the rebellion of the latter from time to time we see the action of the self-regarding instinct manifested in opposition to the commands of God. The action and counter action are clearly manifested in the history of this people, viewed in the light of present knowledge. For amongst them the belief in the existence of a God was a universally accepted fact. But to return to our subject; in the revelation of Christ we see that the existence of the personal God, which constitutes the framework of the whole system, is the very idea that Christianity springs from. Therefore it is an utter waste of time which is often devoted to the fruitless attempt to prove the existence of a God or the immortality of the soul, for that is utterly impossible apart from the revelation that has been given us. For there is nothing representing the object concerned in nature to prove the existence of either the one or the other. Moreover, the notion of design used for that end is altogether worthless and useless, in as much as it can only point to a God of force, and presents man in the form of body and mind as the grandest display manifested in the action of the forces at work, with an inspiration and craving after immortality. But what have you when the lifeless body of the dearest friend is presented to your view? Where is your evidence now to prove the existence of a God taking care of the self-consciousness of your friend, and binding the forces together by a law that can be traced and demonstrated before you. Higher than the intelligence of man we have nothing, and this intelligence only procures for us an individual existence, while body and mind remains united in the bodily organism. Hence it must appear to every intelligent, conscientious, or honest mind as an utter waste of time to bestow effort on an argument of which there is no objective existence corresponding to the thing. Therefore the question still rests in an utter impossibility to prove the existence of a God apart from revelation. But let it be fully understood that to say we cannot prove the existence of a God apart from revelation, is very different from saying that God does not influence the mind of man apart from revelation (understood as Bible truth). For most certainly God does express Himself, and the man that worships Him through nature is sure to find Him.

Theodore Parker presents the highest form of such I can think of, and the God he found in nature was perceived by him as his father and his mother too. What a devotion gave birth to that thought! What a fount of love these words include, and what utter loneliness they imply regarding human sympathy, as he finds in God his ultimate. That God he has consecrated his all to, and we call him a sceptic and an outcast. A sceptic we certainly are justified in calling him, for he was an unbeliever, and therefore he did nothing from love to Christ. But see the other marks Jesus would have us judge by, how brightly they stand out (Matthew vii. 20-21) in producing this fruit! Yet he is no Christian, for his fruit springs from self-preservation as the desire of immortality increases. But the Christian's consecrated life is the fruit of his love to Christ as his Saviour and Redeemer, and though in his case much of the same fruit is produced, yet it rises from an entirely different motive. The Christian is saved and one with Christ in God, whom he will or must serve, as being animated by a law which, as faith working by love, must express itself in action. This service to God is the effect of the belief implied in his power to overcome his former bad habits aided by the strength of Christ. The other, on the contrary, is earning eternal life as the fruit of his good works according to the saying, " do this and live." But the believer lays up treasures in heaven in the name of Jesus, and as the reward of service done for his Lord while he strove to attain the perfect state enjoined in Matthew v. 48.

But though man cannot prove the existence of a God, yet those who search will surely find him, as the feeling of the felt expresses the manifestation of the God of nature, which will be seen in the person of Jesus Christ as the objective portion of the Godhead, and as the one who is to be called the God of the whole earth. (Isaiah liv. 5.) But this worshipping of a God of nature and finding Him at the end objectised in the Christ of Christianity is wholly different from worshipping Jesus in the Christian form, and earning for ourselves the reward of having witnessed for Him before a sinful world. Hear the words of our Saviour as recorded in Matthew x. 32. " Whosoever therefore shall confess me before men, him will I confess before my Father which is in heaven." The honour here implied is the highest conferred on our race, or even possible to man. The idea that seems attaching itself to those who profess to believe in Christianity, and yet avowedly teach the impossibility of perceiving God in consciousness, is at utter variance with the teaching of the originator of Christianity, and cuts at the very root of His doctrine. For there is no point that our Lord more fully maintains than this, namely, His felt presence as a state of consciousness intended to maintain the evidence of His power and presence in the church through the individual believer, as the fruit of the new birth, and the manifestation of the spirit that was ever to witness for Him. (John xv. 26, xvi. 7-13, also John iv. 23, 24. To the individual the felt power is of vital importance, as the counterpart of the truth he receives in his Christian faith, and as the influence that stimulates to action in pulling down the old structure, and rebuilding the conscious mind in the likeness of Christ. Thus it created the new man whom Paul points to, and nothing short of this would enable him to rise above the doctrine of necessity, nothing short of the joy that attaches itself to the reconciled child would satisfy him as a believer approaching the Father in the name of Christ, and feeling the warm glow of heavenly love throbbing in every nerve as he points to his eternal home and says, "it is mine; for Jesus died for me, and God is love, I know and feel". Thus does he feel the promise made by Jesus in John vii. 17 to be fulfilled in his own personal experience of the truth of the thing revealed. The Bible proclaims the words of Jesus, and the Spirit applies them to any one *listening* and willing to be taught. For Jesus will only have willing service, in which man does not see his own glory, but the glory of God as seen in Jesus Christ. It is thus when we look to the forces that were combined in an intelligent life as the revelation made to the Jews foreordained to form their promised Messiah, and regard them as the germ brought to maturity through the Virgin Mary, as the root of David presented in the Jesus of history that rose from the dead, and ascended to heaven; it is thus we can say: Behold the man that has demonstrated the immortality of the soul by revealing the personal God!

Chapter V.

THE NEW BIRTH EXPRESSED IN FEELING.

IN our day it seems peculiarly apparent that it is mostly the poor and so-called ignorant that have the gospel thus addressed to them, as they sit at their humble fire-sides and discuss the mystery of the knowledge of God. With the evidence of His promise in the witness of the spirit manifested as a felt power in every heart they feel Christ dwelling in their midst, and dedicate their children to God in Him. They have the experimental proof of their religion throbbing in every nerve in Jesus as a felt power within (Ephesians iii. 17-19), and you may say it is all sensation, mere feeling. But what does our knowledge arise from but the feeling and the felt? And have not the class I refer to the historical Jesus, though they may have never heard of Him, and they are only bewildered if you speak to them of the historical Jesus. They have never doubted, and therefore they have no notion of the historical Christ, but by this they certainly have not lost. For the "blessed are they who have not seen, and yet have believed"; this simple "faith is wholly theirs". We, that have made our religious belief a matter of proof in finding the historical Christ cannot say He is ours in this child-like form, as we fight the battle of life, and having found Him outside the Bible —therefore believe. For He lives outside the Bible as well as inside it, and it only requires one animated by the Spirit of God to get acquainted with the laws that govern the mind, to be able to point out the idea implied in Paul's work of the flesh (Galatians v. 17) as the fruit of the self-regarding interest, and the wave of feeling which issues (see John xvi. 7 as to the origin of the wave) from Jesus, making His presence felt as the idea standing for the Spirit of God in the movement which is first expressed in the new birth, and afterwards in the Christian experience of the believer. Thus, with these two truths separate and combined, the most ignorant of the race, in the possession of the Christian experience, could have presented the truth taught or revealed, as seen in the counter-current; that is, if the laws of the mind had been known to them together with the perception of the feeling and the felt as man's ultimate. The power of combining was certainly within their reach, however stupid they might be. Only, without the experimental knowledge of the new birth all is midnight darkness and nothing in the future certain.

Chapter VI.

THE SOUL AS A GROUP OF SENSATIONS PROCLAIMED IMMORTAL.

I CAN fancy I hear many of my contemporaries saying: well, if the soul is to be reduced thus to a group of sensations, what proof have we that the grouped mass will hold together when the bodily organism falls to pieces? I would answer, the very same authority that we have for the existence of a God objected in the revelation he has presented to us. The counterpart of this we find in the root and offspring of David as the grouped intelligence and the seed of the miraculous conception which appeared in the Jesus of history, being the child of Mary, but the Son of God and the ideal God of humanity. The subjective and objective existence is that which the church has sprung from, just as the sensations arising from the wave of feeling thence originated, have united the individual soul of the Christian believer with its correlative objective whole. The unit which finds its objective existence in the God Man is the only expression we can point to as demonstrative proof that God is, and the immortality of the soul rests on grounds exactly similar. Both rest on the fact that a revelation has been given to demonstrate the truth of both—namely, the existence of a God and the immortality of the soul.

We have seen how the objective Christ was formed,

and came into being as the counterpart of the forces employed in the revelation given by God from time to time to the Jewish race, and having assumed the form of humanity in the person of our Lord, became the God of the whole earth, and the being through whom humanity has procured an eternal existence.* For thus has an individual immortality been secured to every germ which is the product of conception, and the fruit of two lives is seen in the parent germ, the soul being presented and immortalised through the life and death of the Redeemer whom God provided for that end. In the seed of every such germ we have the generalized experience of the race, which is implied in the term humanity. And at no stage of its existence can we prove its immortality apart from revelation. You may deny the formation as the result of sensations grouped together, but you gain nothing by your denial. If you say that God creates each soul, which He implants in an organism, then what reason have you to offer for God providing a germ which in its instinct of self-preservation will, if left to itself, ultimately aspire to possessing the throne of the Almighty? If you present the product of creation in this

---

* This eternal existence undoubtedly is presented by John ii. 2, where Christ is said to have atoned for the sins of the whole world. From this we reason that in the countless ages of eternity the worst will ultimately be rescued from the power of evil in the conscious ego being endowed with power to stamp out the evil as he rebuilds the structure, animated by love, which I hold to be included in many words of John's. It will be apparent, from all that has been said, that evil and good in the abstract must exist eternally apart; that is if the devil, animated by his self-regarding interest —Isiah xiv. 12-14—is to have a continuous existence, and be animated by the same feeling.

156   *Christianity Reduced to Proof.*

form, you present at the same time God in a false light. For as we have before seen the self-regarding interest has been fully demonstrated to be universally the strongest power in man. But now, allow this spirit to be the product of sensational grouping, and the effect produced in humanity as the result of a natural law, with the individual experience of the race presented in the individual soul, and you have a reasonable soul at once, with the character of the individual or personal God present in the religious element evolved. With the grouped sensations presented as the human soul in the light of revealed truth we are justified in proclaiming it immortal. For here we have the eternal mind objected in the unit of intelligent life, built up through the medium of human experience, in which the individual feels he has power (in a certain sense) over his thoughts and actions as the form with which revelation chiefly concerns itself, and as that aspiring thing which would usurp the throne of the Almighty.*

While we proclaim the carnal mind as seen in this

---

* There is a passage in Romans viii. 7-8 which throws light on this point, for there we are told that "The carnal mind is enmity against God: for it is not subject to the law of God, neither indeed can be. So then they that are in the flesh cannot please God." For at this stage, where a revelation is given, aspiring man crosses the path of a mightier than he, who will be obeyed, who sooner or later says to the individual germ, or soul of the race presented thus, "As you judge you shall be judged". Possessing the little superiority which your additional brain power gave you, what justice have men rendered to that weaker portion of humanity, woman, whom the Lord committed to your care as the product of his laws, and marked by a sensitive nature as keen as your own. As you judge, so you shall be judged. (Will not then that iniquitous Contagious Diseases Act speak here, when man presents himself before the Supreme Being?)

sensational grouping to be immortal in Jesus' name, so we view Him in one sense as the propitiation for the sins of the whole world (1 John ii. 2.) In other words, Jesus has secured the individual immortality of the race, when, in the life to come, He, as judge, will mete to each individual according to his own measure (Matthew vii. 2), and shall have power to enforce His judgment. At the same time He has secured immortality to each individual, as a responsible, intelligent unit, capable of reasoning on the past, the present, and the future; fully conscious, moreover, of its immortality as it sees humanity presented in Christ, who is the God Man thus qualified to judge and condemn a race, which is seen to be the product of God's laws while it is insured of an eternal existence. As we present the grouped sensations which embodies the human soul and proclaim its immortality in Jesus' name, we point to Jesus as God and Man, whom as the God of humanity we worship and adore, for He took on Himself a human form, and proved Himself capable of realising the joys and sorrows which animate us, having rejoiced at the marriage and wept at the grave, and in all respects assumed our nature and suffered in our stead.

Chapter VII.

THE THEORY OF THE GROUPED SENSATIONS BROUGHT OUT.

AS aspiring to connect two systems of truth, I present the human soul as a group of sensations which are the product of the organism and its environment, and as yielding a conscious life which dwells in the framework of the body. And thus I say the individual soul bears the form of the body. Here I would say one word to those who may possess natural deformities, which are a cause of a cross to them in this life. If they have glorified God in bearing their burden in the spirit of the " Thy will be done ", then the bodily defects will present the form of treasures laid up in heaven, and be for the individual a triumph through eternity. Not now will they seem as deformities, but as distinguished marks of grace, of course in a limited and Christian sense. A similar impress did our Saviour bear in the marks of the nails on His hands and feet. For the afflicted individual has suffered because of the laws of nature, which is God operating on the earth and producing a form like this. And any one so afflicted may feel when the finger of scorn is pointed toward him,

Theory of the Grouped Sensations brought out. 159

that the finger thus pointed is mocking God, represented in the form produced by His laws.

We are now dealing with the soul as bearing the impress of the body, and as a group of sensations which we claim the right, in God's name, to proclaim eternal, in accordance with the language of revealed truth. Therefore we would lay the foundation of the personal soul first on the sanction presented in conscious life, and next on the serial states of consciousness which form the grouped sensations of the individual soul. It is an accepted fact that our knowledge comes to us in the shape of ideas ; for example, the child, when taught, perceives the dog, the cat, and the table, &c., &c, and the man knows what anger and fear means by the feeling implied, as the perception of the cause that gave the idea birth ; so also he receives the impression into the brain, already prepared as a kind of framework in which the ideas presented in this framework were developed in the parent germ. I thus accept as a fact the notion that the cerebrum of the brain contains the stored up ideas of the individual, presenting themselves as sensations on the sensorium portion of the brain. The shock, herein implied and occasioned by the union of the gases and rendered a sensation, divides its forces according to an established law ; as the wave spreads, one portion of it carries the idea forward to the cerebrum portion of the brain, the other part goes to form the individual soul (or angel, as it is called in the Revelation of John). It will be here observed, that I take no notice of any sensation except such as presents itself in the consciousness of an intelligent being, because this is the only portion that personal responsibility is attached to. Though the actions and thoughts of a drunk man with other similar cases, such as fever and madness, will doubtless be presented in a continuous flow of thought as the life experience of the individual—for I cannot comprehend a break in the continuity—yet of such feelings I take no account and confine myself to the flow of conscious life as presented in the responsible man.

From this reasoning our individual life will present the divided wave in the shape of a sensation causing a shock on the nerves of the sensorium, and this will be the portion presented before the judge as the disembodied spirit, soul, or angel. It will be thus seen that the spirit thus formed presents the appearance of a portion of matter disintegrated from the body as the growing part of conscious life, though doubtless it will also contain in its framework the impression of the grouped forces of the parents which made it possible to act thus, and which were the seed which produced the individual as a whole. I can see no better arrangement than this, as in it we leave the inner brain (or cerebrum) to arrange the stored up ideas according to its own law, by which they will, or may, again present themselves in a new form to consciousness, namely, as thought. Here again the wave divides, the one half being carried back, while the other part goes towards forming the individual soul, and helps to create the big thing which some of our men of science will proudly find to belong to them, as the product of a well spent active life in the search of truth, stored up for themselves in the form of an individual existence. In the union of the gases thus presented we have an objective existence which corresponds exactly with the idea Christ gives of the soul, namely, as an existence where every individual will have to render an account of his stewardship, and as the conscious part of the body made to rise again.

Chapter VIII.

CHRISTIAN RESPONSIBILITY IN THE LIGHT OF MODERN SCIENCE UNLOCKING THE BIBLE.

IF modern science enables us to present the Saviour's words in a form like this, it is time we had recognised the science of Christianity as true to ourselves and others. Feeling that in Christianity we hold the key to the immortality of the soul, as science shows us how the form is built, then we ought to proclaim it in Jesus' name eternal. How selfish we are not to do so, though in looking at Christianity from this point we increase our responsibility ten fold! It would be almost as credible to shun the subject altogether and live in peace, as we allow the experimental knowledge of Christianity to die out, or be so unjust as try to shelter ourselves in saying that the men of science have closed the Bible themselves, and therefore we are in no wise responsible. But Christ will make us wholly responsible in this matter; for they have no opportunity of proving the immortality of the soul, except in the light of a revelation. As Christianity was given for that very purpose to animate man with supernatural power, manifested in his union with the Saviour, for the very end that he may witness for God. As he rises above the necessity doctrine in rising above the things of time and sense; as he proves his belief by a life corresponding to his profession; as one whom Christ has chosen out of the world to proclaim His truth; as one reconciled to God, and responsible as such to God for the impressions his actions produced on the race in revealing God to it; in all these we see the forces which God has applied for that end in view. By their influence the individual may be built up in a form in which he shall not be ashamed to meet the Lord, and be judged according to the deeds done in the body, as one who is responsible for the impression he may have given of the character of God. Of that God the world can know nothing for certain, except through the members of Christ's body, that is to say, individual believers. This then is our position, whether we honestly accept it or not: God in the form of Jesus Christ will certainly expect positive fruit. But to return to the grouping of the internal sensations as the grouping of the human soul. By my way of reasoning we leave the cerebrum free to act; only we are responsible, in so far as we have power to control the circumstances in which we store up our ideas. This we cannot but feel if we keep in view the consequences involved in the words which Jesus Himself made use of. (Matthew xii. 36.) "But I say unto you, that every idle word which men shall speak, they shall give account thereof in the day of judgment." For the form of reasonable soul is the product of the laws of nature, now inspired through the conscious union with God, as the fruit of the new birth, and therefore capable of perceiving truth in the form of revelation, as the wave issuing from a personal Christ. It may be through this medium, acting on the soul in the form of fixed laws, and rebuilding the structure according to the form which the individual soul possesses, that there is presented a result as certain as that of the laws of nature. Thus also it may be that the impression which we receive in consciousness is the result of the former actions, classified according to the decrees manifested in the work of redemption. An action like this, taking place here on what we shall call the outer redeemed mind, as purchased by the Saviour's redemption, and governed by the law of His kingdom, would correspond exactly with the internal arrangement which, we have good reason for saying, is that which is manifested in the action of the cerebrum brain. Thus it sometimes happens with the subject which we were engaged on yesterday, or it may be months ago, and which we left in utter confusion with a sigh of regret at the helpless entanglement of it. When we take it up again, we find that the subject is presented to consciousness with perfect clearness (implied in the words, I see through it now). The ideas are divided and subdivided so that we can take up any point and see where it differs from, and where it agrees with, any other point. In this way we proclaim an eternal truth as the fruit of a reasonable soul, responsible because possessing this conscious knowledge as the result of ideas received as sensations, which were however quite different from the form they now assume, although quite capable of being referred to the forms presented in the separating sensations. For these sensations have by one sense or another proceeded from objective things, or at least things which profess to have an objective existence. Surely then no one will be so unreasonable as to claim the merit of these groupings. With regard to them all that is left for the individual to do is to register the facts, as the means to a yet nobler and higher end. For it is a universal law, that an established fact becomes the ground-work which we use as a means to enable us to grasp something higher ; so to speak, we degrade every thing as a means to attaining a yet higher end in our aspirations. It is so with Christianity. Christ has reconciled us to God as a means to a yet higher end, by causing our service to be rendered in the spirit of love, and our approach to the Christian God with the cry of " Abba Father". Being thus made desirous to glorify God in all things we are enabled to enjoy His conscious presence for ever.

In the view thus taken we have first the sensorium brain, the seat of conscious life ; then we have a divided wave, carrying the ideas inward to the cerebrum brain, and outward to form the conscious soul (in the case of a Christian embodying a unit of Christ's redemption purchase); but over this outer portion we have no control during natural life. The seat of conscious memory is certainly to be regarded as composed of the stored up ideas of the cerebrum. It is to the cortical layer that the molecular wave is directed when we rouse the vasomotor nerves in search of a missing thought. We raise up one train of reasoning after another till we get hold of the notion wanted, which we feel is stored away some where ; and often after a fruitless search with a heavy heart we turn away, as we feel we cannot advance one step without this idea wherewith to close the argument, only to find that after all the thought comes wholly unexpected, at the very time perhaps when we are listlessly thinking of nothing. We feel our cheek flush, and our heart beat, as we catch up the idea so much wanted ; for with it the train of reasoning is complete (we have found the piece of money which was lost). The sensation that presents itself as the " I am " of the individual life, must therefore be sought for in the sensorium, which receives every idea presented in consciousness, in the shape of a sensation, of which the wave divides itself into two halves, the one carrying the impression inward, the other outward ; the whole being regulated by a natural law which binds the ideas together in the single shock in question ; though the latter indeed may be viewed as made into two halves, each doubtless governed by different laws, as the effect of the different conditions under which it originates. For let it be observed, the one half of the before mentioned wave is fixed in the cortical layer of the cerebrum brain, where it usually finds a prepared place, or can unite with something bearing some resemblance ; the other, united as a whole, swings in pure space, so to speak, and is the expression of an imaginary existence, bearing the impress of the individual soul, and is in fact the sensitive thing our Lord addressed in Mark viii. 35-38. There it is spoken of as a responsible thing which may be lost, while yet it is able consciously to perceive the effect of mediatorial rebuke in the particular case of having been ashamed of Christ before a sinful world or generation, and of having thus merited the treatment naturally entailed by such conduct. For the Saviour, in His human nature, feels and acts as a man possessing a perfect sense of justice, and, having procured salvation for all, He had a perfect right to demand to be recognised and honoured accordingly. Believers that refuse this recognition and honour, will nevertheless feel the fruit of it in themselves, in their increased sense of justice as they judge themselves. For though Christ saves His people from the punishment due to their sins, by securing them from the consequenee of the state implied in "You shall not come out hence till you have paid the uttermost farthing", yet the increased sense of justice, as the fruit of our being saved, will become so fully developed, that each will recognise and realise his own short-coming. Not that the Lord will upbraid any, but all will judge themselves according to their works, viewed in connection with their privileges, and the soul will be seen to be the result of our earthly life, conscious memory in it being understood as the chain that binds all our individual experience together, and enables us to judge our past actions in view of present circumstances.

In this objectised soul we present every conscious thought and action. Viewing the thing thus, we may suppose the union of the gases thus formed to assume the impression of the thing implied in the thought; for example, in the form of dissolving views, as scene after scene takes the place of the former one in the order of the impressions received in the course of perception. Suppose the case of two redeemed disembodied spirits, capable of perceiving impressions in this way, one of which had rendered many kind services to the other, every one of which appeared in the form presented, as the impression received in the union of the gases, the shape of ideas being the result of the first conscious meeting, and all feeling in the form of ideas having expressed itself as such, so that the exchange of conscious thought might thus become a very rapid process. This presents itself to my mind as a very natural mode of communicating between two conscious minds; for in this case mind presents itself as such, that is, as a grouped mass of ideas in connection with a conscious mind, capable of expressing themselves or itself so, yet longing for the resurrection of the body, when the powers of the mind will be greatly increased in the consequent reunion.

CHAPTER IX.

A THEORY APPLIED IN REFERENCE TO THE RESURRECTION OF THE BODY.

WHEN we see the selecting power manifested in the animal and vegetable worlds we may well generalise in reference to the resurrection body. In the vegetable world we see the fruit-bearing trees producing fruit, each after its kind; first the flower, and then the fruit. So in the animal world we behold species after species brought forth from the parent germ, the organism of each being included in the molecular substance of that tiny speck from which in time we find the full grown animal presented. A germ containing the selective power, through the operation of which all this is produced, and the different qualities of matter necessary for the ends aimed at in maturity are evolved, we can speak with eertainty about. And further, if the rays issuing from the sun by uniting with waves of the same period can build themselves up in the form of a special crystal with perfect symmetry, as we may justly infer: and if the aqueous vapour, seen at another stage in the ice block, can with certainty be said to have been acted upon according to law; if we can in all this trace the selective power in nature, manifested according to law, surely we may justly infer that the human soul also will be endowed with a selective power, which will be clearly displayed in the possession of the capacity to select and unite with its parent germ in process of time, and this notwithstanding that the germ may have passed through many and great changes during the interval of separation. This resurrection is a promised fruit of Christ's redemption purchase, and less than this will not present the promise fulfilled, and would rob our Lord of His purchased possession.

In the light of present knowledge we may clothe the spirits or angels of the redeemed with the resurrection body, with as great certainty as we can talk of any theoretic conception accepted as a truth in science, even though this conception can only be regarded as a step towards a yet higher conception as our knowledge and intelligence increase. In this way we follow in the footsteps of theoretical science, when in theory we create the resurrection body of the saint; for it is the redemption purchase presented in the individual life we are dealing with. As we use our reason, illuminated by scientific thought learned at the feet of Tyndall, Bain, Spencer, Lewes, and Carpenter, we are enabled to comprehend our Saviour's words. Here and there we gather an impression, and gradually find a growth of bundles of grouped sensations, presented in the form of ideas received, as the result of the union of the gases during the period embracing our earthly life, *i.e.*, in that portion of time in which the human soul or mind was formed, as the result of the bodily organism influenced through the medium of its environment, and expressed in the feeling and the felt, the object and the subject. In dealing with this union, resulting in the renewed mind, we have a something that presents an individual, in which every impression was marked as the result of a change of feeling in the individual, and as the cause of a movement somewhere else, either in the cerebrum brain, or through the senses, as the case might be. Anyhow, we have a something produced in connection with bodily organism. Or, to put it somewhat differently, we have one portion of matter receiving lasting impressions, as the result of being thus related with another portion of matter, from which, however, it has disengaged itself by being absent from the body, but present with the Lord ; for the bodily organism through which the soul was evolved falls to pieces for the time being. Now this germ, which we first find formed as the result of natural laws, was at another stage of its development the conscious subject of a change presented in the Christian records as a state of being born again ; which state was realised as the result of felt communion with Christ. This germ formed from the union of the gases, and including the conscious knowledge of the processes implied in the united series, understood as conscious life, is a unit similar to the intelligence we have presented to our view in the Revelation, as the Angel sent by Jesus, to make known the future of the Church and the world to the beloved disciple in the Isle of Patmos. Christ presents this figure in the form of an Angel in Rev. i. 1, and again, in the sixteenth verse of the last chapter, we find the intelligence thus employed, making His antecedent circumstances clearly apparent in Rev. xix. 10, as well as in Rev. xxii. 9, where occur the words, " I am thy fellow-servant, and of thy brethren the prophets, and of them which keep the sayings of this book ; the result of which is to leave no doubt as to the form of the intelligence implied in the term angel used by our Saviour. In addition to this, our men of science have enabled us to apprehend the full meaning of this phrase, by taking it in conjunction with the words "behold the man". For, because of their hard reasoning and clear thought, we may earn the blessing promised in Rev. i. 3, " Blessed is he that readeth, and they that hear the words of this prophecy, and keep those things which are written therein : for the time is at hand". From these words in the light of present knowledge we may certainly infer that Jesus will make us responsible as to the way in which we apply the teachings of science, in our effort to understand His words in the light of the immortality of the soul as an accepted fact implied in revelation, and lying at the very foundation of its existence. As the fruit of that revelation the Saviour is presented as the Redeemer of the race, reconciling man to God, and influencing his soul in proportion as he recognises a personal God to whom in love he would dedicate all things. This God the man of science may adore, glorify, and worship as the originator of the laws by which finite intelligence came into being, and through the power of which man as an intelligent being can rebuild the universe in theory, laying down the result of his labours at the feet of the Infinite Self-existing Eternal Being, and see in Him the Father of Jesus Christ, the risen Lord, the God of humanity, and the Ruler of the whole earth.

Through the labours of modern science enquirers we can take hold of the disembodied individual life, in the form of an angel, as representing the group of separate experience of an individual intelligent life. It is to this that our Saviour's words apply, when in Matthew xxiv. 31, He speaks of His angels as those who " Shall gather together His elect from the four winds, from one end of heaven to the other". Nor is it to be regarded as other than the expression of a natural law, of which the result will be that the portion of the body which we have laid in the grave as the dust of a departed friend, will again unite with its parent germ in the shape of its former intelligent companion, having every portion of matter before presented in this union, which is essential to procure the end required, and implied in the resurrection body of the saints. In this form our present knowledge enables us to comprehend the matter, by offering to us the body and mind as one substance. On this head the words of Jesus Himself are very instructive, as revealing to us the way in which this process of reuniting is to be effected. " Wheresoever the carcase is, there will the eagles be gathered together." (Matthew xxiv. 28.) We understand that by the eagles are signified the individual souls, and in the carcase we recognise the particles or stuff of the body seen to close with the spirit, or soul, or angel, just as Professor Tyndall's experiment present to our view the play of the atoms in the process of the formation of crystals. As we follow our Lord's words in the light of modern science we see where one law can be applied as well as another, only we cannot call our departed friends out of heaven to show the working of the process as Tyndall can in his experiment. Nevertheless, we do not feel in any degree less secure on that account, as we repeat the words of our Saviour,

"Heaven and earth shall pass away, but my words shall not pass away". (Matthew xxiv. 35.) And indeed it would be very inconvenient for our friends, safely lodged in the arms of Jesus, to come back at our bidding to enable us to prove our theories, and thus to help in the work in which we may sneeringly have refused to be helped by them when here, because we thought our knowledge far superior to theirs.

What portion of the dust that we lay in the grave will be needful for this end we cannot tell, only it would appear by Paul's reasoning that it depends on the quality of the soul. (1 Cor. xv. 38-41.) In the passage referred to God is said to give the soul "a body as it hath pleased him, and to every seed his own body", and therefore we must view man in the sense here presented, as the product of God's laws, and confine man's responsibility to the possible in man in the light of his organism and environment. From this point of view Christianity implies a terrible responsibility, as in the light of that revelation we view the possible in man; recognising, as we have to recognise, in the objective Christ the elect of God, with all as elected of God, where the ideal Christ, in the form of our Saviour, appears in the subjective Christ as part of the individual mind. From this point of view we have no notion of what the possible in man may include. All we know is, that through this union humanity is presented in the form of body and mind and spirit; the last being regarded as of the form of a wave of motion, issuing from the Infinite and passing through the medium of the Saviour to animate the human soul, and to express its presence to the individual mind as a new state of consciousness. Through this spirit God is addressed as a reconciled Father in the "Abba Father," in the wave of feeling as motion sent back. As Christ is the elect of God, being the fruit of revelation seen in the forces employed in the process working according to law, so, in the very same sense, are we the elect of Christ, according to the language used in Matt. xxiv. 31, where we are told that his angels, in the form of the redeemed disembodied spirits, gather his elect, in the shape of the redeemed body belonging to each spirit, from the four winds; for Christ's redemption purchase includes body and mind, and therefore he must collect his elect in the form of their bodily organisms, which helped in forming his image. Nothing seems more intelligent than the truth presented here, as we follow Paul in his reasoning in the light of present knowledge; and the difference in the fruit thus raised may include a difference to be expressed in celestial and terrestrial bodies, possessing different degrees of glory, in accordance with the view of the possible in man. When we follow this line of argument, and view the Christian man as endowed with the potential energy implied in Paul's words, "I can do all things through Christ, which strengtheneth me," (Phil. iv. 13)* who can say what is the possible in man, as we consider the impressions received through the sensorium brain (or portion of brain), and know that through this origin the will pre-

---

* I would have it understood that I make a great distinction between those who have been born again and others simply holding the truth in the form of an intelligent conception, though both classes are entitled to the name of Christian.

sents itself in such a way as to make it possible for man to have the power over the two sets of muscles taking their rise here, and enabling him to act, or not to act, as he views the consequence of each action in the light of revealed truth ; as well as giving him power to think, or not to think, on any subject which may be presented to his conscious mind ; for he has the power to select, by dismissing the one and retaining the other idea, except when the mind may chance to be taken possession of in consequence of a great sorrow or a great joy, which for the time may prevent action. But in this latter case both extremes are guarded against through the influence of Christianity, for in the most trying circumstances we may see the will of God, and say that all things work together for good to them that love God. And in the highest state of earthly joy we may see, that what the worldling lives on is the expression of a state of mind which includes our promised inheritance in the home to which we hasten, and therefore may treat it as a common thing. But, in the light of all this, it must appear to every thoughtful mind, how careful every Christian ought to be regarding the food he provides his mind with, both in regard to the books which he reads, that is to say, the ideas which he imbibes, or in regard to the outward life, in so far as he has control over the circumstances connected with it. For the Christian has the certain knowledge of the future consequences before his eyes, as they have been revealed in the Christian records, and it is in the light of these, and the effect produced by Christ's life and death, for all springs from that point, that the Christian's profession will be judged. But with those who are converted individuals, the case is somewhat different, if we understand by these those who are living out their professions, and thus have the power of selecting their own bodily substance, which will include the degree they are qualified to occupy in the state of glory, as sinners saved by grace, and rejoicing in the treasures it laid up in works done from love to Christ. With them in the next world the element of justice is so fully developed, that they are enabled to comprehend with perfect accuracy the part they have acted toward others, while they condemn the actions of life that are worthy of being condemned, humbly desiring to make amends if such be possible. For surely heaven, or the state of being saved by the Vicarious Sacrifice, cannot include less than this. Paul tells us in 1 Cor. xi. 31, "If we would judge ourselves we should not be judged". But if it is so on earth, surely we may infer that this high sense of justice, with a desire to make amends, is included in the fruit of the redemption purchase, as the individual sits in judgment on himself or herself. From this point, it is very essential that we realise our responsibility in reference to the potential energy stored up in the mind in the shape of gradually accumulated ideas.

It is here that we find the intelligence of the race treasured up, and accordingly it is the cerebrum brain which must rise again in the shape of conscious life, first in the portion of the human race raised at the first resurrection, but ultimately, at the final resurrection when all will rise to answer for the deeds done in the body.

Chapter X.

TWO SETS OF TRUTH CONTRASTED IN THE CEREBRUM BRAIN.

THE treasure box of stored up ideas in the cerebrum brain, alluded to in the last chapter, is the birth right of the race, and is capable of being divided into two groups, being the product of two distinct sources, through both of which knowledge in the shape of sensations come to us, and divides itself as it forms the ideas which include conscious life. One portion of the cerebrum brain, according to my reasoning, is stored up with knowledge that comes to us in the shape of what is earthly, that is, which has regard to our movements on the earth. The other portion of the cerebrum is stored with revealed truth, dealing with a state of existence succeeding this life. This, we may say, is the revelation contained in the Scriptures, because in them we have grouped together both the ideas of revelation given from time to time in the past, which have now been fulfilled, as well as information regarding the future of the race. Thus, in accepting the truth here revealed as containing absolute truth, we receive the conscious knowledge of revelation in impressions received into the brain. Through this medium the ideas present conditions, which either have an objective existence in this life in some sense corresponding to the impression implied, or must have an objective existence in the world to come or, yet again, they present scenes which have still to be acted out in this planet. In this sense then, we find the element of history blended with the element of prophecy, the knowledge thus presented in the Bible being taken as coming from God, and addressed to man. This is the medium through which man may gain the knowledge which will enable him to unite his soul in conscious union with God, who represents the objective portion of the Infinite, which has risen out of the revelation given, and now occupies a point in space in the form of the risen Lord—the God-Man who is the developing intelligence of the universe.

It will be seen that the set of ideas coming to us from this source, is wholly connected with a revelation that deals with a state of existence we have no means of knowing anything about except through revelation, so that the ideas stored up in connection with this subject are purely of this nature, and therefore may be termed collected truth, or knowledge of a peculiar nature. Hence the form of energy which has been employed in building up the brain in this respect, is not in one sense concerned with the products of earth in this formation. For in the way in which I have put this subject, the Bible, or the truth contained in the Bible, is principally the environment employed to build up the organism, in the form at least in which Protestants are most concerned to have it built up. And in this connection I would add one word of infinite importance to the individual Protestant. Our religious belief deals with the individual as such, holding each man as responsible for the formation of his individual existence, whereas the

Roman Catholic Church upholds a system which takes little or no notice of the individual, but leaves the Purgatorial fire to act upon the individual. And though I rejoice in my Protestant independence, I cannot help recognising much truth in this system, if wrought out in its purity; but alas! alas! viewing it in the light of a book recently published in America, "The Priest, the Woman, and the Confessional," by Father Chimoëny, it seems the bleakest spot upon earth.

Having stored up one portion of the brain with ideas got from the truth contained in the Bible, I would point to the environment which encircles the organism on the earth as that which furnishes the ideas stored in the other part of the cerebrum brain. In this division I would be understood to deal purely with natural phenomena, not meaning to take account of such things as the loaves and the fishes, &c., &c., as an environment, seeing that these only appeared as such by the word of Jesus This portion of the brain is stored with ideas which may be tested in the form of objective existences, or as theoretic conceptions which may be tested in this form. The universal ether cannot be tested as such, but, if we agree to accept the fact, we may procure a basis through which demonstrative proof may be presented in another form, as when we see the white light refracted or broken up into the coloured light, and presented as coloured light, and again, when we see one colour absorb another, as is shown by experiment. In this way, viewing this portion of the brain as stored by ideas, which are the result of the organism and environment, we may say

Two Sets of Truth Contrasted. 181

that the sun's energy produced the impression and also the appliance.

If we view light as a quality of matter, and also as the medium through which we apprehend matter, we have the transparent gas* presented to us as the result of the union through which all our knowledge has received an objective and subjective existence. The expression of feeling may be pointed to as containing all the elements of matter issuing from the sun, and known to us in the form of intelligent life. For is not this the process implied in the formation of conscious life, as each form of existence presents itself in the form of many compounds. Sometimes we pick the idea to pieces, and build it in a new form, calling it by a new name, or we leave out one of the elements and present the idea as a new thing. During all these changes does not the gas unite in order to bring about the new form, as if it were a little sun burning in the human brain? Anyhow, whether the sun has produced all the stuff we call matter as well as the energy we call force, is really of little moment, for it has produced in one form or another all the elements from which the brain has been built up. For indeed nothing is more certain than this in our day, as we view revelation in the light of science, and know that science itself rests on demonstrable proof. Let us call revealed truth God's truth, as we find it presented in one portion of the brain, while the facts of nature resting

---

* Although transparent to light, observe this gas is far from transparent to *heat*, and I believe on this point the Roman Catholic doctrine of Purgatory will chiefly rest.

on demonstrable proof are man's truth, as seen in another portion of the brain. Thus is truth, as presented in the flesh, found to be contrasted in the cerebrum brain in the form of matter as human intelligence.

Chapter XI.

CLERGYMEN RESPONSIBLE FOR MODERN SCEPTICISM.

VIEWING the portions of the brain built up of a purely earthly form as the things of earth and time, let us as Christians try to realise how we stand indebted to our men of science, as of late years in their search after truth they have stored our minds with new ideas. Now the effect produced through the two systems of truth—truth in revelation, and truth in nature—will and must stand out in bold relief in the individual as the effect of different laws acting through different mediums, yet both of God. Under this heading we shall advance still farther in the question of contrast, as we present our men of science in their devoted search after truth in contrast with our Protestant clergymen professing to proclaim the truth of the immortality of the soul, with all the consequence attached to a responsible life. Well, what sort of contrast do these two sets of individuals present in the amount of energy, generated by personal labour, given to the work each class has voluntarily chosen to devote their earthly life to. For there can be no doubt in the light of present knowledge, that every grain of the sun's energy includes a measured portion which will and must reappear in the new form it has assumed, just as each soul will present the measured portion which the individual carries into eternity with him, as well as the forms in which the forces thus objectised were generated while here. The truth of this reasoning must be apparent to every honest mind. From this point of view, I would ask what appearance will some of our Clergymen make as they stand contrasted with our men of science, each class assuming the form of intelligence which they may have developed while each individual of the two classes is in possession of a separate system of truths standing contrasted? Thus I view the contrast in such a way that every grain of force used up will proclaim its own work. I feel God will demand a reason from our Clergymen for the cause of the scepticism of the age, because the immortality of the soul is the truth they have specially taken in hand to deal with and proclaim, while that is a form of truth that our men of science are no wise responsible for. For the truth with which they concern themselves presents an objective existence, and the expression of the spirit, as such, only lives in the bodily organism, and they have no means to trace it there. Revealed truth alone deals with the immortality of the soul and the nature of the evidence attaching to that subject. Moreover, this is concerned with that personal experience which arises when the individual has been brought into direct communion with the Saviour, and has undergone the change implied in "born again," which proclaims its power in producing the state of mind referred to by our Saviour in John vii. 17. In what is there stated all may recognise that personal fruit, arising from Christian belief, which enables the individual to present himself as the inspired and taught of God, and therefore as possessing the personal experience which proclaims the individual so endowed as being in personal communion with the Infinite, in consequence of being in union with Christ. Further, having thus learned truth for himself he is enabled to teach it to others. Hence he meets the unbelieving man of science with the consciousness that, as a Christian and as an individual, he possesses a state of thought and feeling wholly absent from him (the unbeliever), and different from any experience he has had, so that he is often found beseeching the unbeliever to be reconciled to God in Christ (or united to God in Christ). But if Christianity does present something so distinct as this, why not proclaim it? For God in Christ will most certainly expect this at the Clergyman's hands, as he professes to be taught of God, and takes on himself the responsibility of teaching others in proclaiming the immortality of the soul—an immortality that can only be known to have demonstrative proof when it comes in the shape of the feeling and the felt, and can point to the risen Lord as the Jesus of history. Therefore with all this as within the scope of a Christian experience the Clergyman is surely greatly responsible for the scepticism of the age.

Chapter XII.

THE CONSEQUENCE OF WASTED ENERGY IN VIEW OF THE CONSERVATION OF ENERGY.

THE doctrine of the conservation of energy is now recognised as an absolute or demonstrated truth. We have seen our men of science weigh and measure the energy or force stored up in a ton of coal; they tell us that it is the converged rays of the sun's bounty, absorbed in woody fibres ages ago. By the aid of modern Science this energy is liberated and measured; and though it appears in a different form, and is called by a new name, we find that the absolute quantity remains the same. Throughout the different changes it has undergone, the original force has neither gained nor lost in quantity; and doubtless every grain of energy used up in conscious life will bear demonstrative proof of as rigid a nature. Thus the services rendered by the poor in ministering to the luxury and comfort of the rich will all be presented in due course, as each individual must, if humanity is to be judged according to the deeds done in the body. In view of all this we would ask, what obligations do those incur in our day who are great consumers of such energy, though producing no useful work in return? How different will the relationship that now divides the rich and the poor then appear, as they change places, and the words of our Lord are fully understood: "Woe unto you that are rich! for ye have received your consolation". (Luke vi. 24.) A like remark applies to the terrible responsibility attaching itself to wasteful extravagance of every description. Consider the price paid in human energy in producing coal as a necessity of life, in the hardships the collier has to endure in his daily work, as he provides for the members of his household depending on him, while he enables the race to advance because such as he will and must work. How little do we think of all this in the wasteful extravagance we display in regard to our coal, which was first the product of the sun's rays in bygone ages, and now is procured by much *labour as human energy, the brain and muscles of humanity, both examples of muscular force, liberating the sun's energy, and making it possible for the race to advance;* for what would all our mechanical appliances be without the use of coal? As finite intelligences we rise higher and yet higher, but we may say that we are able to do so only by the aid of the collier's hardships, as he earns an honest living. The hand of such, many would feel degraded if expected to grasp in recognition of the best service rendered, as if the money earned by such can in any way repay the obligation received in procuring such results as our coal enables us to make. Notwithstanding all this we still continue to waste, heedless of the consequences which our waste entails, and of the load of obligation we are brought under to a class whom we may have treated with contempt, just as if we thought that honest labour degraded humanity. How changed all this will become when we meet before the throne of God, with the Saviour, the carpenter of Galilee, seated on it as judge, bearing the marks of the labouring man, while his hand and his arm are stored with potential energy, as the fruit of the thirty years' toil, and his brow bears the marks of the sweat of such labour!

And just fancy the human energy that, from first to last, has been used up in producing that ball dress, which is intended to be worn for one night only, while the wearer of it dances away more energy in those few hours than possibly she ever devoted all her life to work—work, that is to say, rendered as the fruit of love, and in the service of the Saviour whom she professes to serve, as she devoutly kneels at the communion table. She is careless of truth like this, but nevertheless she must render an account of the energy she has used up, as well as given out, in that other way; for every grain of energy will proclaim itself in the formation it appears in as the process implied in procuring and presenting that form. The blacksmith's right arm will proclaim his calling in the muscular fibre presented to the eye of sense, and the sensitive muscles of the tongue and larynx of the throat yield a proof, equally direct, of the nature of the energy there stored up in the form of these members of the body, which made it possible for man to proclaim his thoughts in vocal sound, as the symbol of his thought.

There is nothing we may be more certain of, than that concealment of any kind will be utterly impossible in the state of existence which succeeds this life, where the thing formed will proclaim the process employed in forming it, as the evolved soul of individual man is objectised, in that grouped mass of matter which stands disembodied, we call the soul.

Chapter XIII.

THE RESPONSIBILITY ATTACHING TO A CHRISTIAN PROFESSION.

IN viewing the poor and the rich in relation to the human energy of the one class being used up by the other, I would remark in passing, that I do not think the rich as a whole are so tyrannical as the poor. That is, in the possible event of their changing places, I believe the poor would tyrannise fully as much as the rich do. Hence, in the light of Luke vi. 24, we must believe that it is their circumstances and not their nature that gives them the advantage, sheltering them from the woe that falls on the rich. One thing is very apparent, that the old landed gentry often do display great forbearance and kindness to the poor on their properties, even when the poor are very ungrateful, as sometimes happens.

Christianity then presents the distinction I have stated, both in regard to its source, and in regard to the process implied in the personal experience which it manifests when it proclaims its divine origin. In the same way we view our ultimate knowledge as coming to us in the double shape of the feeling and the felt. If we regard our Saviour's teaching, as for instance, in the Sermon on the Mount, and especially in that part of it contained in Matt. v. 39, where He says to His elect, "That ye resist not evil ; but whosoever shall smite thee on thy right cheek, turn to him the other also ". Regarding this we cannot say that Christ's teaching presents a state of endurance beyond what He is quite justified in expecting from the individual in possession of eternal life, and having the prospect of a glorious future provided for him. For the latter has to bear witness in a world where the believer's actions, in the prospect of the immortality of the soul, are the only testifying declarations which God has provided the race with on that point. For the revelation contained in the Bible is evidently intended by God to be objectised through this means; the ideas there revealed regarding the other world being first received into the brain, and then embodied in the action of the believer's life, being presented to humanity as his testimony to the truth contained in revelation. To point to the Bible and proclaim it as the Word of God, means nothing in our day, except we can show the fruit arising from it in some way. As a theoretic conception it only presents the appearance of a mere assertion, and simply goes for nothing. If we are not prepared to endure all that is implied in Matt. v. 39, we are quite justified in not submitting to such usage, and may prefer to divide our inheritance between time and eternity, by having less treasures laid up in the shape of works done for His sake. In this matter we have a perfect right to choose; for our Lord will only accept willing service. Only, let us be honest enough to confess that we keep this back, as we would demand from others what is *due to us*, confessing that we are so influenced, and prepared to take whatever consequences may follow. All this is right and just; we wrong no one in this except ourselves in our eternal glory. But in the face of the words of our Saviour, contained in Matt. v. 39, let us be honest about it, and say plainly, the words are indeed these, but we are not prepared for the sacrifice they involve, and thus act an honest part *to the world, to ourselves and to our Saviour*, and not seek to act such a hateful part as would lead us to explain away the message in our desire to excuse ourselves. For whether we believe it or not, we, as professed believers, shall alone be made responsible for the acting out of the doctrines taught in the Christian records. Than this nothing is clearer to us, as we view Christ's teaching in the light of present knowledge. In the light of the necessity doctrine, with no possibility of proving the immortality of the soul apart from revelation, the teaching of the Lord is perfectly intelligible. For example, take this statement of our Lord's, " For whosoever will save his life shall lose it, and whosoever will lose his life for my sake shall find it ". (Matt. xvi. 25). How meaningless and absurd it is to expect or suppose that these words are addressed to any but believers, when we know that humanity at large have no certain authority for believing that there is another life. Doubtless, in both worlds the believer alone will be judged as condemned or acquitted, in the light of Bible truth ; as professed believers they must suffer the consequence of being lost as such, if they neglect their soul's salvation. Doubtless also, viewing all *unbelievers* as Gentiles, we cannot but think that an additional responsibility attaches to those of the latter who have chanced to live where the Bible was presented as the Word of God. With this, however, their responsibility ends, for they will be judged according to conscience. Even so, however, they shall, alas! find that they have refused the inheritance of the adopted children of God, as they are judged according to conscience, and must abide by the consequence all through eternity. They had a revelation within their reach, which, with their superior intelligence, would have enabled them to compare revelation with modern science, and so they might have taken a high place in proclaiming God's will on the earth. Thus they might have had many treasures laid up as the fruit of love to Christ, having accepted Him as a Redeemer, and so been brought in contact with God as God. Such then is the light in which I would treat Christianity. That is to say, I would first divide all men into two classes, the believers* and unbelievers, each class possessing an entirely different experimental knowledge. Then again, I would divide the cerebrum brain of the believer, by marking off the portion of it occupied by the truths coming through revelation. In this resides the ideal Christ, rendering the possessor capable of holding communion with Him, a developing intelligence, as a power within the brain. The knowledge here stored becomes conscious knowledge, *only* when it proclaims its message on the sensorium ganglia though stored with His words in the shape of ideas, distinctly presented as revealed truth. In connection with this point I would refer to the teaching of our Lord (Matt. x. 19, 20), " When they deliver you up, take no thought how or what ye shall speak; for it shall be given

* Generalising so broadly as this, we must attach the state of being born again to the term believers here.

you in that same hour what ye shall speak. For it is not ye that speak, but the spirit of your Father which speaketh in you ". This presents a case where the course of action is vastly different from an individual having command of the two sets of muscles in the sensorium brain, and deals with the spontaneous character of the individual in the action of the cerebrum brain, when the vaso-motor nerves are roused, and when the self-acting, leyden jar (as we may call this part of the brain), gives off the effect of a previous experience, we shall say in the form of electricity, manifesting the effect of our Lord's words in the 20th verse just referred to. The other portion of the brain may be fully stocked with the ideas coming from modern science, and there demonstrated truth is accepted as God speaking in nature—as the thoughts of God manifested in nature. From this point of view the theoretic conceptions of modern science are regarded as involving consequences which may throw light on revealed truth, and are to be viewed in connection with it, though of course not accepted as absolute truth. The believer, however, as an individual, is perfectly justified in accepting the conclusions of theoretic science, as feeling them to be the best explanation yet given of the things and operations by which we are surrounded, thus vindicating his claim to private judgment, while he seeks to give his reasons for so accepting them, even though they are not confirmed by demonstrative proof. Viewing his scientific conceptions in this way, in the light of revealed truth, the believer may help to confirm theoretic science, and secure for it a permanent place or basis; yet always let him follow *as a believer* in the footsteps of modern science, being only desirous to get more fully acquainted with the teaching of Jesus as it stands revealed in the light of God's dealings in nature. We would, therefore, recognise the importance of individual liberty, while proclaiming the truth of revelation in word and deed. At the same time we are conscious of the difference that divides the believer and the unbeliever ; only we would leave others free to choose their lot in eternity. Inasmuch as the believer makes the distinction that divides and thus clearly defines the two classes, he feels that with this his responsibility ends. For if he has received an advantage from the other's labours, he has offered a definitely marked experience in exchange, with a life corresponding to his belief. And yet one step further he can go ; he can insure to his unbelieving brother the immortality of the soul as absolute truth, which his position enables him to proclaim. How helpful would Christianity in this way become, if each believer realized the responsibility attaching to the individual life in the light of an endless immortality. It is only when the two truths are accepted in this way, and mingle freely in the individual brain, that the full advantage arising from Christianity will appear with power on the earth, and Christ will be honoured in being recognised as our Lord.

Chapter XIV.

THE FREEDOM OF THE WILL DEFINED, AND THE EFFECT OF THE ORGANISM.

IN the light of modern science we are wholly justified in proclaiming the freedom of the will and the sovereignty of God as manifested in what is possible to man. In dealing with this subject in the meantime, we will take no notice of the responsibility the Christian belief confers thereby increasing the responsibility of the individual a hundredfold. In view of the necessity doctrine the responsibility in man is greatly less in consequence of so many elements coming into play, in shape of the antecedents of the individual, the early training, and the circumstances in which he is placed, and over which he has no control. From this point of view man's responsibility is a question that the wisdom implied in the Infinite alone can determine. For each grain of energy, moving in connection with conscious life, can be taken account of by Him, the Infinite One. The energy in every form will proclaim the condition through which it assumes its present form and place in the individual life, and whatever responsibility is attached therewith, it being always borne in mind that it is a law of the organism, that a pleasure is snatched and a pain avoided without any regard to consequences, and that to act in accordance with this rule is always the natural law of the mind's action. The so called freedom of the will is determined by many antecedent circumstances, and principally rests with the power the *individual has acquired over the two sets of muscles taking their rise in the sensorium brain, which will enable him to direct his energy according to deliberate choice.* But that there may be a proper use of this high attainment in having a complete control over the power of these muscles implied in the execution of the will, their exercise must be accompanied with a high sense of justice, in the light of individual responsibility, before this power will morally affect man's actions. In the light of all this, how little responsibility can we justly say attaches itself to many actions which our laws punish with the greatest severity. For example, take the case of a drunkard's brawl, in which, let us suppose, one man kills another. Well, I hold that the former is wholly irresponsible in this case ; the so-called murderer had no control over his actions, he had no power to withhold his hand ; his was an action as much determined by previous circumstances as the result of any of our laws of nature. The whole guilt attaching to this act rests in the power the man had over his inclination in regard to getting intoxicated. And as I follow that man through the few succeeding scenes of his earthly life, from the prison to the court of the *so-called justice*, and hear the judge sum up the evidence, leaving the jury simply to say in one word what he implied in many words, that the prisoner is guilty of murder ; as I see the judge assume the black cap, and in mock justice condemn the man as a murderer to death, while he expresses a hope that God will have mercy on his soul, which doubtless will be fully fulfilled in view of all the circumstances of the case ; as I follow him to the scaffold, where through the carelessness attaching to some one the hanging process may have to be twice performed, the rope having broken, and the man requiring to be hoisted and hanged a second time. During all these different stages the poor man is thought of as the guiltiest wretch on earth, while the family of which he was a member is branded, because it has chanced to be in connection with such a wretch. The fact of the matter however is, that the man is a martyr to circumstances over which he may have no control, or over which his power may have been very limited indeed. Certainly in regard to the last act for which he and his family and friends suffer all this misery, he is wholly irresponsible, and dies a martyr to the so-called law of justice made in the name of a Christian state, and in the light of the certain knowledge that the automatic structure of the individual renders the action of that individual, when under the influence of passion or drink, wholly automatic. Individuals who suffer thus will doubtless find the measure of justice meted out by a God of mercy wholly different from man's. And yet man asks God's blessing on such a state of things, and calls it justice in the light of Christ's teaching, with the words ever before our eyes, "With what judgment ye judge ye shall be judged". (Matt. vii. 2.) No one will deny *that society must be protected*, but dare we, in the name of Christian justice, protect it at such a cost. Indeed, viewing our criminal class as a whole, we feel that our sense of justice in the light of their responsibility is wholly at fault; we must give them a new organism before we have a right to punish them as we are doing, and *this new organism Christianity provides.* The scenes that sometimes takes place in our convict prisons are of a nature that would paralyze the half of humanity, if there were any one to care for the poor convicts, and draw public attention to what they sometimes suffer. But a convict seems to have no claim on humanity; for no one heeds his grief. Yet true is it that in many cases he suffers as a creature of circumstances; while the circumstances surrounding him in prison often, if not always, tend to harden him yet more.

I was informed of one punishment administered in the convict prison either at Portland or Portsmouth, in 1875 or 1876. It was of this nature. One of the convicts had six dozen lashes given him in consequence of having spit over the balcony on one of the officers (a medical officer I think). This dreadful punishment so shocked me when I heard it that I was quite unnerved for days. I have since then prayed hundreds of times for the man that suffered so, and look forward to meeting him in glory, (for as a Christian of course I believe in the efficacy of prayer as a means to an end). Now if the officer so used, who must have been greatly provoked, had simply forgiven the man this personal insult, which I fancy he as a head official had the power to do, but which perhaps he could not have done if it had happened to an official in a lower position, how the cord of sympathy would have vibrated in a heart treated in this way! The man would have stood self-condemned, whereas the punishment suffered for such an offence must have paralyzed every human feeling that might linger in his heart. And how the prompters of such a punishment are to stand before God, to have the same measure in some sense measured to them again, is a *matter which concerns themselves only*. The future certainly does hold in store some such position as that for them whoever they may be, and I for one do not feel that I have any sympathy to offer them, seeing that, when they had the power to act mercifully, they showed so little mercy to the erring but weak.

What mockery the form of prayers offered up in behalf of the convicts, in convict prisons, must appear before God, in the light of such cases as this! How useless to pray, where no sympathy is given! Prayer is as much to be valued as a means to an end in going forward to our work, as the end itself which is ultimately to be attained. When we ask the Giver of all Good to touch the heart of any one, we ought also to ask to be able to help that one, by having our own heart beating in sympathy. I am informed that Ladies, while engaged in their works of mercy and labour of love, have been excluded from convict prisons, because they were too sympathetic and were giving the authorities trouble in regard to the punishments. In this I may have been misinformed, but at any rate there is little power brought to bear so as to soften the convict's heart. However, as I think of the future in connection with our convicts, I can find comfort in the assurance that, where man has measured out their punishment, God's justice is testified, and they must stand acquitted before a merciful God, so far as the offence they have suffered for is concerned. They have sinned against man, and man has punished them, therefore the God of love is sure to acquit, for we find this law established in relation to his capacity as a judge, "an eye for an eye and a tooth for a tooth". It is only to the Christian that the words of our Saviour, "Resist not evil" can apply (Matt. v. 39). As I follow our convicts to the judgment seat, I can see every grain of energy stand out in bold relief, in the shape of suffering exacted by man, but taken account of by the God of humanity as he appoints to them their place.

As the judge pronounces the sentence which he thinks equivalent to the offence commuted, in the view of revealed truth, we would remind all such, that the words of Jesus stand as eternal truth, "With what judgment ye judge, ye shall be judged." When the criminal and the judge change places, and the former, though he has sinned, has at length wrought out his punishment, will not the other, in the name of *national justice*, await his sentence? *

---

* In connection with this subject, I would draw the reader's attention to a book just published, "Five Years' Penal Servitude," by one who has endured it. The misery that arises from the working of the system is too terrible to imagine, as we follow the author through the experience he gained, where everything seemed to be so managed in the form of a punishment as most effectively to crush every feeling of humanity out of the convict, as he satisfies the demand of English justice, and by this determines the position or system that nation will occupy in eternity; for they must be judged according as they judge. I can look forward to the time when a man who had strayed into temptation, and sinned and suffered, and in consequence of suffering, like the author, found forgiveness and repentance—when such will be as much respected and admired as they are now *despised* and condemned. This state of things must succeed the time when humanity is enabled to conceive God everywhere manifested in

In the conduct of our convict classes we see, how very limited is the power which they have acquired over the two sets of muscles taking their rise in the formation of the will; for they suffer again and again for the same offence; in many cases they almost seem to have no control over themselves to enable them to resist a temptation. In consequence, therefore, we must view the freedom of the will as it is seen in the formation of two sets of muscles,

His laws. But now I would raise my voice with the author in behalf of the weak, the erring, and the downtrodden, as we try to follow a case or two. Page 210—A young man gets five years for embezzlement, and leaves a wife and child. The wife supports herself, and the child dies. She quarrels with her mother, with whom she lives, writes her husband to ask his consent to leave the protection of her mother and go into a lodging house, but he is not at *liberty to write* for *four months*. The chaplain will do nothing to enable him to write *at once*. The next he hears of her is that she has left her mother, and the end is a gentleman has *seduced her*, and she is living with him in style. She was a young pretty creature, of nineteen, to whom her husband was devotedly attached. Fancy his despair—an inmate of a convict prison, his child dead, his wife seduced! Surrounded as we find him, is it possible for him to reform? Observe the chaplain, who had pledged himself before God and man to devote his time to convert the convicts. He might have helped him, but he refused. Page 349—Two men are told to lift a stone, and told if they do not the officer will report them for laziness. One of the two men's turn for writing home came next week; by a report against him he would lose the privilege of writing, as well as getting a letter in reply. He puts forth his whole strength, injures himself internally, falls to the ground, and, before he could be taken to the infirmary, is dead. See the doctor and apothecary on their rounds (page 197), and the ointment left on the side of the author's plate in the middle of his dinner, and fancy being obliged to swallow castor oil while at dinner. Page 383—A man gets seven years for stealing 12 eggs. In this case the *judge is one of the great unpaid*. A postman, five years, for stealing a few dozen of stamps. Page 142—A decent old man, from Lancashire, who bore a previous good character, five years, for receiving 10s. of postage stamps, which turned out to be stolen goods.

over which the highly cultivated and developed man sits in judgment, as he deliberates in view of the past, the present, and the future, in his choice of the course of action he is about to pursue. Viewing the soul as purely material, presented in a group of molecular motion (destined as a conscious thing to live for ever), where each part is the product of previous action, the possibility of the capacity to act or not to act having been evolved through the product of two such sets of muscles, we see that man, when fully developed, is in the possession of a power corresponding to the idea included in the freedom of the will, while at the same time the laws of nature, as presenting the will of God, are definite and independent. Yet man may be seen in the form of a finite God, possessing complete power over those muscles, as he deliberately chooses his future destiny in time and in eternity; a very God knowing good and evil, and presenting the form of demonstrated proof, which was implied in the words of the serpent in Gen. iii. 5, " Your eyes shall be opened, ye shall be as God's, knowing good and evil ". For man, when he possesses full power over the Will, as seen in the form of the two sets of muscles (in view of the future of the race revealed), may, as I said before, choose for eternity as he deliberates on the past, the present, and the future.

CHAPTER XV.

A THEORY APPLIED TO EXPLAIN REVELATION AND ITS EFFECTS.

IF we are justified, as I hold we are, in maintaining that a special agency, made known in revelation, was to reconcile man to God, and procure for him personal good, which man was destined to receive in being made a friend of God's in and through Jesus Christ, the mediator provided for that end, so that man might serve God in love in consequence of having been redeemed by the blood of the Son of God, then the ideal Christ and the actual Christ unite in the brain of the believer, and express their union in the new birth. This is the action and counter action determined of God, viewing Christ in the form of his elect and all as elected who are united in this way to Him, or in other words who believe on Him, as when the gases have united in the brain in forming the impression implied in the ideal Christ, and the impression received manifests itself as demonstrative proof in the felt communion implied in the realization of belief, as stated in 1 John ii. 27. The wave of motion, personified in the spirit, carries the impression generated at the centre outward through space, first as it issues from the eternal in the form of revealed truth, and now as it issues from the objective Christ, as the expression of that revelation. In the light of present knowledge, we may view revelation as presented in a very intelligent form, if we accept mind as a quality and form of matter, and call it the highest quality of the stuff fitting space, which we call matter, while our senses are the means through which we get acquainted with this stuff, filling infinite space as matter and force. This latter we shall, for convenience, term the material part of God's existence and the medium which he makes use of in his communications with man. We view man therefore as a product of God's laws, and as originated for the very purpose, we shall say, of procuring His ends, so that through this means God might procure a comparison for Himself. This was the personal end God had to serve, so to speak, in producing the form of man according to law, from the very lowest form of existence; and in order to produce this form a revelation concerning future events was necessary. Through this revelation the whole human race have received infinite advantage and eternal benefits, which procure for the race individual and eternal existence. Well, in view of our universal medium, matter in form, or matter and force, which has been called stuff, is thus a very easy process, implied in revelation, which at some future time is to occupy a certain place and form, and which at present exists in some place and form. Now suppose that, in the form of revealed truth, the same portion of stuff that now exists somewhere should assume the form which it will at some future time appear in (according to law), then we shall have demonstrated the revealed will of God, as it is presented in the form of revealed truth. For example, in the Revelation of Saint John in regard to the future of the race we have only to suppose that the stuff, which was at a future stage of development to appear as such, assumed that form for the time being, as it presented the actual existence which was to appear in due course according to law. All that is necessary here is, that the stuff, as matter and force, or matter in form, has an actual existence.

We are thus enabled, by the help of modern science, to present a theoretic conception, implied in the decrees of God, and understood as the laws through which forms are produced ; our view being that the freedom of man's will is included in the power he has attained, or may possess, over two sets of muscles taking their rise in the sensorium portion of the brain, over which man in his highest development may preside in view of the past, the present, and the future, as he chooses the course of action he will pursue. And I hold that this attainment includes the very highest development possible to the race—the very highest form which the circumstances could produce, and certainly the very highest which my reason can comprehend. I would have it here distinctly understood that Christianity does not come to us professing to deal with such a form as this, though it contains enough to satisfy such a form.

Christianity, as personified in Christ, may justly be viewed as the product of the Jewish nation, to which a revelation was given, and over which I expect the Saviour will yet come, for a limited time, to reign in Jerusalem, when He appears as the Messiah of the Jews. From this point Christ is seen in his mediatorial capacity, wherein he was decreed to reconcile man to God by suffering in his stead, so freeing mankind from the consequences of guilt on certain conditions.

Our Lord so presented is understood to come to any nation in which the existence of a God as an Infinite existence is an accepted fact, and in which men realise their responsibility to this God, and their liability to punishment in consequence of their actions.

To humanity in a state of development corresponding to this, Christianity proclaims its glad tidings in the form of a free gospel, where Christ is presented as a substitute to all who will accept Him ; where all who as sinners accept Him thus are reconciled to, and through Him, approach God in the spirit of the "Abba Father" of the Christian God. It will be thus seen that it is by *increasing the emotional element*, or producing action in consequence of emotion, that Christian action is produced. As the heart of the individual is filled with gratitude and love, then to give out energy in the shape of service is a natural consequence, and in its essence is purely automatic. I hold that the very adoration implied in the "Abba Father" of the reconciled child, is of the highest form of service ; and surely all will allow that that expression, as the outburst of emotion, is purely automatic, is simply a quality of matter, beating in sympathy with God, and breathing the language of heaven, personified in the felt presence of the Spirit of God, and wholly of God. We might say that it is the brain vibrating at the rate of motion implied by Paul in 1 Timothy vi. 16, as a quality of this stuff known to us as matter, which surrounds the immediate presence of God in the place we call heaven, wherein God manifests His presence. It will thus be seen that Christianity *simply provides a motive* and stimulus to action in a certain direction, so to speak, through the process implied in faith working by love. The Christian work produced in consequence of this love, according to the Saviour's teaching, assumes the form of treasures laid up in heaven, in the form of works done from love to Him, and it is these that determine the position of the eternal inheritance which the believer has a claim to as the fruit of his earthly life ; so that from this point it is the motive which produces the action that God as Christ takes cognizance of, or accepts as sacrifice. We thus see how the individual becomes possessed of a new organism in connection with Christianity, as we view Christ in His double form, presented in the ideal Christ and the actual Christ, in the form of organism and environment. For the ideal Christ moves the feelings, and the feelings build the inner man, in the form of the new man referred to by Paul, 2 Cor. v. 17. As our men of science theoretically rebuild the universe so we rebuild the Church theoretically ; for they have taught us to apply laws as they do, and to see that laws will apply to one case as well as to another. We see this automatic action of Christianity in the life of the devoted believer, as the heart vibrates in love, and animates the organism, *as the brain may be said to act in obedience to the heart, supposing the heart to mean feeling, and to be the motive power, while the brain is the machine.*

But if Christianity proper takes no account of works, except such as flow from love to Christ, and if the sinner is saved by grace from the consequence of punishment for sin, that is, as a sinner for whom Christ died and who is accepted in Christ. We must take into account the element of justice in such as are fully developed, so that each individual thus saved, in reviewing his earthly life in glory, will be fully conscious of the consequences of their actions, and of the effect their actions have produced on their neighbours and the race. In consequence of this element of justice being fully developed, a desire to make amends to those we have injured, where such is possible, must have a powerful effect on the individual in procuring a spirit of humility, as well as influencing us in many other forms of action. Hence though to a certain extent an unrighteous act in this life may be forgiven, yet the effect in another sense must follow us to heaven, where we shall be conscious of the effect our actions have caused, and shall see the effect that an unkind word has produced in the loss of energy caused by the pain it gave. We might follow the effect of all our actions thus, and see the terrible consequence a selfish life will have caused, as the stronger power triumphs over the weaker.

I would end by adding one word in reference to our duty toward the heathen. With a Christian religion, which contains all I have stated, is it not high time that the gospel should be proclaimed in every land? We are using up so much of the heathen's life or energy in consequence of the luxurious state of our living, seen in the foreign products made use of, and this must present itself in the form of human energy given out by the heathen in producing it, and capable of being weighed and measured by our Lord as the God of humanity or the God of the whole earth. In view of the energy here referred to, what appearance will be made by our Christian efforts put forth to secure their salvation. This is a serious question, in view of the fact that every particle of human energy will proclaim itself in the work it has done, for at the final end it must do so when humanity appears at the judgment-seat of Christ.

CONCLUSION.

THE treatise I thus present to the public requires no apology or qualification. If the union of two truths already existing in contrasted ideas produce new thoughts, including a spiritual experience which in its essence includes God, making his presence felt in consciousness, then we are presented with a state of things in which every individual unit may enjoy the proof of the truth implied. Therefore our religion can no longer be called a religion of faith, if faith is looked at as a negative quality apart from any experience of the thing implied. Thus I present the truth of revelation as capable of expressing itself in consciousness, in a feeling corresponding to the promise made by our Lord to His followers in John xlv. 21, " He that loveth me shall be loved of my Father, and I will love him, *and will manifest myself unto him.*" This test removes the knowledge held by the individual believer from a state of theory to a state of certainty, which may be defined as a positivism resulting from Christian belief. The truths of religion, therefore, are presented as truths open to proof from this point, and, as the result of the union of the mind with Christ, are expressive of the objective and subjective in the form of the wave of feeling, that unites the redeemed soul with the Redeemer. Viewing feeling as man's ultimate, the statements put forward in this treatise are indeed capable of proof from one point at anyrate, and consequently requires no qualification. Therefore, I would say to all believers—prove the truth of the statements made to you, for the Christian theory does indeed admit of proof. (John vii. 17.)

Our Protestant faith was founded on or rose out of justification by faith, and so we rely on absolute truth, trusting to a crucified Redeemer *as the seed of God in the soul of man* proclaiming itself eternal. This doctrine of justification by faith is peculiarly a Protestant doctrine, if not *the* Protestant doctrine. According to its essence the individual may inherit all things, and in laying up treasures in heaven he possesses the power of reaping the fruit of his love to Christ, as he rises higher and yet higher in his knowledge of God as seen in his laws, through science illuminating revelation. But as the Protestants stand here accepted in Christ by God, we need to pause while we try to answer many questions requiring to be clearly defined. To many of these the Roman Catholic Church* has given an answer, while we attempt no explanation, but simply dismiss the subject. For example, what explanations are we to give to the words of Jesus in John xiv. 13, 14. "Whatsoever ye shall ask in my name, that will I do, that the Father may be glorified in the Son. If ye shall ask anything

---

*In reference to the Roman Catholic Church in the work she prescribes to her clergymen, if honestly executed, it includes much merit, which doubtless God will not despise; for in honour to Him they are thus working out their own salvation, in the form of duty prescribed by their Church, calling itself by our Lord's name; so that viewing God as the universal power manifested in the uniformity of the laws of nature, we are only just in our reasoning in supposing that the "Well done, good and faithful servant," will at the *final* end be spoken to many of them.

in my name I will do it"; and so with many texts pointing to the same meaning elsewhere? Well, are we to assume that the power and efficacy of this promise ceases when we fear that some one dear to us has died without being born again, and we know that such a change is not possible under the circumstances? Nevertheless, may we not hope that the prayer of faith may yet prove in some sense effectual, as we thus follow our departed friend, and read our Lord's words in John xiv. 2, 3: "In my Father's house are many mansions; . . . I go to prepare a place for you". Here we realise that the *place* Jesus has prepared for such of us who have been born again and are living for Christ, will bear a more extended meaning than a single mansion, for we may have many mansions in a place. Thus may we not hope that a mansion may await our friend? Viewing mind as a quality of matter, we have the certain knowledge that mind is progressive, so that we may hope and pray even after our friends have ceased to occupy a place in time. May it not be just possible that the Roman Catholic notion of a purgatory represents some corresponding state of existence, though a state not *essential* to Christians, when as believers they make their calling and election sure by walking with God in Christ; whereas believers living an *indifferent life* may make such a state essential to the securing of their future well-being before they are qualified to use their resurrection body to the glory of God. When we view the Church of Christ as presenting a first and second resurrection (Rev. xx. 6) this state seems very possible.

There are many such questions which must be answered

in the future by the Protestant Church in view of a progressive immortality; and one which will agitate the Church of the future will be to define the meaning to be attached to Jesus' words in Matt. xix. 11, 12 in comparison with Rev. xiv. 3, 4, 5. As we listen to the words from the lips of our Saviour in Matt. xix. 12, " He that is able to receive it, let him receive it," we feel that the question of celibacy is to be discussed in the light in which mind as a quality of matter will be viewed in the future. For from this point of view we are very certain that a life of celibacy presents that quality of stuff, which we call mind, in a state peculiar to itself, and therefore demanding an explanation from the Protestant minister that takes the position of *unfolding* the Word of God as he finds it revealed in the Scriptures.

In the light of all this we shall have to view Paul's teaching in 1 Cor. vi. 18 in connection with an impure life, where man is said to sin against his own body. All these questions, with many more, will be raised in the future, and the sooner we try to understand revelation in the light of scientific truth, the better will it be for individual man, so that each may make the best possible use of his life on earth in view of a progressive immortality.

In the light of our present knowledge what a fount of truth is proved to be included in such a verse as this (Prov. xxii. 6), " Train up a child in the way he should go, and when he is old he will not depart from it ". When we find that impressions received in youth in a peculiar sense grow with the brain, and such impressions remain there, we ought to remember that the future destiny of the individual life will be influenced by such impressions, as it proclaims itself immortal, just as when we cut our name on the bark of a young tree we find it grows with the tree.

And again, let us refer to a passage in the Revelation (that book so much questioned in our day, and cast aside by many Christians as utterly unintelligible) in regard to the new Jerusalem—Rev. xxi. 11—where the city is pictured as " pure gold, like unto clear glass ! " Now, gold is the only metal known to modern science that is transparent to light, and here we have the material substance of the heavenly city, the new Jerusalem, presented as transparent gold, and therefore capable of transmitting light and heat, as the city in the light of which the nations of them that are saved are to walk (Rev. xxi. 23-24). Science surely unfolds the Scriptures here in presenting a metallic base of this order, where we may interpret the term city as possibly implying an intelligence of the highest order, in full communion with God and with Christ, and thus giving out light and heat, a source from which the nations referred to may be capable of generating an increase of energy. This and much more in that wonderful book of Revelation is worthy of notice, and will be a subject of inquiry in the future, when science teaches us to read it, for doubtless it was given to explain the working of the laws of nature in the light of revealed truth. Therefore to make the individual to understand it, his mind must be stored with experimental Christianity in the shape of a personal experience, as well as with an intimate acquaintance with modern science, which includes mental powers of a high order. This is a quality of mind which we have a right to expect in the Protestant clergyman, as he proclaims to a doubting world or race the doctrine of the immortality of the soul, grounded on a Christian faith, based on an objective Christ, occupying a point in space known as heaven; for faith in the Scriptures is a term which implies a something which has an objective existence, manifesting itself under certain conditions. For example, the Christian will find the objective Christ as the disembodied spirit gravitates toward Him, its centre, while the soul quivers in love, as it nears the personal Christ.

In conclusion, I would draw attention to Rev. xix. 10: "And I fell at His feet to worship Him, and He said unto me, See thou do it not; I am thy fellow-servant, and of thy brethren that have the testimony of Jesus: worship God: for the testimony of Jesus is the spirit of prophecy." In the truth included in these words *(the testimony of Jesus is the spirit of prophecy) we see the Lord as a developing intelligence revealing truth*, the meaning of which we realise as we reason on revealed truth in the light of modern science; therefore a Christian striving to unfold God's word of truth may be understood as striving to unfold *(or predicate)* future events, much of which will appear to the natural man as mere assumption, as they thrust the ideas presented aside, (just as many of this class are doing with the truth contained in the Bible —truth, which is eternal as God, and it is this very truth which divides the human race); consequently if we proclaim an apparent new truth, we may expect to be abused, while the new way of putting an old truth is being sifted and weighed, and at the end accepted as absolute truth. So we Christians labour and wait, as we rest in Christ our Lord.

Until I read the book referred to I knew nothing about modern science, and cared as little, being happy and contented in knowing Christ as my Lord, and only determined to acquire some knowledge of science when I perceived it would *better* help me to understand my Bible. This knowledge I have acquired exclusively through books, and in this form absorbed other's thoughts. Knowledge thus accumulated through the medium of so many differently constituted minds may fairly claim some slight consideration from others having greater advantages who may criticise the work. But however *erroneous* the conclusions I have formed may appear to some, I would remind them that I have drawn my conclusions from *two legitimate sources, and therefore I am justified in demanding a better explanation of the facts I deal with before they condemn my reasoning.*

APPENDIX.

The Appendix includes an account of what to me is a special or prophetic Revelation, and the theory that has proceeded from it.

THIS Appendix has been made necessary from various causes. First, in consequence of the book having been in a way suppressed when it was issued in February, 1878, though this was concealed from me at the time. As this was a private matter, there is no occasion to refer further to it here. Secondly, because I feel it my duty to detail what to me implied a prophetic revelation (in the form of a truth which will affect men in all ages), and the theory which has risen from the revelation.

The distinctive character of the book may be fairly estimated by its dedication to the memory of the late J. S. Mill, and likewise from the complimentary way in which I have felt it my duty to write of the startling work of the Duke of Somerset, on " Christian Theology and Modern Scepticism," *even although it cuts at the very root of our Christian faith.* While I answer the question put in page 148, " Is faith in God the faith which Jesus taught ? "

or, " Is Christian faith more complex in its manifold requirements?" by showing that Christian faith *is more complex in its manifold requirements;* thus I lead the intellectual *believer* step by step onward until I produce in my *willing pupil the much to be desired* mental condition which combines the conviction of the intellect with the obedience of the heart, made apparent in *faith working by love,* or, in other words, action flowing from feeling, which, in its essence, includes union and communion with God in Christ, being the final issue involved in Christianity.

The work, as a whole, is intended to point out that Christianity anticipated the discoveries of modern students of nature. I address myself to the intellectual believer in a religious system which springs from the conviction that a revelation has been given, in which God has revealed His will by manifesting His presence from time to time in a special manner—where the term or idea involved in "prophet" is understood to affirm or predicate that revelation addressed to an individual enables such an one to *grasp a truth applicable to men in all ages.* In our Protestant Church, the Bible is understood to include the truths principally resting on what is termed the miraculous, *all* of which the believer is unhesitatingly to accept, though his judgment (or common sense) is expected to be his guide in all other departments of knowledge, with the exception of being warned against the views put forward by modern science. Instance, Professor Tyndall's Belfast Address,

1874. Yet, in whatever form the Bible reveals the miraculous, the Protestant believer is expected to accept it, though revealing facts so startling as that man for the first time appears or was called into existence only about seven thousand years ago. Two thousand years later the earth is ingulfed by a flood, but, fortunately for the work of creation, the whole *animal world*, including eight *souls*, are saved by means of an ark which took one hundred years in building. Later on, fire from heaven consumes the Cities of the Plain. In course, the ten plagues of Egypt follow, with the Israelites escaping by the sea dividing, in which their enemies are ingulfed; with all the miracles of the wilderness, during forty years' wandering, in which we are told neither their clothes nor their shoes waxed old upon them. Perhaps, to us, the most startling of all is the sun and moon standing still. Yet, an interference with what we, in our *infancy*, call the laws of nature, may have no place here, for the Protestants all allow that anything is possible to the God they serve, as the Intelligence at the heart of everything, by whom we may infer all is regulated according to law, being the truth involved in the decrees of God. Nevertheless, in the face of all this, the destructive nature of my book must be very apparent, as it only claims for the one miracle of the resurrection of our Lord, the place of unhesitating acceptance freely granted by our Protestant Church to all the others, while I offer substantial proof for the truth involved only in this one.

If such an author comes forward with the startling intelligence that, in consequence of truth, *first perceived* in the form of a prophetic revelation, including truth capable of being demonstrated, comprising in the perception the physical basis of mind, therefore, truth which must affect men in all ages—a revelation capable of bearing out all this—would surely be hailed by the Protestant Church as of vital importance. For, if the author can prove all this, it will secure for the individual the intellectual freedom involved in the Protestant term "right of private judgment," being the perception our Protestant Church rests on, yet preserves in the Church all that is essential for individual development, being the idea included in faith working by love, which manifests the individual's sanctification—thus making him fit for the Master's service. The simple story, including this startling prophetic revelation, is told further on. The truth which it involves is wrought out in this Appendix, finally taking the form of a theory, including ultimately the possible salvation of the race, being capable of demonstrating the physical basis of mind in its relation to a bodily organism; and this does much to prove the theory advanced by Dr. Carpenter in his "Principles of Mental Physiology," dealing, as that book does with a special department of knowledge, presenting a system of truth which includes mind in the abstract, although it was not issued when the prophetic revelation was given. If such a startling announcement can be verified by facts it must involve great gain to the *liberal-minded Protestant.* I only read Dr. Carpenter's "Principles of Mental Physiology" at the close of 1876, and I confidently affirm a careful perusal of that book was absolutely necessary before I could fully comprehend the nature of the prophetic revelation, so as to enable me to present the truth included in the form of demonstrated truth, so that I might define, in the fullest sense, the limit which the natural man is entitled to (as seen in his form of body and mind), as he reasons on the possibility of a future life, when the bodily organism is broken up at death. For, doubtless, it is only when we can refer to a revelation—instance Christianity (as it includes Christ in his divine and human form and nature, thus presenting the God-Man as the refuge for sinners) that we have a right to apply the term *absolute truth.* This, therefore, is all I contend for in using that term, which in some quarters has been used as a powerful weapon against me, so that my ignorance might be made apparent in my professed admiration of J. S. Mill, the strenuous upholder of the elasticity of knowledge. This I hold rather to reflect credit, in consequence of this author, in his last work, "Nature—the Utility of Religion and Theism," *limiting the bounds of his class,* as they reason on the truth included in a Christian revelation being entitled to no higher *aspiration* arising from that *glorious dispensation,* than the dim hope that a revelation has been given to lighten the midnight darkness which separates the dead from the living; positively excluding his class from having a right or title to any higher aspiration—in this manifesting his usual clear perception, in thus limiting the subject dealt with, *by marking the limit that divides the two sets of intelligent life, defined as unbelievers and believers. This coming from him,* leaves the Christian Church in no doubt how it stands related to the world of Nature—with man in the form of body and mind as the crowning intelligence at the head of the system. For a sceptic has, in what I would term *his crowning work,* clearly defined the relation in which the Church stands towards the world, in proclaiming Christ's divinity, thus alone giving it the power and honour to proclaim the *absolute truth* included in our Christian revelation, *therefore entitled to exclude Doubt, which is the very element included* in my favourite author's definition of *Hope.* I, therefore, ask any candid mind if there could be a more full inclusion or exclusion than J. S. Mill has enabled the *true Church* to make, as it proclaims Christianity *capable* of securing a condition of mind that *excludes doubt*; yet, leaving each intelligent man and woman free in their own silent consciousness to answer God in the language which will manifest the class they belong to, defined as a believer or an unbeliever. In this little book, I can have left no doubt in the reader's mind to which class I belong, as I claim for the Christian Church alone the power of proclaiming truth in a special form, justly entitled to be defined as *Absolute Truth.*

The Protestant Church is based on the full conviction that God's Spirit is a felt power in the *renewed mind*—sanctifying and revealing truth of a spiritual nature, where the feeling involved in this experience can always be defined to a sympathising mind. This state of mind is implied in Peter's "Be ready always to give an answer to every man that asketh you a reason of the hope that is in you with meekness and fear," 1 Peter, iii. 15, and refers to the discriminating power of the intellect, enabling the individual to define a spiritual experience to a sympathising nature in language clearly intelligible. This experience, in the fullest sense, proves the power and presence of the Spirit of God. It is this spiritual experience, therefore, as a felt power within, which makes it safe for the individual to derive knowledge from all quarters,* and turn all to a practical account, in view of the eternal existence which springs from our present life—a life to which great responsibility is attached.

As we have gained much knowledge from the ideas advanced by Modern Science, therefore, I hold our men of science had a perfect right to expect the Protestant Church to point out the physical base of mind in the quality of the stuff which includes conscious life, as the ego of the individual being the formation procured by the oxygen of the blood

* For unless the individual realised his union with Christ in felt communion, there might be a danger in acquiring knowledge from sceptic books of his becoming an unbeliever.

and the carbon of the system uniting in forming and fixing the ideas or mental images, and is the formation which will ultimately include the human soul, as it passes from the body. But the definite perception included in this process, can only be perceived when revelation is illuminated by taking possession of the thought put forward by Modern Science enabling us to perceive the idea or mental image involved in the term "soul." If we stand so related to Modern Science, we are only just in saying that our Protestant Church has, by her conservative notions, *robbed the men of science of their birth-right, including the assurance of eternal life, and all that such involves.* Am I not, then, justified in saying the Protestant Church owed them a debt of gratitude which was clearly within the limits of the Church to repay? And does not the slavish *fear* manifested in the nervous excitement breathed out by the whole Protestant Church imply much unbelief, if the Bible is touched ever so mildly by the friendly hand of criticism, as if our Protestant Church did not secure for us the full assurance that God's Spirit, as the absolute source of inspiration, was a felt power in every *renewed heart*, inspiring men now as ever with love to God in Christ, clearly defined in the beautiful words I so often quote from the thirty-sixth answer of our Presbyterian Catechism—" an assurance of God's love, peace of conscience, joy in the Holy Ghost, increase of grace, and perseverance therein to the end," which supplies the individual with a far surer test than though every word of the Bible could be proved to be literally inspired; for in this internal evidence we possess in the Spirit of God the source from which all revelation comes, which is all that is needed to ensure the fact that eternal life, *is a continuation of this life.* Therefore we may hear the Angel, of *Revelation* x. 6, proclaim that time shall be no longer, which is the answer to what I have stated, sounding in our ears "*time is no longer.*" This we are enabled to do when we call in the aid of Science, by turning to practical account the ideas advanced by such authors as Dr. Carpenter.

I will now proceed to describe the prophetic revelation referred to. It occurred in 1873, though I was obliged to conceal it until I made myself acquainted with the subject, which enabled me to turn the truth involved to practical account, by perceiving where Christianity and Science may be said to form the counterpart of each other, in Christianity predicting the discoveries of modern students of nature. By this means I hoped to shield myself from censure; otherwise, had I not taken this precaution, as a member of the Protestant Church, I would have incurred the merited rebuke of casting pearls before swine, while the community would have turned to rend me, as that Church wholly ignores the probability of God manifesting His presence in a special or prophetic form, and so implying that the book of revelation is closed. Had I belonged to the Church of Rome, I would have been in a wholly different position, as that Church holds the conviction that God does manifest His presence from time to time, in what is popularly called the miracles.

But to the point of the prophetic revelation. Soon after "Christian Theology and Modern Scepticism" was issued, I read the work, to find out immediately afterwards that I, too, began to question the truth of Christianity. I, therefore, determined to make myself acquainted with historical Christianity, and seek to establish the truth from that point. This course satisfied my intellect so completely that not one trace of unbelief remained. From this point, Christianity acquired a new and powerful influence over me, for, in the truth it taught, I saw truth of infinite importance— *in fact, the one thing needful for time and eternity.*

About this time, I formed a slight intimacy with a family where the gentleman was an avowed sceptic; as such, I felt exceedingly concerned about his salvation, and, after once or twice referring to Christianity, we arranged to meet and discuss the question. This meeting lasted about three hours. By this interview I felt I had made very little impression on him, but he had left a lasting impression on me, for I found him one of Nature's truest sons, highly endowed with the religious element, as in reverence he acknowledged, worshipped, and adored the God of Nature, while the moral element was so fully developed as to be strong enough to hold all low, grovelling, selfish ends in check. The feeling left on my mind after this interview was that, from the point of personal merit, my sceptic friend was, in God's sight, entitled to a higher place than I, for his religious nature was more highly developed. Nevertheless, from Bible testimony, he was an unbeliever and, therefore, wholly unsaved. For some time after the interview, the question, Can such as he be eternally lost? was ever present in my mind. This question I felt utterly unable to answer, for the Bible, to me, seemed to say he must, as an unbeliever, be eternally lost. From this time, my burdened mind sought to find relief in a term that would fully define the distinction that separated his class from mine (defined as believers and unbelievers) and mark the difference, by words clear and definite. This state of mind lasted until one Thursday evening, as I sat silently thinking, when all at once the thought flashed into my mind that such as he could never rise above hope, either in this life or the next. They live, and they hope to live. Hope is to them their ultimatum, therefore, I concluded, Life is Hope. *With this generalization, the burden was lifted from my troubled mind.* My intellect was satisfied and relieved. *I had found a real distinction*—in life is hope, as that idea stood contrasted in my brain with its opposite, realized in the state of being assured of eternal life, this being my own realized condition, in the sight of God, as a believer, therefore, a sinner saved by grace and entitled to eternal life. Had I not, then, found a real distinction in the contrasted ideas so related? Now my whole being quivered with intense joy, for in this generalization the hell of my infancy disappeared, as I perceived a state of hope excluded despair, and the worst, as I reasoned, may have hope. But this was not the source of all my joy, for now I realized that all believers were, in a sense, saved, and that it was *Christ in them, the hope of glory, that ensured eternal life to them.* How bright and happy heaven and earth seemed then, as in gratitude and love I sought to adore God. My spirit breathed only holy joy as His Spirit thus revealed truth.

This state of joy, as the fruit of a clear intellectual perception, lasted with more or less intensity up to Sunday, until late in the evening, when I began to question the *enclosure,* and reasoned thus :—*Can God intend all believers to be saved?* adding, Can those who live a wicked and impure life be saved and fit for heaven, though they do believe? With this question unanswered, I thought, and thought, and felt constrained to admit, that it certainly could not be so revealed in the Christian doctrine that all believers were saved and one with God in Christ. In the early morning of the day following, when giving expression to this thought, all at once the words, LIFE IS HOPE, were stamped on my sensorium brain in letters of light, just directly at the back of the left eye. This was the form the impression was made to take in conveying the truth involved in the generalization I had previously made ;* the truth which I was about to efface by my

* Which was to the effect that a state of hope is the highest point

reasoning, namely, that God could not intend all believers to be saved and one with Christ. But God prevented me, and *thus stamped the truth which is of infinite importance to the race on my sensorium brain, so as to confirm it to me as absolute truth.** In the formation effected thus, the "L" and the "H" were capital letters about an inch and half long, the others small type. The impression lasted a second or two—just long enough to make a vivid impression on consciousness, in conscious mind—then faded away so as to give place to another thought. I got up immediately, and observed it was a quarter to four o'clock on the 17th November, 1873, as I took a note of the thoughts that succeeded the impression, which I copy, and was as follows :—" 17th November, 1873—He, the Spirit of Truth, has sent me to tell you, O, men of science, it is all mind over matter till you take Jesus as God reconciling the world to Himself, and the seat (part) of the brain you will find it (mind) in is just beyond (behind) the eye—it may be only the left eye, it may be both eyes, but you test and try, and you

---

man can rise to as he reasons on the possibility of a continuous existence, and that this mental state of hope is equivalent to life; so that hope, in this sense, may be made to include eternal life.

* Observe, hope is the mental state which separates the believer from the unbeliever—all believers being entitled to eternal life as the fruit of belief; consequently this revelation, when fully understood, concerns unbelievers only. But it enables us to place in contrast the mental condition the two classes are entitled to—the believers being assured of eternal life, whereas the unbeliever lives on in hope as the equivalent of life.

will find it visibly written there; for mind, my Master, King Jesus, has told me. Search and try and you will find it true. I have it by faith, but you will have it by sight. That is all he has sent me to tell you—the seat of the brain you will find mind in,* just the seat of the brain you

* It will be necessary to add a note of explanation here. In the cerebrum brain we find a quality of stuff which has come into existence as the product of thought or mental life, as the quality of stuff which includes the mental images, or ideas, of the race—consequently, a material holding intelligent life in the concrete, as the stuff built up of, and held together by, the mental images, which includes intelligent life in its ideal form. This quality of stuff, by my reasoning, both forms the tree and the fruit, in having the power to present, as ideas in the form of thought, on the sensorium brain, all the fruit the tree contains where the ideas will express in the notion or conception of the sentiment, or thing, all the knowledge of the subject dealt with which the individual possesses. For example, if religion is thought of, the conception in the concrete deals with all we know of God, and our relation to him, as the knowledge which has been gathered by the race, and treasured up in the form of an element or conception in the cerebrum—a conception which may be broken up into parts implied in these words:—"This phase of religion is peculiar to this race, and that phase of religion to that other race." By this process, the individual breaks up the religious sentiment and analyzes it in perceiving what was peculiar to one race, and what to another. I hold that the quality of stuff capable of producing all this is held together in the cerebrum brain, built up in this form, containing the soul or mental life as the experience of the race—the action of which will be manifested, doubtless, by the laws peculiar to the stuff and its conditions. Such action is sometimes manifested in the preconscious action of the individual soul, where the subject we dismissed in utter confusion, when taken up again is presented with clearness. But, observe, every sentiment or idea as matter and force governed thus has been evolved through a brain, and is the product of intelligent life, bound by laws as eternal as God. How this stuff, as the element of thought, stands related to the individual is the matter in hand. Its relation is, that it forms impressions, as thought in ideas on the sensorium brain, and is the inner world from which that organ receives impressions.

will find mind in. I have seen it written on the brain with letters of light, and like a little fluid it faded away as soon as the impression was given to make way for another thought. Prove for yourselves."

In communicating these facts I feel my responsibility ends; as, if any credit should be reflected on me for the knowledge I may have gathered, the source of it will be seen to have come from this impression, which, in one sense, only concerns myself, *though the ideas involved in their contrasted relationships are of infinite importance to humanity*—the question at issue being, Does belief ensure eternal life, and, therefore, exclude doubt, as this experience stands contrasted with its opposite, including a state of doubt as seen in " Life is Hope"?—the hope referred to here having arisen from man's previous experience, in view of the past, the present, and the future, which state of mind certainly does include or involve doubt. How these two contrasted ideas* stand related to humanity is the question that concerns the Christian Church and demands an answer.

> On the sensorium brain, a joint alliance is formed between the internal source of knowledge I have described above, and the external source, as the impression made on our senses by object existences. It is by means of these two sources, as the springs of intellectual life, making their influence felt on the sensorium brain, that the individual soul is formed, and is the explanation I give of the term used, "seat of the brain you will find mind in." Observe the office which the sensorium brain performs is taking on impressions from two sources, and transforming them into thought, as soul or mental life.
>
> * Which present the two mental states—the one including a state of doubt, the other resting in full assurance.

It now remains with the men of science, on the one hand, to say if mental life can be defined as thought, by the impressions presented forming an idea or mental image in the form of a sensation on the sensorium brain, as the oxygen of the blood and the carbon of the system unite; the union thus formed would *contain each impression* in the form of thought, and, that thus grouped, unit, would ultimately be presented in what we are justified, as Christians, in calling the individual soul. *The forces so generated would include conscious mind as the individual unit* produced, where we are to suppose the gases unite in photographing every thought as the unit forming conscious mind. Whereas, the question to be answered by the other class as believers, specially including the Protestant Church, will be, does Christianity raise the believer above hope, by *insuring* him of an eternal existence in union with Christ our Lord in his relation as the Son of God?

The question which concerns humanity is—how does the truth involved in this prophetic revelation *stand related to known truth? for it is only when contrasted with known truth that it concerns the world of intelligent life.* Observe the different stages I passed through. First, Christianity is unhesitatingly accepted and realised as absolute truth (for I was converted in early life.) Then a period of doubt follows, when scepticism makes the truth of Christianity to be questioned. Here the historical evidence of Christianity steps in and establishes its truth. The effect of which is manifested in the conviction stimulating the emotions, and feeling is profusely poured out in the form of a strong desire for my sceptic friend's salvation.

Now, an entirely *new element is perceived in the high, moral, and religious character my sceptic friend presents,* in consequence of which, my *intellectual conception is confused,* as the question rises, Can this man be eternally lost? which must have remained a week or two unanswered, until at last the *discriminating power of the intellect perceived the distinction between the two classes (as believer and unbeliever).* This is clearly defined in Hope presenting the highest point in view of eternal life to which the unbeliever can ever attain, as he reasons on the past, the present, and the future, in the light of eternity. Therefore, I concluded *"Life is Hope,"* as onward through eternity the soul that has been produced here will continue to live under different and altered circumstances, and still hope to live, as age succeeds age. While the believer, through all these stages, enjoys the full assurance of eternal life, as he realizes life in union and communion with the Son of God, seen in his Lord and Master, Jesus Christ.

I arrived at these conclusions by the *force of reason alone.* Up to this point there was no revelation properly so called. Doubtless the joy that ensued was an expression of what the Protestants define as the Spirit of God revealing truth. The Spirit was thus fulfilling his mission by verifying the words of the Saviour, " He shall guide you into all truth, for He shall not speak of Himself, for whatsoever He shall hear that shall He speak, and He shall show you things to come," John xvi. 13. The work of the Spirit will thus be understood to present the truth of revelation, as it stands contrasted with truth in nature. The intelligence of the Christian would, by my reasoning, enable such an one to perceive truth from two points, and unite the truth from both points under one head, in a generalized idea.*

The physical cause of the joy I experienced, however, is the very same condition which our men of science would define as joy derived from an intellectual perception or insight; the strain on the intellectual power being removed in consequence of having secured the generalization desired, the object wished for *was attained*, and the energy is poured out over the system, manifesting an emotion of pleasure in all the members of the body rejoicing together as one great whole. Up to this point, I had evidently anticipated what Christianity reveals, and the conclusion the Protestant Church should have arrived at ere now. There was no need for a prophetic revelation being given if my brain had been *big enough to hold the truth in the form of an intellectual perception, grounded on the full meaning of the term "belief" in its concrete form*, as a term used

---

* Life indicates movement, and hope progressive movement; but, in the assurance of faith, both conceptions or ideas are combined under one head, in eternal life being realized by the believer, where life and progressive movement are doubtless included.

to include the state of mind involved in acting with as much energy for an *intermediate* end as for an *immediate* end, which is the *scientific way of putting faith working by love.*

It will be thus seen the forces already present in our *Protestant faith* were enough to produce this effect by presenting revealed truth in a *clear form, demonstrated as the intellect and the emotions performing their separate functions, animated by love,* for the work is clear and different from a *Protestant* point of view. While I rested here, all is *well,* for the joy and glory of Protestant Christianity are *realized.* God is adored in having given His only begotten Son to redeem the sinner.

Here I would have it clearly observed that it was in reality the most subtle form of *Egotism* that necessitated the prophetic revelation. Take notice of the question I am trying to solve—when the impression was made on my *sensorium brain*—namely, Can all that believe be saved—the worst and the vilest? Possibly, *though I am not aware of it,* I was mentally comparing my own life with that of others living in known sin, and, therefore, I must exalt myself *and those of my class* by maintaining the old position, that faith must be substantiated or accompanied by good works, implied in—all that believe can not be saved. Although this error was at the root, *and is the most subtle form of Egotism,* yet, doubtless, it springs from not having clear views of what faith or belief really *includes in its essence,* which I would again state is a mental condition that ensures working for an intermediate end with as much energy as for an immediate end, which is simply other words; for firm, strong faith will always produce a blameless life, or at anyrate, a desire to live a blameless life. I had not clear enough insight to perceive all this, therefore our Lord must present the truth that separates the believer from the unbeliever in his own language, as Life is Hope, by the impression made in letters of light on my sensorium brain. The fact being that, though I held the truth in an intellectual perception, I had not brain enough to hold all the parts separately as a logical whole. The physical cause was the oxygen and carbon in the system united, forming an impression as an idea, including truth that applies to the race, in thus proving what science has revealed, enabling us to take hold of their ideas, and state the case thus—our mental life, in ideas as mental images is the formation which has been effected in the union of the gases which hold the forces together in the laws which include the individual soul.

The question now is, Has modern science taught us to comprehend the full meaning of revealed truth? as we make the acquaintance of such authors as H. Spencer, H. Lewis, A. Bain, and Dr. Carpenter. To my judgment, the last-named distinctly implies, in his "Principles of Mental Physiology," that the mental life of the individual is "played off," or produced, in the impression made on the sensorium brain; and we have only to add, when the oxygen of the blood unites with the carbon of the system *under this condition it includes in the shock* the ideal impression then present in conscious mind; so that, in the light of revealed truth, we are justified in holding up the continuous mental impressions thus formed as the *soul of the individual.* All must admit that this is a fair and logical course to adopt, as we reason on revealed truth in the light of the ideas put forward by such authors as I have here quoted, who teach us to comprehend how the individual soul is formed. The process being, the gases forming the impressions unite in holding the mental images together as they are presented in their ideal form (or as ideas), destined to contain the mental life or mind of the evolved soul, being the unit of a system that includes the intelligence of the human race. Observe, instead of having the brain-organism, or function, we have the compound in the united gases *bound together in the mental images they include,* presenting the conscious "ego" of the individual, or we may perceive the brain containing our individual mental life as the impressions received that form the series in the united gases. Could anything be more simple and definite to realise than the union of the oxygen and the carbon, thus formed, held *together by means of the mental image* that includes knowledge as mind or mental life ? While the union of the same gases taking place in any other part of the organism or body, in consequence of the *mental image not being present,* therefore, the union effected in all other portions of the body would include an entirely different form of matter. This last formation may ultimately present the bodily organism in the form of crystallized carbon, over which the *will of the individual* would be understood to exercise complete control, as the ultimate form which the resurrection body will take, including a unit of intelligent life which was produced on this planet.

With this explanation, I am hopeful the obscure parts of my book will be rendered more intelligible. For example, page 159, all I contend for is that the shock which accompanies the union of the gases includes the mental image at that moment present in consciousness, and that consciousness is always accompanied by this shock and union, which form the physical counterpart of consciousness or mind, forming the "ego" of the individual which has been evolved, and is the product arising from a bodily organism in its relation with its environment or surrounding. The bodily organism thus possesses the power of taking on vibration and transforming the vibration thus received into an intelligent perception of the thing or object causing the movement or vibration.* For example, we communicate our thoughts by intelligent speech, the physical cause being atmospheric

---

* By means of the movement which is caused by the objective existance, the object is transformed into the subjective state, so that, by this process, the "ego" is formed. This is the meaning I attach to the terms objective and subjective, which I use in my volume—terms which, I contend, include man's ultimate knowledge, and, therefore, his intelligence.

air taking on certain vibrations, interpreted as sound, which convey and include the ideas or mental images the speaker represents in the terms he uses. By this means, impressions are transmitted to other minds, by the organism taking on the vibrations, including all this. Therefore, is not the "ego" the product arising from the organism and its environment in the bodily organism being so effected by its surrounding as to produce this "ego," as the intelligence of the individual, included in the shock that accompanies or causes consciousness, as the carbon and the oxygen unite on the sensorium brain holding the impression formed together. With this form of matter, understood as the "ego" or conscious life of the individual, we have a physical base presented in the brain organism which I hope to turn to good account, as I strive to elucidate the obscure part of the subject, and give the meaning I attach to the different terms dealt with. The "ego," presented in this form, will be understood to include the units of conscious life, grouped together so that each unit is, in a sense, related with each other unit, forming one great whole. However, in this whole, we find some of the units more closely related than others; for example, the groups defined as the moral and religious *groups* or *elements*, the social group—the love of country and kindred, and so on.

The religious element I would define as a group, which specially includes, and springs from, the belief in a God, or that there is an Intelligence at the heart of every thing.

Therefore, all adoration, worship, reverence, including submission to and acquiescence in the will of such a being governing, according to his own good pleasure, are included in this germ or group, as it *vibrates* in worship, so rendered by, or through, the individual. possibly presenting the special emotion in the colour seen by the phase of vibration. I likewise assert the possibility of each individual holding communion with God, as the human soul in adoration seeks to approach the Infinite; and I hold this feeling, proceeding from the religious element, to include man's ultimate knowledge of God, except where a special revelation is given in some form. Under such circumstances, man's knowledge of God must ever remain exceedingly limited and vague, or obscure, except where a special revelation is given, and such could only apply as a general rule to man individually. Nevertheless, man has a craving after the Infinite, as in aspiring adoration, a feeling which I hold may fill the inner man with joy, and presents man in his natural state — instance Theodore Parker. Such an element as this being present with more or less intensity in the race, I hold to be demonstrated, or manifested, in the experience of the race as a whole, having arisen, or sprung from, a desire in the lowest intelligence to be led by a higher intelligence, increasing until, in a way, God's felt presence is realized, and through this, presents the highest form of worship possible to the natural man. Observe, it does not ensure eternal life, and the highest point that can ever be obtained by such is a hope that life may be continued through eternity. We may thus perceive how feeling after feeling has crystallized round the centre unit, and produced such men as we sometimes find in the heathen world. To meet the requirements of a race possessing such an element as this, Christianity presents all that can be desired, when it is viewed in connection with the moral element present in the race also, having been evolved, possibly being first seen in connection with the tribe or family, hence the social relationship connecting itself with the interest of the individual, inducing man to do justice to fellow-man, in exacting only his due, while he would recognise service rendered, and strive to give an equivalent. Until a social state is reached, where each realizes his individual interest as included in the weal of the general whole as a race; doubtless this feeling will ultimately include the weal of the intelligent universe as a whole, *viewed in the light which Christianity forecasts.* This social and moral element, merging one into the other, is a sentiment, in some form or other, universally present in the race. Where it exists in the highest form, the individuals so possessed feel they have a common interest in the well-being of the race as a whole, as each renders to each other their due; and while the moral element has been forming, the germs have been crystallizing round the centre unit, and by this means the part ultimately presents the "moral element," manifested in humanity, even although the forces thus combined are often powerless when combating against the self-regarding interest of the individual. Nevertheless, in every case where the self-regarding interest is held in check, this power is fully manifested in the moral element, as the force proceeding from this group of brain matter; the function of that group being to perform moral actions. Again, it is with a race thus possessed, in which such feeling is present, that Revelation in the shape of Christianity, making known to man in what relationship he stands towards God, in consequence of being in possession of a moral element, and, therefore, an Intelligence to whom God will ultimately show himself all powerful, addressing one and all of the race in the words used by our Lord, *Matthew* vii. 2, "With what judgment ye judge, ye shall be judged; and with what measure ye mete, it shall be measured to you again," having power to enforce the condition implied; for this includes all, in one way, that Revelation demands of the natural man, and is fully included in the Jewish law of "an eye for an eye and a tooth for a tooth," which includes the fulfilling of the Law.

It is with the moral and religious element, as the crystallized unit, which I have here defined, that Christianity specially takes to do. And observe how my reasoning is illuminated by the *prophetic revelation* referred to (as the words were impressed on my sensorium brain in letters of light—*Life is Hope)*, showing how every thought of the mind, as conscious life, has been photographed in the form of an impression by means of the gases uniting, in forming and fitting the impression which includes the physical basis of mind, as a portion of matter, where the mental life of every individual is held fast in the forces that have combined to form and fix the impressions included in thought.

Observe, that the crystallized mass of conscious matter, thus defined, is held together in such a way that each separate group expresses itself in the form of an element having a special function. For example, the emotions of adoration, worship, and reverence, proceed from the group defined as the religious element; and, observe, the emotion proceeding from it may be either presented in the emotion of pleasure or pain, as when man realizeth the awful responsibility attached to intelligent life, he may so dread the consequences as to be filled with fear, approaching to despair, in realizing the position in which he stands to the Almighty as a responsible intelligent being, who must render an account. And, again, he may be filled with joy, as his heart swells in adoration and love to the Supreme, Eternal, Self-existing One; therefore, either a pleasurable or painful emotion may, for the time being, be presented in consciousness as proceeding from the same source or element as the consequence of the intellectual perception that part may assume, for the time being, felt as either pleasure or pain; always bearing in mind that it is a law of the organism that pleasure and pain cannot be represented in consciousness at once. For example, if the animated mental mass is vibrating as the response of the pleasurable emotion, for the time being, pain must be absent or neutralized, because, in its *essence*, it contains a sentiment producing results entirely different, and, doubtless, manifested by a phase of vibration entirely different, possibly made apparent in the colour *forming* the vibration then present. Therefore, in their essence, the emotion of pleasure and pain present conditions totally different, and are the very conditions, *humanly speaking*, which either procure for the individual a continuous existence, or deprive him of a continuous existence, in the sense that pleasure increases the vital action, and pain diminishes it. Nevertheless, the two contrasted emotions can only include *for the human race an equivalent for life and death*, in consequence of eternal life being ensured to all by revealed truth in Christ's sacrifice; therefore, death, in the abstract, must only mean, or stand for, a lowering of the vital action, *though certainly not a taking away of conscious existence*. Thus we reason on the physical causes of things, and talk of the grouped intelligence as mental life, and see that its life-giving property is included in the emotion of pleasure, and its death-threatening property is included in the emotion of pain.

I hold I am now justified in assuming that I have established the physical bases of mind or conscious life in this grouped mass of intelligent life, held together by the forces that have combined in forming and stamping the impressions received as mental life. The qualities of matter which present the united substance are carbon and oxygen, transformed by the process into carbonic acid. In this material the mental life of every individual is presented in a series of ideas bound by laws lasting as eternity—personified in the decrees of God as the combination His laws have produced. In thought, I thus transform mental life, formed in the brain organism, and present it in the form defined above, this being the form which presents the human soul, for which Christ has secured an eternal existence. 1 *John* ii. 2.

When we view the human soul in its concrete formation, we may separate the special parts as groups, and define the groups as the structures of the different functions; the function thus defined having the power of raising in the conscious "ego" either the emotion of pleasure or pain. And, observe, pleasure and pain are the contrasted emotions which determine the moving power of the "ego," and are the germs from which all movement springs; these movements include the law of the organism, where the vital action is ever increased by pleasure and diminished by pain. Therefore, pleasure and pain are to us the equivalents of life and death, and are the roots which have quickened into intelligent life, enabling us to perceive the means that will secure the end desired—the vital power derived from pleasure being ever sought after as an end, until Christianity steps in with its pruning hook and strips the germ of its power during this life, for Jesus' sake, by inducing the converted and sanctified individual to choose suffering, so that the Redeemer may be glorified and His race increased on earth.

All our knowledge being derived from contrasted ideas, and our judgments formed by the discriminating power of the intellect, which enables us to classify our knowledge in generalized ideas, by perceiving where one object or emotion differs from all other objects or emotions, in consequence of the discriminating power we derive from this mental condition, we may divide and build up in a new form. For example, just fancy all that the two words, matter and force, include to our men of science, as they perceive in mental life the ultimate of matter, because the knowledge of this stuff comes to us by the effect it manifests on our bodily organism, and the mental conception growing from the contact includes all we know of matter. Therefore, in the brain organism, have we not mental life in the ideal form, as the abstraction of all we know of matter—the discriminating power of the intellect having done its work of putting down and building up, where the ideas, thus formed, are stored away in the brain organism, to be reproduced when wanted. In this form, the whole concrete mass is included in the terms, subject and object, as the joint alliance which has been formed on the sensorium brain, including the mental conception, forming intelligent life, this language being only intelligible to our men of science, as in mind or mental life they perceive all we know of matter and force.

Whereas, to people not acquainted with the subject, the words hardly present a definite intellectual perception at all, in consequence of the discriminating power being less fully educated on that point. In this, we see how differently the crystallized mass of intelligent life has been *made to combine* in one class compared with the other, whereas, our men of science presenting intelligent life in this form, enable us to understand in its fulness, the *idea our Lord wished to convey in the term "Flesh,"* where he includes this very condition, in the words, "that which is born of the flesh, is flesh," John iii. 6. Does not our Lord in this predicate or reveal what students of nature now prove, while He would have us point to this crystallized unit of conscious life as the natural growth which has been brought to maturity, through the influence of self-preservation, acting as the force which has produced the whole? But a force which is now hurtful to the further development of the individual, and necessitates the change involved in conversion, or in being born again, a change which cuts at the root of the self-regarding interest, by inducing man to desire God's glory in preference to his own glory, and thus making man willing to suffer, so that God in Christ may be glorified, while the change which has produced this, includes a new state of conciousness, defined as a spiritual experience, realized in union and communion with God in Christ.

It is now necessary to refer to the law that governs the conscious "ego," being the desire to secure a pleasure because of its life-giving property, which is [1] the principal force that stimulates the individual to pursue a self-regarding course, where selfishness is at the root of every movement, and is the power which so influences man's actions as to make it impossible for him to resist a temptation beyond a certain point. The case may be otherwise stated thus— in consequence of the law of his organism, compelling him to pursue a selfish or self-regarding course, there is a certain point beyond which he has no control, because at this point his course is fixed or regulated by the law of his organism, which compels him to choose a selfish course, whoever will suffer or whatever may ensue. Consequently, men in reality have only a limited capacity to resist a wrong course, and they cannot therefore be held wholly responsible in the eye of the Almighty, *far less in the eye of his fellow-man, being conscious of how often he himself falls.* This, then, being the law of the organism, there is only a limited power man can possibly acquire over his destiny, even although the moral element is most assiduously cultivated, for even in this form there is always a point beyond which man is liable or *compelled* to act from the instinct of self-preservation; whereas, when the moral element is, as often happens, left almost wholly uncared for or uncultivated, the power to resist a temptation is very limited indeed. The question is, how far have antecedent circumstances limited the individual's power of resistance. Anyhow, to the natural man, there is a point beyond which he is utterly powerless, and it is at this point that Christianity proclaims its divine origin, in raising the individual above the influence dealt with, *i.e.* selfishness and raising him above the influence of earth and the things of earth. This is effected when he realizeth his union with Christ in God. This union insuring him of a happy eternal existence, raises him above the surrounding circumstances which before formed his temptations and compelled him to choose a selfish course.

It is to produce this state of feeling I aim at in the first part of the book, where I strive to create the mental states which combine in making a Christian a willing servant of God's, and in training the believer to stimulate the perception included in Christianity, by so pouring the emotion of love into the conception already present in the term belief, as to fill the conscious life, or "ego" of the individual with love to Christ, being the source from which the highest form of Christianity springs. I thus sought to stimulate the emotion of love so as to absorb every other feeling by compelling all earthly interests to possess only a limited power instead of holding the principal place. Observe, the book is not addressed to *unbelievers,* but principally deals with the professing Christian in dealing with the fruit that proceeds from Christian faith, or felt communion with Christ. As I strive to give expression to the mental process that accompanies and produces this fruit, in showing the intellectual believer that the highest form of Christianity is only attained when the soul is stimulated by the emotion of love, as the individual clings to, and rejoices in a *personal Saviour* manifesting His presence in the soul thus possessed, and filled with the new set of forces springing from belief in the Christian faith. Thus, then, I hope to inspire the individual believer with the Christian love and zeal that animated John and Paul over eighteen hundred years ago, this being the means by which the dead image of the ideal Christ held in the form of an intellectual conception, would be animated by a force containing in its essence the spirit of God and capable of rousing the dead image into a living form, strong and powerful enough to animate the believer with the fire and zeal present in the souls redeemed in glory, as they raise the song of triumph to the Lord who bought them. And I am fully persuaded that the course enjoined at the beginning of the book, if pursued in the spirit of *real desire*, will animate the Christian believer with true joy, as his heart responds to the full conviction included in "*Christ is mine, for God is love, I know and feel.*" And where such aspirations as these are the daily and hourly experience of the mental life, are we not justified in saying that the world has lost its power, and, with it, *the power of temptation is gone*, for the joys that this life or the world has to offer have lost their power. *Therefore, man is redeemed and consecrated to God in Christ.*

This, then, was the object I had in view in writing the book, when I found, in the ideas put forward by the authors I have referred to, the fits I required to enable me to perceive what the physical basis of mind included, as the portion of conscious life our Lord defines as "flesh." As I thus point to the physical basis of soul, in the united forces which combine in procuring and fixing the mental images of every thought that has passed, or will pass, through the mind during our earthly life, I would ask, are not our souls worth more care in cultivating for eternity than we bestow on them? In view of God having provided for us a Saviour to rescue us from the penalty and power of the self-regarding instinct, by animating us by new sets of forces which proclaim their divine origin, by filling the soul with an assurance of God's love, peace of conscience, joy in the Holy Ghost, increase of grace, and perseverance therein to the end. Justification by faith secures for the individual, at conversion, the power to procure the form of mental life enjoined—to whom Christ is to become all and all. But where the course which will insure success is not followed, we may infer that such a state will induce or entail suffering in the next life. The full blessing being only promised to such as *overcome*, by striving to regulate their lives in accordance with Christ's teaching, as the fruit which will flow from love to Him when the individual is wholly consecrated to the Lord. Viewing the physical basis of mind in the light I put it, all must allow that it is the truth put forward by Modern Science which has enabled us to form a conception of the physical basis of mind or soul, enabling us to understand how matter, as conscious life, becomes possessed of a new mental experience, manifested through our Christian belief, made apparent in the words I will again state—"an assurance of God's love, peace of conscience, joy in the Holy Ghost, increase of grace, and perseverance therein to the end." This glorious experience unites us with heaven in uniting us with Christ. All this springs from our Protestant doctrine of justification by faith, being the germ from which the emotion of love can alone in its purity proceed, and procure works fully acceptable to God; because such works, as a natural consequence, flow from love to Christ in spontaneous energy, where the individual looks for no reward. Much confusion has arisen from the Protestant Church failing to perceive, with clearness, the idea involved in Paul's conception of it being possible for man to attain the state of glory included in his term of "glory of God," showing that, though the possibility of attaining to this high state *is included in the fruit that may flow from conversion*, nevertheless, from various causes, few Christians care to attain this high state, which is only secured where the life is wholly consecrated to God in Christ; but in this state of consecration the idea included is the natural fruit which flows from love to Christ, for in this state the individual is filled with the fulness of God, therefore, full of the glory of God. This fruit, in its highest form, does flow from, and secure, a fully consecrated life, because fruit, so rendered, includes both cause and effect, *or the final cause*, thus making it possible for man to attain to the condition conveyed in

Paul's conception, which includes that to be filled with the glory of God is made possible to man, *and is the condition which is attained when the life is fully consecrated to God in Christ*. Much confusion has arisen from our Church not perceiving, with clearness, that, though conversion makes it possible for man to attain to this high state, nevertheless, that change does not often produce the high form of Christianity included in Paul's conception, *which, however, is only made possible through conversion*.

I hold that, though the individual has been converted, where the life is not fully consecrated, the law of the organism, in such a condition, will necessitate suffering in the next life; but that this suffering will spring from the voluntary labour which the individual will choose to perform, as fruit flowing from love to Christ, and that the pain he suffers is in consequence of his organism not having been perfected by means of a consecrated life while on earth. But though the willing service such an one will now render will be accompanied by pain as an offering of love—yet, observe, this is pain voluntarily chosen. Nevertheless, that such a condition does and will include suffering, *is all I contend for in the notion I hold of the conception included in Purgatory*, or an intermediate state of suffering, which is a doctrine held by the Church of Rome.

I will proceed by stating my theory as briefly as possible. I can have left no doubt in my reader's mind of the meaning I attach to the physical basis of mind, held fast in a portion of matter we call fixed air, being the product of intelligent life in the human system, by which the ideas are formed as mental images comprising the conscious "ego," or we may state the matter thus—*As it passess through the brain organism, under certain conditions, the physical basis of mind is formed in fixed air.** This quality of matter is held together by the ideas forming mental life which it contains, and, in consequence of these impressions, as mental life, it must endure, and will possess the power of reproducing, at will, the whole series or any portion of the series of the individual's conscious life on earth. The mental life here referred to has sprung from, and formed itself into ideas, rising from conditions which have an objective existence. This objective existence, which forms the counterpart of the subjective state, is the object which gave the subject birth, and which is now formed into an idea, as the mental image which has sprung from this objective source, and which has thus been made to form the mental conception of the object, *including all the knowledge we possess of the object.* I hold that an object so related to a subject will, under certain conditions, have the power of rousing the ideal expression of the subjective state which springs from this objective source. For example, suppose the object which had roused the feeling of anger again present the "ego," which I always associate with a bodily form,

* Because the mental images thus formed are to be found in the fixed air.

might assume the expression of anger in the compressed mouth, the frowning brow, the erect figure, with the feet firmly planted on the ground, or might assume any of the various expressions indicating that passion, and that the objective existence which gave this feeling birth, might always have the power of raising this state, though, doubtless, under many conditions the sensation of anger would be absent, though the expression was present. What I have stated might be presented in the phase of vibration indicating anger. Matter or stuff possessing this power, surely we are justified in defining as the physical basis of mind, as it holds together in this form the concrete mental life of the individual, where each individual life so defined is in possession of a moral and religious element. Elements, in this sense, will be understood to present the matured ideas included in the terms as the products of evolution, therefore, capable of progressing.

I would have it fully understood that the very highest meaning I attach to the term *Civilization* is manifested in the highest degree where the character of the individual displays *the "moral and religious" elements most fully developed*; because my subject deals with a state of existence in which the well-being of the individual will depend on the care he has bestowed in cultivating his moral and religious nature.

In close relation with these two elements, we find Conscience, which includes the knowledge of right or wrong, a sense which enables the individual to form a judgment between right and wrong, not ultimately, but from his own point of view. For example, supposing some one pursued a course of action which caused another to bear the consequence of an unmerited rebuke. I hold that the individual who caused another to suffer this, as a general rule, would feel the injustice of the course he had adopted, and, except where the temptation was very strong, he would avoid such a course in the future, being convinced it was a wrong course; so that, by this means, a notion of right and wrong would be formed. Conscience so defined will, as a matter of course, depend very largely on the character of the individual; and I hold that *Guilt* will only be attached to such an one where the conscious feeling of having acted wrong exists. Thus, then, it will remain entirely with the individual to pursue the course he may approve of, always bearing in mind that such an one is understood to have conceived the truth and accepted the fact involved in there being an *Intelligence* at the heart of everything, *to whom he is responsible for his actions, being liable to punishment if he fails in his duty*, where the degree of punishment will be based on the principle involved in our Lord's word, "Do to others as you would have others do to you; for with what measure ye mete it shall be measured to you again." Though, doubtless, the surrounding circumstances of the life will greatly add to or take from the responsibility, nevertheless the responsibility of all such (for I am dealing with the natural man) will be limited, in consequence of the law of his organism compelling him to choose pleasure at a certain point, because of its life-giving property defined as self-preservation—the effect of such a condition being that, up to a certain point, this selfish course may be kept in check by various causes; but when a certain point is reached it will disregard all consequences in the effort to attain a continuous existence —words equivalent to saying, *if the temptation is strong enough all are liable to fall, or, indeed, must fall.* So that with such a force at the root of intelligent life there can only be a measure of justice possible or of responsibility attached, as the individual ever craves for a higher state, and where the desire to attain it will, at a certain point, render him careless of who may suffer if he can secure the end desired.* The selfishness which leads man astray seems to be anticipated in, or closely allied to, a course sometimes recommended in the phrase " regulating your conduct according to *expediency.*" This course, to my judgment, implies that man is only to think of his own convenience by using every means to attain that end whoever may suffer. Where this is the meaning attached to the phrase, and where the course is recommended and pursued, we may expect the very worst issue as the end of such a course. For the

---

* This reasoning leads to the conclusion that, if to do right is the guiding principle that animates the individual, God may say of him "he has done what he could."

motive implied in expediency so rendered rises wholly from selfishness; and as the motive stands for everything in rendering the action good or bad in God's sight, the motive in this course being purely selfish, therefore wholly bad. The truly bad effect which must proceed from this course is very apparent to a race where the best is sure to fall if the temptation is very strong. Nevertheless it is so with the natural man, as the intelligence God purposed to redeem, by securing for him, under certain conditions, a happy eternal existence, in virtue of another's merits, through whom the individual is rescued from the power of selfishness, which includes conscious guilt, both having risen from a desire to maintain a continued happy existence, being the notion included in, and rising from, the emotion of pleasure, which increases the vital action, by inducing the desire to attain a yet greater flow of vitality whoever will suffer, which course is sure to entail a selfish course. However, the selfish course is checked when the individual realizeth that his eternal life is secured, and perceives the obligation this includes. This being a state of mind which will induce gratitude, and a desire to show it by being willing to suffer so that the Saviour may be glorified, who has redeemed him from the consequences of a selfish course, which eventually, if not checked, must have led him to ruin. When the individual realizeth all this, the gratitude which proceeds and includes love becomes the strongest power, and induces a self-sacrificing course, which eventually takes the place of a selfish course, and, by this means, man is redeemed. I further assert that, in one sense, Christ's atoning sacrifice has secured or redeemed the race by securing for the individual an eternal existence, which will, under certain conditions, animate man with the emotion of love to God, so that each will only desire an eternal existence in union and communion with him. My theory is, that even where Christianity has been rejected, but where the life has been regulated by justice and truth, in so far as that is possible to the natural or unbelieving man, the blameless life of such will, in virtue of Christ's atoning sacrifice, secure deliverance from the penalty included in "You shall not come out thence till you have paid the uttermost farthing."—*Matt.* v. 26. And that, in virtue of the deliverance thus secured, the individual will be animated with love to Christ which will produce a desire for a future existence, only in union with the Redeemer. Self-preservation will thus, in the form we find it, be neutralized. For if we view intelligent life as acting according to law, this self-regarding instinct must be overcome by a force which will conquer it, and such a force we find included in Christ's atoning sacrifice, which operates by so increasing the emotional state as to compel the individual to act according to a certain course, prompted by love to God, where, in its fully developed state, all the actions proceeding from this source will be in harmony with the will of God, being fruit flowing from love to God.

In saying a good life, in virtue of Christ's sacrifice, will save the soul from the consequence of sin, as seen in *Matt.* v. 26, nevertheless, it is very apparent the relation Christ stands in to the class saved thus is totally different from the relation He stands in to believers. To the believer He is Brother and Redeemer, a Saviour and Deliverer, sent of God, to whom all believers are joined, and with whom all believers work, in showing forth His glory on the earth, where He is reviled and despised, and called an impostor, or at best, a self-deceived man in regard to His mission. It is while such abuse is heaped upon Him that the believer is honouring Him in proclaiming His Divinity, and in being willing to suffer for His sake—their mission being to proclaim an absolute truth, involved in Christ having a permanent objective existence, as the counterpart of the ideal Christ, which is presented in every brain. Further, believers help to build up a system of truth, where Christ, as the God-Man, is the developing intelligence of the universe, and to Him the believer is brother. Observe, unbelievers, though rescued, have never honoured the God-Man on earth, and because they have not honoured Him when He was despised is, I believe, the difference which will distinguish the so-called saved and lost through all eternity—these being the two classes the race will ultimately be divided into; for take notice, the ideal Christ, in the God-Man, as the fruit of revealed truth, *has not* been formed in the soul of the one class. *Though they are saved they are not fully equipped*, therefore, have not the power of believers, for what the believer held in faith was an absolute truth, and will be manifested in the God-Man, as the developing intelligence of the universe. Thus it is apparent that being delivered from the consequence of sin is totally different from being members of the true Church, presenting the Church of the first-born, where the ideal Christ, in the form of the God-Man, brightens every brain, shining forth in the form of a little sun, diffusing light and heat, and wherever the influence is felt, developing intelligent life. I hold that to be rescued from a self-regarding course is absolutely necessary before a soul is fit for glory, because, *among the pure and the holy, one selfish act would pollute the place.* But who can tell what terrible retribution will be necessary before a wicked life can be rescued according to law, as doubtless all are under law; however, if we find man has only a limited power of resisting a temptation, surely we cannot infer that he is to be eternally lost, though doubtless there will be an eternal distinction between the saved and the lost, viewing the unbeliever as lost and the believer as saved.

I can have left no doubt in the reader's mind that no works coming from the believer are acceptable to God but where they are the fruit of love, as action producing work flowing from love. The source of action indicated here alone will make the work acceptable to God. I, therefore, infer, when we view the future of the race from a Christian point, that the works proceeding from love, as the work rendered by the Church of the first-born, will ultimately ensure the salvation of the race, in the form of fruit flowing from love, in gratitude for personal deliverance, acting according to law, as each member of the ransomed Church united by love to Christ hastens on His errand of mercy to the erring and weak, to proclaim the glad tidings of "he that overcometh shall inherit all things"—*Rev.* xxi. 7. All this I hold to have been included in the eternal purpose of the redemption purchase, ultimately destined to animate the worst with new life, as the birthright Christ has procured for the race, including the glad tidings delivered for the second time, as the Church of the firstborn proclaims the tidings in every ear, which are destined to animate every heart with love to Christ, as the individual strains every nerve to overcome, in the strength of him that is all powerful; while I ask will not we of the Church of the first-born be the willing messengers of such tidings which will animate the face with hope now clouded with despair, and ultimately enable each one to triumph in love, as they strain every nerve to make themselves worthy of Him who includes even the worst in the kingdom that will be delivered up by our Lord to the Father at the final end. This, then, is the result I anticipate from the redemption purchase, which you and I, believer, may now, and ever, hasten.

In adopting this course of reasoning, if I have erred, I

have erred in mercy and not in judgment, as some of my contemporaries have done, by proclaiming eternal punishment. To my judgment, in our present state of knowledge, we may hear the voice of our Saviour proclaiming in every ear the words delivered to St. John—" He that overcometh shall inherit all things, and I will be his God and he shall be my son"—Rev. xxi. 7. *I would draw particular attention to this verse, for here it is Christ as God we have presented, where they that overcome are to be His sons*, whereas to the Church of the firstborn, He stands in the relationship of a brother. In this distinction, we may have the separation that forms the eternal distinction—separating the two classes dealt with. I thus form my judgment in forming new ideas, and by this process I mentally divide and build up in a new form, careless of others' judgments, only responsible for myself, and willing to abide by the consequences. In what I have stated, *I see all the promises of God fulfilled in Christ*, as in Him they are yea, and in Him amen, unto the glory of God by us—2 Cor. i. 2.

But let us look at this subject from another point. Suppose I make the salvation of the human race a matter of prayer, resting my claim on the words of the second Psalm —" Ask of me, and I will give thee the heathen for thine inheritance, and the uttermost parts of the earth for thy possession." (This, in our present state of knowledge, includes all intelligent life, past, present, and to come, in view of the material soul being purely of the earth earthy.) While

I plead the promise given by our Lord—"All things whatsoever ye shall ask in prayer, believing, ye shall receive"— Matt. xxi. 22—the fulfilment of this promise wholly rests on belief as the condition that secures the end. Now, supposing I have strong enough faith to believe I shall receive all I pray for, how do I stand related to Christ in the promise? Observe, I have got the faith; will that secure the condition? Let the doubters say yes or no to this question, for, as a Christian, I have asked the salvation or deliverance of the race, past, present, and to come, and have strong enough faith to believe I will succeed; or, in other words, that I am only filling God's decree in asking all this. *Anyhow, I rest in full expectation that the promised condition will thus be secured*, in the ultimate deliverance of the race, and all that such includes. Observe how the salvation of the race is effected. Man, as we find him constituted in the power we term Will, has power to choose a certain course of action up to a certain point, beyond which he is utterly powerless, being compelled to adopt, at any cost, the course that will ensure self-preservation. It is thus seen to be a desire to ensure self-preservation that leads the individual astray, so that when his self-preservation is secured by the merits of another, and when the individual realizeth that it is so, he will adopt a course of action in harmony with the will of God, which will include the ultimate well-being of the individual. This condition is secured when the individual realizethh that his lifeis in union and communion with God. In this condition the emotion of love is ever present to stimulate action in one direction, the course being ever guided by a desire to glorify God. This course is stimulated by gratitude, because of the deliverance secured over a self-regarding instinct, which must ultimately have ended in the individual's ruin, or, at least, have limited his attainments in consequence of the desire being present to secure individual well-being, independent of any regard to the will of God as the intelligence at the heart of everything. Now, I hold that, stating the cause of the existing evil, which is selfishness, and securing a remedy, or perceiving a possible remedy, is all we are justified in attempting as finite creatures.

In the forces which have combined in forming the intelligent mental life bound together and presented in fixed air, we have the action of the individual soul, or the spirit of man, in the "I am," "I can," "I will," which we call the unit of the system forming intelligent life, as the germ that has sprung from the earth and its surroundings; and we may fairly infer the character of the unit will be perceived in the phase of vibration it presents. Supposing the individual stimulated by self-preservation, which will cause a selfish course, red might be the colour distinguishing the individual so influenced, where violet might distinguish the character of one striving to glorify God *in the face of many difficulties;* finally, the pure white would manifest the character which had secured the victory and rested in Christ, being capable of performing any service, because the phase of vibration which could produce pain has ceased to have any power or effect on a character where all changes have been effected according to law in obedience to the will of God; *being the form and character which Christian influence was intended to produce* through the course prescribed, acting according to law; this course would be personified in the decrees of God as His laws.

In the way I put the subject, the phase of vibration which produces the colour, under certain conditions, would likewise include the character of the soul. In the red we have a slow phase of vibration, capable of giving out this one colour; in the violet or mauve we have a very rapid phase of vibration, therefore we may infer that the intelligence capable of vibrating so rapidly as this would possess the power, up to this point, of increasing or retarding the power of vibration at will. Whereas in the pure white light we have the condition which includes all phases of vibration, therefore the soul whose natural condition is to produce white light, which includes the most rapid phase of vibration, could at will assume any phase of vibration, so that under such conditions pain would be impossible, as pain will be understood to be caused by the individual striving to attain a more rapid phase of vibration than the one natural to him in a state where the phase of vibration indicates the degree of intelligence the individual has attained. The most rapid phase of vibration would thus indicate the individual possessing the greatest intellectual capacity, *by enabling him to combine ideas most rapidly*, therefore possessing great intellectual power.

To put all I have said in a more concise form; this fixed air, which includes intelligent life, and which has the power of vibrating more or less rapidly, where the phase of vibration distinguishes the degree of intelligence arrived at. The most rapid vibration presenting the highest intelligence, because the more rapid the phase of vibration, the more quickly can the ideas be broken up and combined into new forms and relationships, *being the process that includes intelligent life*. Here I only deal with the powers possessed by the conscious "ego" over the matter defined as fixed air, which include intelligent life. But, to look at the subject from another point of view, as the quality of stuff which forms the human cerebrum brain, the substance, in one sense or another, is formed of, and held together by, the intelligence of the race, taking the form of generalized ideas. For, observe, this substance, in forming the mental images, has passed through a brain organism and contains the intelligence of the race, and, because of this, is defined as the physical basis of mind; for, in one sense, it both forms and contains intelligent life, which is equivalent to saying that the cerebrum brain contains, in generalized ideas, the intelligence of the race. But, although all this is contained in the cerebrum of the brain, the power included is only perceived when the idea makes an impression as thought on the sensorium brain. This being the portion of brain where the conscious mental life of the individual is played off or produced by the subject and the object forming a joint alliance here, and, by means of this alliance, conscious life is produced as the intelligence of the individual in an ideal form.

Whereas, in view of the material way in which I put the subject, the impressions coming from the cerebrum, in the form of ideas as thought, may be as fairly classed by the name of objects presenting an ideal form, as the impressions coming through the senses are the effect of outward things or objects The consequence of all this is that the sensorium brain presents the medium which connects the two sources from which our knowledge comes, and by means of the union effected on the sensorium brain, the conscious "ego" is produced, as the unit of intelligent life presenting the spirit of man, the action of which, as I have before said, is manifested in the "I am," "I can," "I will," which action, in a limited sense, includes the individual's power to choose, in view of the past, the present, and the future. Observe, by my reasoning, the cerebrum is stored with the ideas as the frame-work from which the intelligence of the race springs, because the grouped unit of the thing implied is held in the form of an idea, including all the knowledge we have of the thing, or thought presented in the grouping, where all such groupings are supposed to have an objective existence from which they have sprung, and to which they apply, and must thus include, in the ideal form, the subject and object which form the frame-work of intelligent life. The parts called elements, because of their uniformity of action, are formed by the units which resemble each other grouping themselves together (in what we may term cerebrum action as the pre-conscious action of the soul), and presenting what we term the religious and moral elements, including the social element, and so on. In few words, all this is presented by the law of inheritance, in the fruit-tree bearing fruit after its kind, to which we must all bow.

From all I have stated, you will observe the action of man's soul or spirit in the "I am," "I can," "I will," is manifested by the impressions made on the sensorium brain, and through that medium alone makes its influence felt in any form. By means of the connection thus formed, manifesting the action of the individual in the "I am," "I can," "I will," making its influence felt on the sensorium brain, a communication is established with the outward world by which the action of the will of the individual is manifested, when, up to a certain point, it is possible for the individual to choose between two courses of action. Where to gratify self is the motive inducing one course, and what he feels to be his duty to another being the motive inducing the other course, where up to a certain point man has the power of choosing what to his judgement is the just and proper course for him to adopt, therefore, because of possessing this power, man has freedom of action, manifesting freedom of will, however limited in many cases the power may be, nevertheless the *germ is there, which includes the term Free Will*. It is a terrible responsibility (in having power to choose) *that the term Free Will confers on the human race;* for, in the power to choose, the individual's *destiny for time and eternity is involved*. This is made very apparent in the plastic matter forming the sensorium brain, because it is in that part of the brain organism that the tracts or muscles are formed which enable the individual to act from deliberate choice, being the action included in Free Will. It is thus very apparent that by choosing the right course the tract inducing that course will be strengthened, so that action that first cost an effort will by-and-bye become an established habit, and will enable man to rise higher and yet higher in the moral scale. By this means the very weakest moral nature may ultimately attain the strength of a giant, in adding moment by moment to the tract which bears moral fruit. But where it is possible to build up our moral nature thus, it is also possible to choose the opposite course of action, where selfishness, regardless of how others suffer, will lead to the very worst course, and where this course is followed, the result will be most apparent in eternity, where the judgment implied in "as you judge you shall be judged," will in one way or another be exacted from us all, in the name of eternal justice. It is from the point involved in personal responsibility, that Dr. Carpenter's work referred to speaks with terrible power, by enforcing the necessity of choosing the right course of action.

In dealing with Christianity, I am dealing with a quality of matter as mind, where the ideal Christ is stamped with all the force of a fixed idea, because the idea thus formed comes from a *permanent objective existence*, thus containing the quality which ensures " *absolute truth*," whereas conversion, in the abstract, may be said to include a force which animates this dead or dormant image, by infusing into the group of forces forming it, movement or life, by animating this intellectual conception, with the emotion of love generated by gratitude, in the individual having realized, in its fulness, the relation which exists between him and the objective Christ (as the counterpart of the ideal unit), in having rescued him from the penalty, according to Scripture rendering, attached to sin, likewise insuring him of a happy eternal existence. Conversion, in the abstract, will appear in the emotion of love stimulating an intellectual conception already present in mind, in the form of the ideal Christ as the Son of God sent to redeem the sinner—*John* iii. 6. This being the conception Christianity includes in conversion, where the intellect acts in obedience to the heart, and is the conception that is included in the Protestant doctrine of justification by faith. And certain it is that, when fully understood, no conception could bear out the principle of action more fully and forcibly, because, in starting from this point, the individual at once realizes his right and title to all the benefits arising from the redemption-purchase; and, when this is realized, gratitude and love fill the soul, so that, by this influence, the believer may attain complete control over his bodily organism in the unhesitating surrender of his will to the will of God. This being the condition included in the redemption-purpose, which represents the elect or counterpart of God on earth, as a people in which the Divine will is substituted for the human, the emotions being ever stimulated by love to God, which is other words for stating the intellectual conception included in being filled with all the fulness of God—*Eph.* iii. 19. For, observe, Christian action, *viewed from the highest point or in its highest form,* is not the choosing between two or more modes of action, which is the conception included in duty, but a stimulus, in the form of an emotion, compelling the individual to take a certain course of action, arising from love to God in Christ. That is to say, the highest motive which prompts to action in a converted individual is love to God in Christ; the intellect and will is only used or brought into action to enable the individual to use the best means to attain an end, where the end to be attained, prompted by love, ought always to be God's glory. This, you will perceive, leaves great scope for the individual effort of the intelligent responsible agent, guided by the Spirit of God. Any one must see how difficult the course here is, as self is to be lost sight of in the effort to glorify God; hence the experience of Paul—*Rom.* vii.—becomes more or less the experience of each converted individual, though the victory is secured in the "I can do all things through Christ which strengtheneth me."—*Philipp.* iv. 13. Even where the organism has come to its maturity, by following the natural course of self-preservation, *which, up to the point of conversion*, is a just and proper course when the rights of others are properly regarded; even when this is the case at conversion, if the bodily organism is wholly stimulated by love to God, this new influence will insure the individual's sanctification, and so make him fit for the Master's service and work.

All this is included in conversion; for, from that moment, the forces are present in the *organism which are capable to effect this change ;* therefore, in the broadest sense, conversion fits the individual for heaven, or, to put it in other words, puts him in possession of the forces which govern and animate the redeemed in glory, and is the end decreed by God, to be attained by means of the *redemption-purpose*, including the believer's sanctification or full consecration to God. But, alas ! how little of this consecration is seen in the lives and conversation of the Protestant believer of to-day. Therefore, I ask, is it not very probable, as the consequence of our living as we are doing, that we are guilty of acting a part which will unfit and deprive us of being among those who are to enjoy the happy condition of being raised at the first resurrection, over whom the second death will have no power—a class defined as blessed and holy ?—*Rev.* xx. 6. Blessed, doubtless, all believers are. But, alas! how little have many of us of the holiness that proceeds from a consecrated life, the absence of which will, in my judgment, entail suffering in the next life, on the *consideration that, at conversion we were put in possession of the power capable of producing the effect required* to fit us for the first resurrection, which condition, to my judgment, includes our bodily organism *bearing the impress of a consecrated life in obedience to His revealed will;* where love to God has animated the structure, as the Old Man presented in self-preservation was being burned out, so that the new form might be made to take his place, and thus make it safe for us to be entrusted with a bodily organism, because it is built up in the form God would have it built up in. For, in our present state of knowledge, we have to deal with the physical basis of mind as well as body, and, therefore, in justice to the Christian martyrs, we are obliged to look for a distinction representing the two classes of believers.

How few of us can say we are wholly consecrated to God, though the condition is present in conversion which could have effected that end, for the forces involved in the conception perceived as conversion include, and will produce, the course of action defined in faith working by love. The faith here stands for the full conviction that the individual is entitled to forgiveness and eternal life, in virtue of the benefits secured by Christ's atoning sacrifice being freely offered and accepted ; when this is realized, the natural fruit flowing from this conception is gratitude or love. But, observe, the stream of action flowing in love, from a clear conception of the deliverance secured, is marred and quenched if doubt arises as to the individual having a claim and title to the benefits derived from this source. Where this doubt is allowed to make way, the fruit, which is the action of love flowing in its purity, will cease, and where this mental state of doubt is allowed to go on increasing, the individual will only hold the conception dealt with as true in the abstract, *but will cease to apply it individually*. In this state of mind he may be said to retain the shadow in the dead conception, but he has lost the substance in the fruit flowing from love as the natural and vital action flowing from, or implied in, conversion; but where the vital action is retarded, we are only just in supposing that, because of spiritual deadness, the element of regret may mingle in our song of adoration as the rejoicing spirit, not yet clothed with the resurrection body, joins in the millennium glory.

Thus, in the light of known truth, is my theory illuminated by the impression, " Life is hope," as this full thought presents the mental state of an uncertain future, which stands contrasted with the assurance of eternal life as the realized experience and heritage of every sanctified believer. It will thus be perceived that the two states dealt with present two totally different mental conditions—distinguishing the saved and the lost, *where despair is, or ought to be, wholly excluded; for the worst may have hope.* A title to hope being surely included in the future of a race which, in this life, has been fettered by a conditioned existence, in perfection being impossible to an unconverted man.

We may infer that the truly consecrated will respond to the voice of love in the " Come up hither."—*Rev.* xi. 12. Or, to put this truth in another form, let us suppose, while I write, the shout is heard, "The bridegroom cometh; go ye out to meet him." How few of the redeemed Church might be supposed to respond, while all that hesitated would be unprepared for the blessing included in the state implied "Blessed are they which are called unto the marriage supper of the Lamb."—*Rev.* xix. 9. For we are dealing with a condition where the response of the willing heart is the only acceptable offering. You perceive, that this point would be decided by what we *might call the will of the individual as he clings to the earth and its surroundings.* Whereas, in the highest form of Christianity, this influence is intended to be powerless, which is the mental condition or idea included in John's words—" Love not the world, neither the things which are in the world. If any man love the world, the love of the Father is not in him."—1 *John* ii. 15. The responsibility of attaining this state must, I feel, be attached to all believing in Christ as the son of God, when viewed in the light of the Christian revelation, which insures eternal life, realized here and now.

From the view I have taken in expounding the highest form of Christian life, it will be seen I deal exclusively with the intellect and the emotions, whereas the will which stands for everything in a system of duty with the Christian, is *simply merged into the will of God,* leaving the emotion to stimulate action capable of producing the highest Christian form as the fruit of the emotion of love. *Where service as a duty is, in a way, excluded,* the will of the individual may be said to possess a very limited power, indeed—the individual being supposed to be guided by the emotions of love to God, where a desire to glorify him is the only concern. That such is seldom the case is no answer. The question being, *will the means secure the end ?*

In justice, we may say, the will is the power God will specially deal with in judging the *non-Christian world as a race, where, up to a certain point, they have the power of choice,* a power which enables man to direct his energy by deliberate choice. To attain great power over the will so as to direct its action in the service of justice and truth, should be assiduously cultivated by the natural man, when we know the physical basis of the mind is embodied in a material substance which he may wield at will according to deliberate choice, being the freedom of action expressed in, "I ought to do so and so," or, "I ought not to do so and so," which must include man's liability to punishment, when the wrong course is deliberately chosen. *For certainly it is the motive that prompts the action, which will ultimately be proclaimed good or bad.* For example, if the desire to do right is present, but nevertheless, because of the trouble such a course might entail, the right course is not adopted, has not the individual, in that case, erred from deliberate choice, and, therefore, become liable to the consequences included in such a course of action ?

My theory may be stated in a few simple words, and starts from the accepted truth that a revelation has been given, including that, except a revelation had been given, we could know nothing of the future life, not being certain even of so much as that there is a future life. In my judgment, revelation includes all knowledge of eternal life. This revelation I hold to be included in the Christian faith, and, therefore, presents Christ in His capacity as Redeemer, and also proclaims the necessity of conversion as the means by which the emotion of love is kindled in the believer, so that the fire of love to Christ may be kept constantly burning in gratitude for deliverance secured, and, when this is so, the life will be wholly consecrated to God, as the soul realizes its title to eternal life in union and communion with Christ its Redeemer. In this case, body and mind are consecrated to the Master, whereas, when this fire is allowed to dwindle away so that only occasionally love to Christ is realized, earth and the things of earth take the place Christ desires to occupy, and the converted believer, in consequence of this half-hearted service, will so mar his heavenly glory as to necessitate suffering in the shape of repentance, which may include work done as willing service in the shape of retribution rendered to those he may have wronged. It would thus be the emotion of love to Christ stimulating the redeemed soul to action that would raise a desire to serve his Lord, while he ever realizes how sure his eternal wellbeing is in virtue of Christ's sacrifice. And, take notice, this state may include actual suffering in the form of willing service, even after the resurrection of the body. This, to my judgment, is implied in *Rev.* xx. 6, where we are told it is only them which are raised at the first resurrection over whom the second death has no power, which surely implies that being raised at the second resurrection includes the possibility of suffering, and, as suffering to the redeemed can only be the result of a self-chosen course, we may infer it will spring from a desire to benefit others of the race, and especially those our influence or actions may have injured during this life; but this service can never take the form of duty, and must come from love to the Lord as the fruit of repentance. I further hold that the blameless life made apparent in justice and truth is the form our Lord points to as the course of action that is to manifest the children of God.—*Matt.* vii. 20. Wherever this fruit is apparent, we may point to such and say the fruit is good, therefore we have the authority of our Lord to call the tree (the individual) good. For, in virtue of the atoning sacrifice, I hold all such will be rescued in the next world from the consequences involved in "thou shalt by no means come out thence till[1] thou hast paid the uttermost farthing."—*Matt.* v. 26—and that, when the individual realizes that the benefit arising from this is secured by Christ, his heart will swell with gratitude and love, so that he will henceforth only desire an individual existence in union and communion with Christ his Lord, and that he will show this spirit in the service he will now render as an offering of love. But observe, though the individual has saved his soul, as the fruit of a blameless life (so far as such a life may be possible to the individual), in virtue of the atoning sacrifice, nevertheless, at bottom he is wholly saved in virtue of Christ's merits as Redeemer, and that the one rescued thus has not one offering as a love-token to bring in treasure laid up as work done from love to Christ. Whereas, it is treasure in this form, as the fruit of conversion, which is the very condition the *Elect of God, as the Church of the First Born, rest on,* being elected because they are made capable of producing such fruit, in obedience to the law that governs love, in honour of Christ as the Son of God.

My theory also includes that, ultimately, the whole human race shall be redeemed by Christ from the consequences of evil, which are the fruits of selfishness, and that this end will be effected by raising humanity above the self-regarding instinct in securing the eternal well-being of the race in virtue of His sacrifice, so that, through this process, by stimulating even the worst with love to God in Christ, the race will be rescued; for are not the worst always more to be pitied than blamed, being more the creatures of circumstance than we are often willing to allow. Therefore, at the end, I believe, when the kingdom will be delivered up to the Father, *the whole human race will, in one form or another, be included in it as the fruit of the redemption purposes*, though, doubtless, there will be an eternal distinction between the believer and the unbeliever. Likewise, there will be a marked distinction between those who have lived a consecrated life, *and so earned the fruit of having overcome*, and those who have lived more for the world than for Christ, to which former condition the Saviour attaches so many promises in addressing the Seven Churches in the Revelations. Observe, it is from this class of lukewarm Christians, who have lived more for the world than for Christ, though converted individuals, that much mischief springs, where their lives imply no higher motive—directing their choice or influencing their actions—than the earth, and the things of earth, while they use up much of the energy produced by others, and give out no useful energy as work done from love to Christ in return. By this, they incur a debt of gratitude to those of the world, and we are justified in supposing their own sense of justice will be so much increased in the next world as to induce them to own the obligation, and stimulate them with a desire to make amends, if such be possible; when they realize that it was in consequence of Christianity, presented in this cold, heartless form, that Christ's race was not increased on earth, which would be the result of a natural law if all lived consecrated lives, in being filled with zeal and love for Christ. Therefore, we are surely justified in saying that such as they *mar Christ's glory* humanly speaking, and must take the consequences, which, for all we know, may be the means of much good ultimately, in the form of voluntary labour bestowed in the next world on the so-called unsaved. That it will be so I feel perfectly convinced, as we view revelation in our present state of knowledge. This firm conviction has arisen from what, to me, presents a prophetic revelation (and, if really so, includes absolute truth applying to the race), in the impression formed in my sensorium brain—"Life is Hope."* When the truth presented in these words stands contrasted with the assurance of eternal life, the birthright of belief is realized in conversion, being the heritage included in the Protestant doctrine of justification by faith. I would again state that the two mental conditions dealt

---

* This prophetic revelation bears a rational explanation. The idea which was previously formed as the fruit of a very wide generalization was lodged in the cerebrum brain, in the forces which had combined in forming the perception, and, therefore, included all this. These forces were afterwards used in forming the written character "Life is Hope," thus presenting in a new form, the generalization I had effected by the force of reason alone. It was thus clear that the same forces which had previously combined in the generalization now completed in forming the letters on my sensorium brain, and by this means (to me) confirming the generalization as absolute truth. You may observe the forces which had been previously prepared for special work, by passing as intelligent life, through a brain organism, are now made to assume different forms under different conditions, as the forces which include conscious life.

with present states totally different. *The one, in assurance, conferring a boon of immense importance, the other fettered by the uncertainty of hope, though longing for assurance.* My theory is that, ultimately, assurance will be made to take the place of hope, and, by means of this deliverance, love will be generated and neutralize the effect of sin, which I hold to arise from selfishness, and that, through this means, it will be made possible for the unsaved to atone for their sins. In the same sense, I hold that a good, just life will, in virtue of Christ's sacrifice, rescue the unbeliever from the penalty of his sins. In holding that assurance will be made to take the place of hope, while this is being effected, it is thus quite fair to suppose that the believer would be very useful to the so-called unsaved, in stimulating the other *to overcome;* for observe at the *final end*—" He that overcometh is to inherit all things."—*Rev.* xxi. 7. Take notice, it is he *that overcometh*, addressing the individual at the *present moment.* Surely this implies much in the light of present knowledge.

These words being addressed by the Saviour to the race after the final resurrection and last judgment is past, where each individual of the race shall appear in the garments he has woven for himself on earth, as the form his actions have moulded his bodily organism into during his life on earth. In this new system of things (the new heavens and the new earth), we have all that remains of our present system. And in this new condition Christ is presented as God in developing intelligent life, calling the class he is addressing his sons, and stimulating them to overcome, including a promise in the words—"He that overcometh shall inherit all things." In this form our Lord *proclaims the gospel of glad tidings for the second time.* This time he stands in the relation of a Father to all of the human race, where personal effort accompanied by pain has to be endured by the individual in securing his well-being, as he overcomes the established bad habits which are the effects of the selfish course he adopted on earth. And who can tell the terrible suffering that will be absolutely necessary before the effect of an evil life can be atoned for and the individual rescued according to law, which must be effected before the Saviour can deliver up the kingdom to the Father? This, therefore, I believe to be the final end decreed of God to be secured by the redemption purchase; while the *true Church*, personified in the Saviour's ransomed bride, will be the willing messengers to proclaim the infinite power conveyed in Paul's words—"I can do all things through Christ which strengtheneth me" (*Phil.* iv. 13). Because this was the power that enabled them to overcome on earth, and is the power by which the race shall ultimately be redeemed by Christ; for the idea cenveyed in these words is now and ever true to the human race, and will invigorate every nerve—where the weakest and the worst will take hold of the idea conveyed by these words in their effort to overcome, so that they may inherit all things. *In all this I proclaim no new Gospel, but simply extend to another system of things the power included in the old Gospel, which is held in potential energy and applies to the condition referred to by Paul* in 1 *Cor.* xv. 24-28, where our Lord must reign till He has put all enemies under His feet—the last enemy being pain—which is the idea conveyed in death to a race insured of eternal life. Pain will, by this means, be neutralized.

Christianity, in its concrete form, simply procures a motion which stimulates the individual to purify or sanctify himself, and, by the force of example, to purify wherever his influence is felt, so that, where this influence has been limited in the individual appearing, in the form of a self-seeking spirit, in the light of our Lord's teaching, to all following such a course, there must be a penalty attached in some form; and, in my judgment, it will be manifested by a desire to render voluntary service toward those who may have suffered from their influence or example, or otherwise. Forces so directed by voluntary choice would be only making an effort to undo what their action or example had done during the previous history of their career, and the forces present in Conversion may involve all this. At anyrate, the forces in Conversion include power to produce a blameless life, showing itself with powers as the fruit of love to Christ; but when the forces have been restricted or limited, the condition I have stated as the after consequence, would only be voluntary service rendered in the form of retribution, as the effect which a just view of previous conduct would entail, where the sense of justice was fully developed. And we may surely infer that the sense of justice will have attained to that full development among the sections of humanity defined as "the Redeemed," or "the Elect," or "the Church of the First-Born," or by whatever name you may choose to call the ransomed Church of Christ. This, therefore, is what I hold to be the germ of Christianity in its essence, *securing voluntary service rendered, so that God, the Eternal I Am, seen in the intelligence at the heart of everything, may be glorified by this means,* being the *design He had in view when He originated the forces which were destined to combine in producing this form of action.*

Here we have to think of another form of intelligent life which revelation reveals—the Devil and his angels, as a section of intelligent life over which the head or king seems to have implicit power. Any candid mind may see that the self-regarding instinct we have present in humanity, and defined as selfishness, would ultimately work itself out by producing an intelligence of that form in which the head would attain unlimited power over the whole tribe, the service of which he would thus retain, because those inferior intelligences enabled him to secure his end, while they may be supposed to have an individual existence only in connection with him. Now, in the light of our present knowledge, are we not justified in supposing God's ultimate decree may eventually be to *rescue* even this intelligent section, which, in reality, must be the products of His laws, from the power of this self-regarding influence, and limit their bounds? Even this, as an ultimate end, is not beyond what I would desire to see accomplished, in view of the past, the present, and the future—in the light of eternity. Ultimately, I look forward to the race being saved or redeemed, and the Devil and his angels rescued. Anyhow, if I have any power given me in the future to help to attain such an end, I would ask that God, in Christ, would give me power to aid in securing this, even at the expense of personal suffering, where God, in the fullest sense, was present with me.

Again, may we not say, during the period of our earthly life, when all these thoughts are passing through, and forming our minds, that the physical condition of mind in those who are rescued from selfishness may be made to take the form of carbonic oxide, which is lighter than fixed air, and, if it is so, we are safe to say, that the disembodied spirits, thus equipped, apart from any power used from within in the form of choice or intelligent will, would rise above atmospheric air, in obedience to a law of nature, because the physical condition was such. Let us suppose, just by way of contrast, two souls, the physical condition of the one being carbonic acid, and the other carbonic oxide, where, as a matter of course, each substance included

the conscious life of the individual, in the same sense that our intelligent life is treasured up during natural life in our brain organism. Supposing also, under such condition, a special phase of vibration to indicate special emotions, with the will *either powerless from choice or inability*; under such conditions, in virtue of a natural law, the carbonic oxided soul would free itself from the earth and the trammel of earth, as it bounded along, containing, in this form, the intelligence of a redeemed human soul, as it nears the personal Saviour in adoring love; whereas the other soul, whose physical condition was heavier than air, would, therefore, be bound to the earth and the things of earth, so to speak.

The theory I advance leads to the assumption that the human soul is the product of evolution, therefore destined to an endless life of progress, where system after system, out of which it has been formed, pass away, while the soul takes on the impressions of every system holding the form fast, though the substance pass away. Nevertheless, the substance in the ideal form shall ever remain, forming the link between the past and the present. The soul will thus grow in knowledge and likeness to the God-man in his capacity of developing intelligence, where He (the Lord) will originate system after system in which He will perceive the end from the beginning, where each system will include worlds capable of still farther development. Thus age will succeed age, bringing with it its yet farther development. The first system of this glorious future, which is to take the place of our present system, we find revealed in the Revelations—"As the new heaven and the new earth, wherein dwelleth righteousness, *and where sea was no more.*" In our present state of knowledge, no words could more clearly indicate this new condition than the words "there was no more sea."—*Rev.* xxi. 1. Under conditions like this, does not the fixed air, which contains our mental life in an ideal form, stand us in good stead, while we grasp the new system revealed in these words "there was no more sea," and quietly walk over dry shod, as in thought we take possession of the system of which we are to form part? In doing so, we can identify our past condition with our present, as we realize how the new includes the old in the formation effected here, seen in the fruit we gathered and carry with us, which joins the past with the present, as we take our place in the new system.

In all this the men of science have been teaching us to understand the Lord's words, while we have been robbing them of their birthright, and doubtless have caused many of this class to shed tears of blood, as they viewed the misery that surrounded them; *for, in proclaiming eternal punishment, we clouded the present and the future,* and thus robbed them of the bright hopes they were justly entitled to, whereas we ought to have grasped their ideas, and thus have unfolded *the glorious future the race shall inherit in eternal life, in union and communion with Christ the Lord.* What terrible suffering we might have saved the race if we Christians had followed the Lord fully, as we grasped truth from all points and proclaimed eternal life in eternal hope, which is a truth clearly revealed; for, in this bright hope, we have the intelligence of man held fast.—*Eccles.* ix. 4.

This intelligence is perceived by me and my class as the products of the sun's energy—energy which, in consequence of having been under certain conditions in connection with a bodily organism, is made the vehicle in which the human soul is grouped and held together in the form of fixed air, where every thought that ever passed through a human brain has been treasured up in its ideal form, and is the quality of stuff which is capable of reproducing this energy at any moment in the form of an ideal conception, thus presenting the action of the individual soul. The sun's energy qualified thus is the product of evolution as the "ego" over which the individual will, in the future, have complete control, and will be capable of manifesting that power of action by reproducing a former state of consciousness at any moment. This "ego" is the part of our system which has been treasured up in the forms of ideal conceptions as the product of the earth, over which the individual manifesting the intelligent power of the system will, in the future, have complete control; and this power will manifest itself in the "I am," "I can," "I will," as the action of the soul.

The origin of matter and force as the quality of stuff in which we find the intelligent life of the individual embodied, is the portion of the sun's energy which we may reasonably be desirous to trace through the different stages it has passed, of which it forms part, and from which it has sprung. In doing so we are compelled to look for the explanation which gave birth to the intelligence of man, in the laws that govern the universe, as the birthplace from which it or he has sprung, first manifested in spontaneous generation as the force which gave birth to the first cell, being the product of the sun's energy—energy governed by the laws of nature—which as a disturber of elements was capable of manifesting that power on the inorganic world by producing a new form of force; and as this new form of force developed itself, it has produced all the forms of the vegetable and animal world by which we are surrounded, and of which we form part. Over the organic forces dealt with, the intelligence of man has attained considerable control. This control is possibly seen in its highest form in the selective power man has employed in developing the domestic animals most suitable to the end he has in view. In this way man moulds the organic forces to his will, in moulding the form his intelligence has selected as best suited to the end he desires. Thus he compels the organic forces to carry out his will, by producing a higher and yet higher form. By his superior intellect man thus takes the place of the Creator in forming and fashioning the organic forces, as he builds up and pulls down. This power is not limited to the bodily organism;

and in the case of the dog, at anyrate, by man's superior intelligence, the dog's mind is made to produce work of a considerably complicated intellectual kind, being moulded partly by fear and partly by affection.

But it is when the savage races cross the path of *the so-called civilized Christian races* that we have most occasion to dread the consequences arising from the power the intelligence of man gives him over the organic forces, in the responsibility this power includes in view of the future life. For the superior intelligence of the one class in the desire to grasp and hold, crushes the other class out. But, alas! in all this the Christian is careless of the terrible responsibility his profession includes, in the truth conveyed by God to the *highly civilized race at the beginning (Gen. i. 26-28)* highly civilized because, when viewed in the light of their responsibility, the moral and religious elements were highly developed; therefore, God addresses them as male and female, created or formed in His image. Thus, blessed of God, they are commanded to replenish the earth, and subdue it. The truth conveyed here, viewed from the highest point, applies to Christians, in union with Christ as co-workers with God, because they are thus capable of creating or forming the lower races, in moulding the organic force of mind *anew in Christ the Lord*, by example and precept—by precept in proclaiming a free pardon in the glorious gospel, as the glad tidings; by example, in manifesting the effect of that gospel in a blameless life. For, in the light of present knowledge, the higher races are endowed with power from on high, by which they could mould the lower races in obedience to the will of God, by the higher intelligences infusing into the minds of the lower, God's words of truth, as the idea implied in Christ being formed in them, their hope of glory. By this means the Saviour's race would be increased on earth, for His likeness would be multiplied in the ideal form. The higher races would thus subdue the lower, by infusing into them Christ's spirit, which teaches them to glorify God in love. In the truth thus rendered, would not the higher races replenish the earth and subdue it, by creating the lower races anew in Christ Jesus, and through this means present them as sons of God, who would be qualified for the very highest place in glory; if the potential energy, included in Christian faith, enables men to live for the glory of God, and to create this spirit in his less highly gifted brother, surely we may infer there is no necessity that the higher intelligence should crush out the lower. However, such being the fact, the cause must proceed from *a law governed by what man has power to effect as the fruit of a grasping, selfish spirit*, and, therefore, he is wholly to blame, for he has power to mould the races he is crushing, and will surely be held responsible to God.* Whereas you often hear the truth

* In connection with this subject, I would draw the reader's attention to the papers on "Convicts and Quakers," in *Good Words*, especially the last paper, August, 1878. The scenes depicted in these papers will justify the remark I make on the terrible responsibility we incur in our treatment

involved in this explained away in words like these—
"Well, it is a law of nature that the lower races must disappear before the higher." In this, man casts the responsibility arising from his selfish course on God; for this is implied in the laws of nature effecting an end, whereas the forces included in the Christian faith enable man to mould

of the lower races. Some of the scenes described are too terrible to allow the mind to rest on, in our present state of knowledge, in view of our responsibility as a *Protestant Christian nation, being a system where each member is made responsible for himself*. From the point of personal responsibility, the labour of the two devoted Quakers referred to in the papers dealt with, shows what two devoted men can accomplish. And, unless for their labours, we might have known little or nothing of the scenes which took place, not fifty years ago, on British soil, and on ships sailing under the British flag. In view of all the labours the Society of Friends have rendered toward the cause of justice and true humanity, the Society have well earned the name of the "Friends of Humanity"—*as the Society of humanity;* for ever since the day George Fox formed the Society, *the members of it have ever been foremost in the cause of justice and truth, always willing to bear the consequences arising from the course they believed to be a right course.* The Society of Friends, I would say, is the only religious body that have any authority to hold up the Bible and call it the Word of God (though we may all say it contains the word of God), for they alone, of all our religious bodies, profess to live to prove that perfection may be attained here below. And we may be very sure a state of perfection is possible to us, *as a state which the Judge at the final end will call perfect*, when the very Founder of our religion leaves us an example of a perfect life and power to follow in his name, with the comment—"Be ye, therefore, perfect, even as your Father which is in heaven is perfect"—*Matt.* v. 48. If we Protestants of Britain are not prepared to live out this doctrine of perfection, we can have no excuse for professing to the world that we believe the Bible is wholly inspired. The Bible most assuredly contains the word of God, but all that is essential to salvation is a risen Lord revealed in the heart of man; and this power, if not resisted by a selfish course, will enable man to attain the state Christ will call perfect.

lxxix

the organic force of mind in obedience to the will of God, by fusing into the lower races the spirit and likeness of Christ, which is the potential energy of the ideal Christ. Thus, therefore, man, being formed in the likeness of God, and having power over the organic forces to build up and pull down, would use that power to secure his own selfish end, and then be unjust enough to refer the effect of this course to the will of God, this being, as I said before, understood in the laws of nature. Nevertheless, God gives man power to create anew, and, as a Christian man, he must be held responsible for the effect he may produce.

Or we might refer the truth included in this to the law that governs heat. In the higher intelligences we have the generalized ideas stored up in the brain, as a quality of potential energy displaying its power in the rapidity with which ideas may be made to take a new form in generalization and abstraction, and in showing how one feeling or object differs from, or agrees with, all other feelings or objects. This power is distinguished by the rapidity with which the brain can be made to give off intelligent life, in energy as heat. And it is by this means that the higher races have infinite control or power over the lower races, either by crushing them out or by fitting them for a higher and yet higher place in glory; because, in the generalized ideas involved in Christianity, the certain knowledge of the two worlds, which *surely includes potential energy as heat of the highest form,* are contained. This is just other words for stating the law which governs heat in the abstract, by showing that the more rapid the vibration, is the more heat is generated, and that matter of a higher temperature affects matter of a lower temperature; and this truth applies most of all to the sun's energy in the form of intelligent life. For, in this form, all we know of matter is treasured up in the conception we have formed of its different qualities, which, in the ideal form, may be referred to the phase of vibration that part assumes in the colour it presents under certain conditions. For it is quite possible to imagine that hydrogen may contain in the concrete every form and quality of the stuff we call matter and force, or matter in form. That is, that hydrogen may have been made to assume, in expanding and appearing under different conditions, all the forms and qualities of matter. All this may be included in the phase of vibration it is made to assume for the time being; whereas, its highest and natural phase of vibration would appear in the phase of vibration which indicates electricity. If it is so, we might say the process going on in the galvanic battery was a process where hydrogen was made to assume its natural element, in being made to take on the form of vibration indicating electricity. And observe, from or through electricity, in one way or another, we can get the solar spectrum, which, by my reasoning, includes all the qualities of matter.

Observe, we may take one of the metals in its solid state, and reduce it to a liquid and to a vapour, in which we find its co-relative in the solar spectrum as colour. In the spectrum it is the phase of vibration as colour which the matter has assumed that we are dealing with, and referring it to, as the counterpart of the metal we hold in our hand; for we have followed it through many forms, and find its birthplace to be the white light that issues from the sun—light which thus makes its different compounds apparent in its phases of vibration, so that, by means of spectrum analysis, we can refer to the metal, and say, with apparent clearness, that matter and force is a something vibrating at certain periods, of which intelligent life in the male and female form is no exception. Where we may yet further generalize, and say man is, or ought to be, principally guided by intellect and will, but woman by feeling, as sympathy. From this we might infer that the perfect state is only possible where the three, "Feeling, Intellect, and Will," can be merged into one, which seems to be the idea included by Paul in the conception he forms of the married state (*Eph.* v. 21-24) implied in "For the husband is head of the wife, as Christ is head of the Church." His notion evidently being that the husband is to be all wisdom, goodness and justice, where the wife is to be moulded by her affection or love in yielding to a higher intelligence. The example Paul adduces is Christ and the Church. .Now, the Church is governed by love. The harmony and wisdom of this arrangement is very apparent, woman having less intellectual power, and less brain matter than man. Therefore, she is more liable to be guided by impulsive feeling, and less qualified to rule, though it appears to me that the quickness of apprehension characteristic of woman is the effect of an exceedingly quick phase of brain-vibration enabling her to break up and combine ideas with wonderful rapidity; though showing no grasp of intellectual vigour in following out the generalization, because her smallness of brain prevents her forming the logical connections necessary to work out the theory included in the generalization she has effected, so that, as a general rule, man reaps the benefit of her efforts in adopting her ideas and making them his own by working them out, which is a just and proper course to adopt, when her ideas are taken possession of by fair means, in referring the generalization effected to her. Which generalization is now wrought out by another. How seldom this course is adopted may be inferred from the general aversion manifested toward the class of women known as *"blue stockings,"* being the class which effects most of the work referred to, and have, therefore, to bear the penalty of being thurst aside and trampled on, while others enjoy the labour that cost them so much. *In this we see the weakest go to the wall; for, doubtless, women, on the whole, are less highly endowed intellectually than men.*

In saying that the experience from which our intelligence is gathered comes from the earth and its surrounding, I state the fact quite correctly, because, in revealed truth,

God made use of the surrounding condition and circumstances in making Himself known through them. God thus used earthly things to interpret heavenly things. For example, we have every reason to infer that the Urim and the Thummim were symbols of Egyptian origin, and were adopted by Moses as the medium God was to make use of in communicating with His people, possibly by illuminating the jewels when the revelation was of a joyous nature, and by dimming the original lustre of the jewels when of a sorrowful one, to manifest His displeasure. Whereas this might have been effected by the truth the high priest had previously imbibed from Revelation, as the effect that truth had made on his cerebrum brain, and by this means affected his heart's action where a joyous expression was apparent, by the phase of vibration the truth was made to effect in producing, a rapid vibration manifested in a burst of light which would illuminate the Urim and Thummim on the high priest's breast, whereas despair or grief might retard the heart's action, and thus be made to dim the natural brilliancy of the gems. Man would thus be made the medium between God and the race in revealing God's will by means of the natural law that governs the action of the cerebrum brain, manifesting itself under certain conditions. The effect proceeding from this action is made very apparent by Dr. Carpenter, toward the end of the book referred to, in the incidents he relates in connection with experiments, where the action of the cerebrum brain was conveyed by muscular action, as when the hands of the operator are laid on the instrument, and by this means the instrument proclaimed the action of the cerebrum brain, manifesting that action by the effect produced by the hands of the operator on the instrument, in communicating knowledge previously acquired by the operator, though not then present in conscious mind " or memory."

This action clearly manifests the pre-conscious action of the soul; and very probably was the means adopted by God, through which the lustre of the jewels was affected on the high priest's breast. And thus God would manifest His will to man by first revealing truth to the high priest, which afterwards affected the action of the cerebrum brain, so as to manifest that action by its effect on the Urim and the Thummim. In this way, God would be making use of the earth and the things of the earth, in the built-up human brain being used as the medium between God and the race.

The different nations mentioned in the Bible are evidently intended to represent or personifiy the different phases of the human character in the phase of intelligence the nature manifests as a whole. By this means the prophecies would be rendered intelligible and applicable to all, by applying to each individual whatever manifested the form of intelligence that his nation was famed for. For example, the high culture of Egypt would stand for the intelligence presented by our men of science, who make it their business to look for the first cause that governs everything in the laws of nature, taking no account of God in the matter at all. Whereas, Babylon might represent a nation where a belief in a God to whom man was responsible was an accepted fact or truth. Nevertheless, where the people were regardless of the responsibility involved, they sought only their own glory in the system their nation presented. If we hold this system to include all the divine knowledge essential for man's salvation, we might say Babylon would represent the human character, where the individual took all the advantage his position gave him, and was careless of how much such a course rendered him indebted to others, provided he could turn all the advantage thus gained as a means to attain a yet higher end, feeling that this higher end, when attained, would render him so much above the class he had benefited by as to render them quite powerless to injure him. He world thus secure his personal well-being, regardless of the well-being of others.* Now, this is exactly what the Church of Rome, viewed from the highest point as a system, aims at, in proclaiming itself the True Church, where the first point taught is that each individual is to work for the good of the system as a whole. In this, the work of the indi-

* It is something very like this we Protestants are doing in the way we act toward our men of science, by taking advantage of all their labours, yet making no effort to perceive where science and religion are, in a way, the counterpart of each other, and thereby show them where they have thought the thoughts of God, in the truth their labours reveal, and that they have thus strengthened the kingdom of our Lord among the Gentiles.

vidual soul is to be work rendered to the system. In this the Church, to the individual, is made to take the place of the Saviour, and certainly it does contain the truth which will save the soul eventually. As a system, it is thus perfect, for each of its members, in the faith which unites the individual to the Church or system, teaches the individual *to worship God in Christ as God.* Observe, Christ, in this sense, is both God and Redeemer—the elect of God sent to save the Church, where all are elected that are in the Church. Observe, this includes and confers on a system all the advantages which our Protestant doctrine of justification by faith includes and confers on the individual, as the fruit that springs from the high position attained at conversion, being the means by which the individual is made a willing servant of God's, in using every effort that Christ may be glorified and His race increased on earth, as an offering of love, where the converted one looks for no reward.

Do you not see that the true or Roman Catholic Church, as a system, has and holds all the benefits included in our doctrine of justification by faith ? *where the individual is reduced to the level of the mass, as he works for the good of the system (a system where Christ as God is head)*—where, as to benefits arising from personal effort, he looks for no reward, as the system grasps and holds all. Where, however, the image of the God-man in the ideal Christ brightens every brain, by sending out its generated lustre to the objective Christ as the counterpart of the faith the system includes, where there is not one unbeliever included, because every soul finds a counterpart in Christ as God.

It is in the advantage which *conversion may be made to include* that the member of the Protestant Church reaps the full benefit of the reward conveyed by conversion on the individual when he consecrates his life to Christ in love, when every effort of this consecrated life will reappear in the fruit Christ refers to in *Matt.* vi. 20 and 21, as the fruit of love. It will thus be seen that the system, as the True Church* or Church of Rome, insures the member of

---

* I would have it clearly understood that in calling the Church of Rome the "True Church," I most certainly do not include in the term "True," all the fallacies that Church has woven into her constitution, very much of which is wholly worthless, besides being greatly injurious, and is nevertheless imposed on the member as duties essential to salvation. The adoration and worship it bestows on the Virgin, to me, seems greatly injurious, especially in putting an obstacle between men and the free intercourse established by the Saviour and the soul He redeemed; for, supposing the mother to have free intercourse with the Son, is it at all likely she would use that intercourse first in behalf of the members of a Church where each individual was freely invited to approach, being assured of the Saviour's willingness to hear and answer every prayer. And again, if a Church so related to the Redeemer as the Church of Rome is, choose to take the responsible place she is doing in teaching her members to incur all the risk involved in addressing the Saviour through the medium of saints and martyrs; she, as a system, is responsible for all the misery that may arise from such teaching. One of the injurious consequences that does arise from this teaching is, that *man, by this, chooses to take a lower place than God in Christ has made necessary.* This is distinctly implied in Paul's warning—*Col.* ii. 18-24. And just fancy the misapprehension that has arisen from the doctrine held in the sale of indulgences, where the Church, in the name of Christ, takes the responsibility of making a system of men responsible for the sins some

eternal life, but insures him of nothing else, while all his work goes to build up the system which secures for each member the assurance of eternal life. It is from this point that the Church of Rome is represented in Scripture as Babylon, in the spirit it manifests in grasping and holding all, whereas she ought to have taught her members that the consecrated life proceeding from conversion secures for the individual at death the right and title to pass immediately into glory, being, by the consecrated life, a member of the Church of the first-born, to whom the Saviour is brother, and that the *new heart so often referred to in the Scriptures is a term to represent the centre where works spring from love to Christ, which is the fruit of conversion presented in spontaneous energy.*

My plea is, that a revelation has been given embodied in Christianity, and, of course, is of God—Christ being the form that has sprung from the revelation—revelation first given to the race as a whole, but ultimately confined. ex-

highly favoured individual chooses to commit; this being what I understand to be included in "Indulgences." However, if the individual choose to remain involved in the responsibility this system includes, simply because it insures him of eternal life, we, as Protestants, are in no wise responsible after laying the condition clearly before him—we have delivered ourselves from all responsibility in the matter. However, my own impression is that the women alone will ultimately suffer irreparable loss in being in connection with a Church that binds its members to a system which, except being fettered thus, woman might aspire to the highest place possible for a created intelligence to occupy in the universe of space.

clusively to the seed of Abraham. That in connection with the Jewish race as the fruit of Revelation, Jesus was formed in the Virgin Mary; thus our Lord took the form and organism of the race as a man, where nothing of Him but the form and the experience He gathered during His earthly life, was of the earth, earthly, excepting so far as the Revelation from which He sprung was wholly in connection with the race, being the design ordered of God through which their ultimate deliverance was to be effected. The reasonable soul having sprung from the Revelation thus related to the race, which was wholly of God, though, doubtless, David combined the contrasted ideas which had previously formed this revelation, and by this means united the units which afterwards formed the reasonable soul. The words of our Lord evidently refer to this in " I am the root and the offspring of David, the bright and the morning star." —*Rev.* xxii. 16.

Christ is thus the centre which, when formed in the human soul, includes the condition referred to by our Lord, in "that which is born of the Spirit is spirit"—*John* iii. 6 —meaning the Spirit and nature of God as the source of a new centre and movement, which is the condition longed for by the author of the 51st Psalm, breathed in the words —" Create in me a clean heart, O Lord, and renew a right spirit within me," words which are literally fulfilled when Christ is formed in the soul, for He is wholly of heaven, with the exception of the form and experience gathered on earth, and will produce heavenly fruit—therefore new fruit.

Further, my plea is that the Bible contains God's revealed will, addressing itself to believers only; that Christianity includes forces which will work themselves out, manifesting the glory of God in voluntary service rendered in love to Him; but where such service has not been freely and fully rendered, the believer, though saved, will be liable to suffering in the next world, as voluntary service rendered toward the unsaved, in the form of retribution, from love to Christ, yet service of such a nature that will entail suffering. Whereas suffering will be impossible after death, where the earthly life, after conversion, has been wholly consecrated, and where life has been so far prolonged as to enable the individual to mould his organism in obedience to the will of God. In this case, the sensation of pain will be quite impossible in an organism moulded thus. Further, that the worst of the race will ultimately be delivered from the power and penalty of sin, in being delivered from a spirit of selfishness or self-preservation, which is *the root of all sin,* and is the germ from which all evils spring, but that, in virtue of Christ's atoning sacrifice, He will ultimately rescue humanity from the self-preserving instinct, and, therefore, from the power of sin, by the human race being made capable and willing to glorify God in love.

All I have hitherto said centres in the few following words. The laws that govern the universe in their connection with the race are forces which have combined in forming the unit, which includes the intelligence of the system in the male and female form of humanity.* The organic centre where the forces producing these forms spring from is self-preservation; and this centre has produced the forms dealt with. This centre of self-preservation we find in the human brain, manifesting its power in individual preservation, as the strongest power in man, and is the centre from which all action springs, being the centre, in the full sense of the word, which produced the natural man. But as the power proceeding from the centre has been abused by the individual, and has taken the form of selfishness, Revelation in the form of Christianity steps in and forms a new centre of action in the human brain, which cuts at the root of selfishness, because the forces springing from this new centre secure the eternal well-being of the individual, in obedience to the will of God as the final cause. This is effected by the new form, which springs from the new centre being made to take the place of the old form, which came to maturity through the influence of self-preservation. Thus, therefore, the old man, from the old centre, is being burned out, while the new man, from the new centre, takes his place in the nature and likeness of Christ, as the form of

* It will be a work of the Christian Church in the future to observe the different works our Lord requires of men and women. It was apparently by the labour of active service that man was required to show his love, whereas, woman was to be most of all concerned in cultivating her emotional nature in love to Christ as the one thing needful, and *the part which could not be taken from her.—Luke* x. 42. In the light of present knowledge, this speaks with much power.

the son of God, which is to endure through all eternity. For, observe, the new form in the concrete proceeds from the Revelation which was given to the race, and manifests God's will in the final cause that was made to produce the form; therefore, this form is wholly of God, and represents the nature of God.

It has occurred to me that some weak one may be encouraged in choosing the course that leads to peace and glory, if I related the simple story of my conversion, which took place in comparatively early life.

My early training was of a strictly moral nature. My religion was of such a nature that if I had gone to bed without going through a form of prayer and reading part of the Scriptures I would have felt quite self-condemned in the sight of God. This, I am safe to say, included all my religion, with the exception of asking God to enable me to perform any work I was to engage in if it seemed to me difficult or arduous; for I always concluded this asking God to strengthen me would secure success —my whole happiness being derived from earth and the things of earth. The fear of eternal punishment sometimes made me uncomfortable; but how I was to secure deliverance was a perfect mystery to me, only I thought deliverance could be secured if I devoted myself to the performance of religious and moral duties. This, however, I did not at all feel inclined to do, because I saw such a life would cut at the root of my enjoyment, and I did not wish to secure eternal wellbeing at such a price; and as to what the meaning of a free pardon secured in Christ by believing was, I was completely ignorant of. That Christ, as the Son of God, was intended to secure man's salvation, I had a vague conception of; but how this was to be effected I was totally ignorant, though a member of the Presbyterian Church, until late one evening, when reading a volume of the Kelso Tracts by H. Bonar, and, as I turned over the leaves, I found the tract "Believe and Live" pencil marked, which raised a feeling of resentment against the friend who had bought the volume for me, and who, I at once felt, had marked the part for my benefit. I inferred this, because at the time he brought home the volume, I saw him looking it over in another room before he gave it to me. I now felt quite indignant when I saw by his pencil mark that he considered I required instruction in religious matters from him. This feeling took expression in the thought, "Well, I am sure I am quite as good as you," which implied I did not need to be instructed by him. However, fortunately, I continued to read, and as I read I gathered at once from the tract marked that Christ had secured a full and free pardon to all sinners that believed. When this idea was formed, I laid down the book on my knee—I was sitting all alone on a low stool before a bright fire, and reasoned thus:—"Well, I am a sinner, and I am willing to be saved by Jesus." With these words my heart's desire rose from a new centre, with, I may say, the first prayer I had ever offered, in the words, "Lord, I believe; help Thou my unbelief," which is equivalent to saying, "I am trying, as a sinner, to trust my eternal wellbeing on the strength of your offered pardon, enable me to do so, and to feel how secure this will make me." The connection was thus formed between me and the Saviour. This prayer ascended time after time, morning, noon, and night, during the months and years that succeeded my conversion. Whenever the thought of the next world crossed my mind, my heart rose to God in Christ with "Lord, I believe; help Thou my unbelief." By this means I became assured of my salvation, as I felt and realized how secure I was in being hid with God in Christ; therefore my eternal wellbeing was secured in and by the Saviour. For I saw in such passages as "He that worketh not, but believeth on him that justifieth the ungodly, his faith is counted for righteousness" —*Rom.* iv. 5—a truth which *wholly applied to me and my class,* "*as sinners saved by grace.*" *I thus learned to rejoice in the liberty with which Christ had made me free, for I was free indeed.*

One thing I recollect during the early stage of my converted life was, that I found no comfort from the Psalms, for they seemed to require a personal righteousness or goodness to qualify for heaven, and I felt I had nothing good in me; just a sinner saved by grace, I had not one shadow of righteousness in me to recommend me; therefore, the Psalms gave me no comfort. For, observe, when I accepted the free salvation offered in the tract referred to, I was neither oppressed with a sense of sin, nor saw any necessity for righteousness. All I realized was that Christ had procured a free pardon to sinners, where the condition was to believe; and in complying with the condition, I had accepted the pardon, and *was, therefore, free as the air I breathed*, with a happy eternity secured, because I was a sinner willing to be saved in Christ's way—a beggar, without one merit to recommend me, for He had provided the very thing I wanted in the free gift, which I thankfully received, for by it I secured a happy eternal existence in union with Him as the Son of God. Some time after, I began to cling to the promise from which new life and peace were to flow. In the old heartless way, I was going through a form of prayer, *really desiring nothing, but simply uttering words in prayer*; when all at once my mind was filled with an entirely new influence, and, in amazement, I expressed my feeling in the words—*God is here.* I was thus filled with an entirely new joyous emotion which I had never in any way experienced before. I cannot tell how long the joy lasted, but when it passed away, it left no impression but the memory of it. Then, I had not learned to love Jesus ; I, as a sinner, was only clinging to the promise which was sure to lead to that. My object for stating this experience is to show it was not joy proceeding from the growth of an affection, to which the religious sentiment is sometimes compared by sceptics, but simply God manifesting His presence in the soul of one striving to get near Him through Christ.

At last I began to feel that I loved the Saviour, and that, unless He was to be with me in heaven, heaven had no attraction for me, for it was the personal Saviour I cared for, to be ever by Him, and with Him, "just to feel He was near," *for His presence then, and now, constitutes heaven to me.* That form alone is all I care for, either in heaven or in earth, for I may say God the Eternal is lost sight of in the Redeemer.

During this stage of my converted experience, Mr. Spurgeon's first volume of Sermons crossed my path, and the way he put the truth in these Sermons affected me so that every nerve in my body quivered in love to the Saviour, as I realized how dear He was to me, and that nothing could separate us either in time or in eternity. I often paused while I read, so that a burst of love and adoration might ascend, as, in spirit, I alone, of all the human race, seemed to sit at His feet, who was, and is, everything to me.

During the early stage of my converted life there seemed little outward change, my life before being, in the fullest sense of the word, strictly moral. The first outward effect was a desire to devote the Sunday to sacred reading, and to give up making calls on that day, for I now loved Jesus so well that I was desirous to know his commandments, and to keep them, though this course was not followed, by any means, from a sense of duty, but was the effect of love to Him. I loved Him, and I wished to please Him, *where fear in any form was, and ever has been, absent. I loved, therefore found pleasure in serving.*

This simplicity of action was only endangered where influences were used from without, when, as a converted individual, I took that position in concert with others, likewise converted. They considered it right to induce me to adopt certain courses of action which seemed, to my advisers, as the right course for a converted one to follow. As, for example, in doing, or abstaining from doing, certain things because of appearances, or rather, because of the injurious influence my example might have. This course, in a general way, I have always resisted, by only acting in any form, or refraining from acting, when I, myself, felt it would be right for me to do either the one or the other. I always had the notion that, to refrain from doing anything, or do anything, from any motive less than love to Christ, *included deception, by professing more love to Him than I felt*, being always desirous that love to Christ would form the pure centre whence all religious work, in any form, would spring.

Fortunately, in a general way, I had enough independence of character to resist pressure from without, where my heart did not move me to adopt the course enjoined. This course of action was strengthened by observing that if I did adopt a course prescribed by others, simply because it seemed to them the right course for one converted to adopt, I was sure to give it up at another time, and thus do the cause I professed to serve more injury than if I had never taken up the position prescribed by others whose religious sentiment was possibly more fully developed than mine. Anyhow, I concluded, however right and proper the course prescribed might be for others, for me it was wrong, because my convictions were not strong enough to induce me to carry out the course implied—the truth, I suppose, being, I had not enough religious sentiment to carry out the course enjoined, and I was clear-sighted enough to see that I injured the cause when I failed, so that, eventually, I rarely attempted to adopt the show of more religious sentiment than I felt, as I found this to be the only safe and proper course for me to adopt. But I always strove to abide by the consequences which my convictions might involve, up to the point of proclaiming, as I have done in this book, the material human soul and all that such includes in time and eternity.

Evolution Illuminating the Bible.

By HERRIOT MACKENZIE.

Opinions of the Press.

"It is not easy to give an idea in a few words of a work like Mr. Herriot Mackenzie's 'Evolution Illuminating the Bible,' full as it is of close scientific or quasi-scientific discussion and reasoning. . . . But perhaps we should not be far wrong if we say that its aim is to reconcile the extremest materialism with religion, and to show that there is nothing in the doctrine of evolution which even the staunchest Bible Christian need fear. 'It is evident,' says the author in his preface, 'that the materialistic views advanced by our leading men of science are causing a class of Christians much anxiety. One object I had in writing this volume was to draw the attention of this class to the fact that our Lord clearly advanced such views when He defined man in his natural state as a unit of Body and Mind—classed by Him as born of the Flesh is Flesh—put in contrast with the new sentiment conversion imparts, defined as one 'born of the Spirit, Spirit.' John iii. 16. Cabannis taught that thought is a secretion of the brain, and Mr. Mackenzie, who writes that 'there is no longer any doubt of the mental structure being of a material form,' seems to stop no way short of this celebrated dictum. The loss of brain substance can so far be measured as a secretion from the brain during mental work; further, the heat developed is perceptible and measurable by thermo-electric apparatus.' Nevertheless, he recognises a spiritual principle under the name of the Ego, a conscious personality, not, however, antecedent to the body, but created by the vitality operating in the blood, yet not perishing with the body but surviving it. To follow the author minutely in his curious speculations *is of course* impossible here. It must be admitted, however, that he seems to have a good acquaintance with recent scientific literature dealing with the relation of mind and body, and must have thought deeply on the subject of which he writes. . . . It is dedicated—without permission—to Professor Huxley, 'as a token of admiration and a tribute to his genius.'"—*Scotsman.*

"The writer of these pages hastens to reassure her readers or rather her fellow 'converted Christians' that Materialism has the sanction of Scripture. She finds the germ of it in the words of our Lord to Nicodemus, and its fuller exposition in the eighth chapter of the Epistle to the Romans. Evolution and the Bible mutually illuminate each other."—*Bookseller.*

From Messrs. Simpson, Marshall, Hamilton, Kent & Co. "Evolution Illuminating the Bible," by Herriot Mackenzie.—"'It is evident,' says Miss Mackenzie, 'that the material views advanced by our leading men of science are causing a class of Christians much anxiety; but the author is not among these. She dedicates her book boldly to Professor Huxley, 'as an admiration and a tribute to his genius,' and though an earnest Christian herself, has written a book to show the class referred to that their fears are groundless; that we have the highest of all authority for accepting the material views advanced by such authors as Spencer, Bain, Huxley, &c.

"Those who are familiar with works on these lines will anticipate the nature of Miss Mackenzie's reasoning."—*Publisher's Circular.*

"Evolution Illuminating the Bible," by Herriot Mackenzie, is an attempt to show that the material views advanced by our leading men of science were clearly advanced by our Lord in His words to Nicodemus about the new birth. The book is not easy reading, and is based on the hypothesis that spontaneous generation is possible. . . . Our authoress regards 'Light as a disturber of elements' the most probable force to originate the vaguest possible form of sensation—which is life."—*Literary World.*

"One of the most singular among the recent books which have been published is Mr. Herriot Mackenzie's 'Evolution Illuminating the Bible.' Mr. Mackenzie is so great an admirer of Huxley, the high priest of Agnosticism that he dedicates this volume to him; and yet his faith in Evangelical Christianity is as devout and unquestioning as that of a Highland Free Church Elder. He is an out and out materialist, and professes to find materialism as one of the corner stones of Christ's teaching. How he reconciles this doctrine with a future state, readers must find out for themselves. It is impossible to indicate in the short space at our disposal the drift of Mr. Mackenzie's general argument. It is able. . . . Messrs. John Menzies & Co. are the Edinburgh publishers."—*Northern Ensign.*

"Miss Mackenzie dedicates her book to Professor Huxley, as 'a token of admiration and a tribute to his genius.' That eminent scientist says somewhere, 'that the crassest materialism is consistent with the airest idealism;' and he confesses to have a lingering affection for the old materialistic view that the brain secrets thought somehow in the same way as the liver secrets bile. It has often been deplored that no writer ever appeared to set about the difficult task of reconciling the theories of the physical philosophers and of the airy idealists, and of harmonising the discordant opinions of Professor Huxley and Mr. Herbert Spencer on the one hand, and of Messrs. Moody and Sankey on the other. By most people it is generally believed that these couples are metaphorically at daggers drawn on such subjects as God, the Universe, and the origin and destiny of man, but in Miss Herriot Mackenzie's opinion such is not the case. . . . . . Miss Mackenzie comes boldly forward and publishes what will be either an epoch making book or the reverse. She concedes at the outset everything to her opponents, postulating only a soulless, godless universe filled with all pervading ether; and at the close she forces the Agnostic into a corner, compelling him to accept without reservation, qualification, or modification, all the doctrines of popular Evangelical Theology. Some critics who look more to processes than to results may be apt to raise objections here and there to Miss Mackenzie's logical methods ; but these are small and insignificant matters compared with the great object aimed at, viz., showing that the principle of Materialism leads ultimately to Methodism, and those of Evolutionary Agnosticism to Scotch Presbyterianism.

"Miss Mackenzie, in the beginning of a book of about 400 pages, shows how the transition from lifeless matter to organism is accomplished by means of the heat and light of the sun. The origin of consciousness is next traced to the simple fact that plants notice the presence and absence of the sun. After this the development of intelligence is easy. All notions of right and wrong follow as natural consequences of sensitiveness to pleasure and pain; while, last of all, the growth of the immortal soul is demonstrated to be connected in some way with the universal ether filling all space. .... When so much is accomplished, the origin of life, of consciousness, and of the soul made perfectly plain to the most rudimentary understanding, there is no need to explain in detail the steps by which Miss Mackenzie at last reaches the conclusion that each and all of the doctrines of Evangelical Theology harmonise with, and indeed are but logical sequences of the principles professed by Professor Huxley and Mr. Herbert Spencer. As our authoress says, after one has followed her argument, 'the process of Christ's resurrection is simplicity itself.' ... Miss Mackenzie has evidently read extensively in the subjects of biology and of organic evolution generally. Her scientific knowledge is up to date. .... Altogether, this is one of the strangest books we have read for a long time. Audacious in its conception and its scientific conclusions. ... Miss Mackenzie's ironical treatise on the Bible and Evolution is certainly the most unique book of its kind."—*Banffshire Journal, Aberdeenshire Mail, Moray, Nairn, and Inverness Review.*

"In admiration of the Disruption it cannot be excelled. It also accepts the rankest materialism, and reconciles it to a very simple evangelicalism by denying to all men any spiritual nature whatever prior to regeneration."—*Dundee Advertiser.*

"'Evolution Illuminating the Bible.' ... The author appears to admit the extremest theories of materialism, as far as Body and Mind are concerned, in order to introduce a third element, as he puts it, 'Born of the Spirit, Spirit.' Several chapters are devoted to a review of Modern Physiology and Physiological Psychology. .... (Example of) the author's style: 'Christianity takes to do with the immortal soul created of conscious states, and we have seen that primary conscious states are divided from the objective world, and carry with them the emotions that accompany them at their origin. I hold it permissible to believe, an Ego or soul, so defined, to be built up of luminiferous ether, which, when disembodied as such in functioning, gives expression to the conscious states developed during natural life, and the correlative of consciousness the phenomena of which conscious states are forms.' "—*Westminister Review.*

"'Evolution Illuminating the Bible' is a study written with a set purpose. The author attempts to prove that there is really nothing in the theory of Evolution which is at variance with the teaching of the Scriptures. 'It is evident,' says Mr. Mackenzie, 'that the material views advanced by our leading men of science are causing a class of Christians much anxiety.' Why this class does not approve of the scientific opinion, he does not understand, for 'our Lord clearly advanced such views when He defined man in his natural state as a Unit of Body and Mind.' . . . 'That which is born of the Flesh is Flesh,' put in contrast with the sentiment 'one born of the Spirit is Spirit.' It is the immense difference between Body and Mind that the author dilates upon, and his reasoning, while ingenious, is very unusual. This remarkable book is dedicated to Professor Huxley 'as a token of admiration and a tribute to his genius.'"—*John O' Groat Journal.*

"The author's object, according to his own statement, is 'to draw attention to the fact that our Lord clearly advanced such views (that is, the material views of leading men of science), when he defined man in his natural state as a unit of Body and Mind.' . . . Classed by Him as 'that which is born of the Flesh, Flesh,' put in contrast with the new sentiment conversion imparts, defined as one 'born of the Spirit, Spirit.' Mr. Mackenzie believes in spontaneous generation—'light originated life, sensation is created by the shock produced in parting atoms of a very stable compound molecule.' 'The vital force inherent in the human form at birth awakens into consciousness, and creates the soul of the first sensation.' The Christianity of the future will be moulded by the operation of the materialistic views, which will explain all mental terms in form of matter."—*North British Daily Mail.*

"We shall not profess to review this work, which is best left to make its own way. The views of the writer are so peculiar that it would require far more time than we are able to afford to enter into their merits or demerits. . . . We would not care to stand in the way of a new light, if new light it is, and therefore would earnestly recommend the reading public to procure the book and judge for themselves."—*Brechin Advertiser.*

"The author wishes to show that the immortal part in man is gradually evolved from material conditions, but being evolved in this life it is then indestructible."—*Independent.*

"This volume gives, undoubtedly, evidence of considerable thinking power and knowledge of biology."—*Glasgow Hearld.*

"'Evolution Illuminating the Bible,' by Herriot Mackenzie, is a praiseworthy and thoughtful attempt to treat the subject, so far as relates to religious matters, in a legitimate way."—*Church Times.*

EDINBURGH AND GLASGOW: JOHN MENZIES & CO.

LONDON: SIMPKIN, MARSHALL & CO.

"This is a singular and remarkable book. On professedly scientific grounds the author has adopted the materialistic views of Professor Huxley (to whom the book is dedicated), Herbert Spencer, Professor Bain, and other scientists—views generally regarded as opposed to the teachings of the Bible, and yet in this book he powerfully applies these same conceptions to the elucidation and enforcement of Evangelical Christianity. The theory of Evolution, which not a few consider to be anti-Biblical, he holds to be illuminated by the Bible, and the Bible illuminated by it. The most startling part of the argument is that in which he applies the Evolution theory to the exposition of our Lord's teaching on the all-important subject of the new birth and its necessity. He finds proof of his thesis in his words to Nicodemus : " *That which is born of the flesh is flesh ; and that which is born of the Spirit is spirit*," and also in the general teaching of St. Paul. On this subject of regeneration by the Holy Spirit he utters no uncertain sound. He describes it as " a change so momentous and of such vast importance, as far to surpass anything that could happen to a human being hereafter, even during that immortal individual's onward existence through eternity;" and he affirms that " much that is said in the eighth chapter of Romans is so plain to the converted—therefore adopted child of God—that he who runs may read. Assuredly," he adds, " to him the mysteries of Christianity are explained in the simplest form of language." Unfortunately, in dealing with these mysteries, the author's style is not simple ; and this, combined with the exceedingly abstruse character of the argument will, we fear, limit his readers to " the few and the fit." Those, however, who will take the pains to carefully study and weigh his arguments and lines of thought will find a rich reward in many a fresh view of old truth and in the confirmation of faith in revelation and in the religion of the Bible. On the great cardinal doctrines of the divinity and atoning work of Christ he is equally outspoken and orthodox. " All that revealed truth ever imparted to our race," he declares " was embodied in the person of our Lord Jesus Christ, who eame to atone for sin by means of vicarious sacrifice ;" and on page 268 he ably shows that vicarious sacrifice " is an eminent law of the constitution and development of the social organism." We regret we have not space to show how, starting from materialistic conceptions of humanity, he arrives at the Christian doctrine of immortality and eternal life, or his treatment of prayer and law, or the application of his principles to the ethics of the Gospel. In all these subjects he shows himself to be not only an earnest believer in Divine revelation, but a *Christian of no ordinary spiritual knowledge. And the freedom with which he handles biological and other sciences in the prosecution of his great and noble object is instructive.* The concluding chapter, entitled " *The Mysteries of Christianity explained in Scientific Language,*" is a fitting close to this singular book. From what we have said our readers must not suppose that we agree with the materialistic views of the author. We do not ; but his object is so good, and his maintenance of the great facts and doctrines of the Gospel is so earnest, that we have been able to speak much more favourably of the work than otherwise we might have done, if noticing it purely as a " scientific production."—*Christian Age.*

www.ingramcontent.com/pod-product-compliance
Lightning Source LLC
Chambersburg PA
CBHW021207230426
43667CB00006B/593